Archaeology
of the Boat

To
John and Audrey Chadwick

ARCHAEOLOGY OF THE BOAT

A new introductory study

BASIL GREENHILL

Director, The National Maritime Museum

Introduced by Professor W. F. GRIMES,
formerly Director of the Institute of
Archaeology, University of London, with
chapters by J. S. MORRISON, President of
Wolfson College, Cambridge, and Sean
McGRAIL, Chief Archaeologist, National
Maritime Museum, and numerous drawings by
Eric McKEE, Caird Research Fellow of the
National Maritime Museum.

Wesleyan University Press
Middletown, Connecticut

Published simultaneously in England by
A. & C. Black Limited, London

ISBN 0-8195-5002-7
Library of Congress Catalog Card Number 76-22928
Manufactured in Great Britain
First American Edition

Contents

Illustrations 7

Author's Note 13

Introduction—by Professor W. F. Grimes 15

Part One   The General Theory

1 A New Study 19

2 Six Boats and their Builders 34

3 Shells, Skeletons and Things-in-Between 60

Part Two   The Four Roots of Boatbuilding

4 The Four Roots of Boatbuilding 91

5 The First Root, the Raft Boat and the Raft 97

6 The Second Root, the Skin Boat 116

7 The Third Root, the Bark Boat 124

8 The Fourth Root, the Dugout 129

Part Three
Aspects of the Evolution of Boats and Vessels
in Europe and North America

9   The Classical Tradition—by John Morrison 155

10 The European Clinker-built Boat before the 174
    Viking Era

11 The Round-hulled Boat before the Viking Era: 190
    A different tradition

12 The Flat-bottomed Boat before the Viking Era 193

13   The Viking Age   202

14   The Viking Ships and the Graveney Boat   207

15   Further Aspects of Viking Age Boatbuilding—by   234
     Sean McGrail

16   The Clinker-built Boat after the Viking Period   250

17   The Cog and the Flat-bottomed Boat after the   259
     Vikings

18   The Mysterious Hulk   283

19   Skeletons Everywhere   286

     Bibliography   302

     Glossary   309

     Index   313

Illustrations

1 Joseph Banks' diagram of a canoe from the Island of Raiatea   28
2 A North Carolina skiff   35
3 A Somerset turf boat   36
4 The building of the *Peat Princess*   38
5 *Nugget*—lines   40
6 *Nugget*—structure   41
7 Fastening of clenched lap strakes   42
8 A clinker-built boat under construction   43
9 Canadian lobster boat hauled out for the winter   45
10 Lobster boat under construction at Jonesport, Maine   47
11 Building a pram   48
12 A Holmsbu pram   49
13 Boatbuilding in Bangladesh—fitting a plank   51
14 System used in edge-joining strakes in Bangladesh   52
15 Boat under construction in Bangladesh   53
16 Completed shell of a boat in Bangladesh   54
17 Frames of a small boat in Bangladesh   54
18 Bows of a frameless cargo boat   55
19 A Bangladesh boat   57
20 Stresses and strains   62
21 American schooners in frame   64
22 Boatbuilding on the Indus   67
23 Indus river cargo boat   67
24 Peshawar valley cargo boat   69
25 17th century Scandinavian dockyard   71
26 Edge-joining methods   74
27 A Pakistan *hora*   76

28 The Gokstad four-oared boat   78
29 Strake diagram of the Gokstad boat   79
30 Conventional lines drawing of the Gokstad boat   79
31 Parts of a dory   80
32 Ferriby boat   81
33 Als or Hjortspring boat   81
34 Björke boat   82
35 Gokstad ship   82
36 Graveney boat   83
37 Skuldelev I   84
38 Norwegian pram   85
39 Hulk   85
40 Font at Winchester   86
41 Bangladesh river cargo boat   87
42 Bangladesh clinker-built boat   87
43 Raft boat   91
44 Skin boat   92
45 Basket boat   93
46 Bark boat   93
47 Dugout   94
48 Lobito Bay raft boat   96
49 Titicaca reed raft boat   98
50 Inflated skin raft from Swat   98
51 A Brazilian *jangada* raft   99
52 Chittagong *sampan*   100
53 Formosan raft   101
54 Small Chinese vessel   101
55 Duck *sampan*   102
56 Chicken *sampan*   103
57 Pechili trading junk   105
58 Foochow pole junk   105
59 Indus punt   107
60 Papyrus raft   108
61 Egyptian tomb model   109
62 Dahshur boat   110
63 *Nuggar*   111
64 Brigg boat   112
65 Ferriby boat   112
66 *Meia lua*   113
67 Jonathan's Cave drawing   114
68 Coracle   117
69 Curragh   117
70 Als or Hjortspring boat   118
71 Kalnes carvings   119

72 Experimental skin boat 120
73 Broighter boat 120
74 Caergwrle bowl 121
75 Bantry boat 122
76 Kayaks 123
77 Beothuck canoe 124
78 Ottawa valley canoe 125
79 Fur traders' canoe route 126
80 Cargo canoe 127
81 Brazilian dugout 130
82 Dugout from Ceylon 131
83 The making of a dugout 132
84 Dugouts at Newport News 133
85 Dugouts 135
86 Extending a dugout—Phase 1 135
87 Extending a dugout—Phase 2 136
88 Extending a dugout—Phase 3 136
89 *Balam* under sail 137
90 Framing of a *murina* 138
91 Edge-joining methods 139
92 Boat on a dugout base 140
93 Strake diagram of a *Yamato-gata* vessel 140
94 Model of a *Yamato-gata* vessel 142
95 Modern *Yamato-gata* vessel 142
96 Maori war canoe 143
97 Canoe from the Admiralty Islands 143
98 Dugout from Ceylon 144
99 Dugout from British Columbia 144
100 Dugout from the Solomon Islands 145
101 Sterns of Bangladesh boats 146
102 A double-ended Pakistan cargo vessel 147
103 A *baggala* 148
104 *Mtepe* 149
105 Log canoe 150
106 Bugeye 151
107 Mycenaean ship of about 1400 BC 156
108 Greek and Tyrrhenian ships in combat: 700–650 BC 157
109 Ram fitting for upcurving prow 159
110 Round boat of 8th–7th Century BC 160
111 Floor timbers in Cheops' ship of 4500 BC 161
112 Attic triakontor of early 6th century BC 164
113 Greek merchant ship and two-level pentekontor
    of late 6th Century BC 166
114 Vase in the shape of a *trieres'* bow 170

115 Clinker or lapstrake construction   175
116 Jagt *Otto Mathiasen*   176
117 Principal discoveries of ancient boats   179
118 Nydam oak boat   180
119 Nydam oak boat midships section   181
120 Nydam fir boat   183
121 Sutton Hoo excavation   184
122 Model of Sutton Hoo ship   185
123 Kvalsund boat   187
124 Utrecht ship—lines   189
125 Utrecht ship in her cellar   190
126 Boat from Sylhet, Bangladesh   191
127 Ketelhaven boat   192
128 East German flat-bottomed boat   194
129 East German round-hulled keel plank boat   195
130 Bruges boat   196
131 Exploded dory   198
132 Gotland stone carvings   199
133 Coins from Birka and Hedeby   200
134 Map of the Viking expansion   206
135 A Viking fleet   208
136 Model of the Oseberg ship   209
137 The Oseberg ship   210
138 Section of the Oseberg ship   211
139 The Gokstad ship   212
140 Section of the Gokstad ship   213
141 The Ladby ship   214
142 Skuldelev Wreck 5   215
143 Bayeux Tapestry   216
144 North European clinker-built boats   217
145 Swedish church boat   218
146 Skuldelev Wreck 3   219
147 Skuldelev Wreck 1, longitudinal section   220
148 Skuldelev Wreck 1, photograph   221
149 The Viking Ship, AD 800–1000   222
150 The Graveney boat after initial excavation   224
151 The Graveney boat being dismantled   225
152 The keel of the Graveney boat   225
153 Working model of the Graveney boat   226
154 Lines of the Graveney boat   228
155 Structure and strake diagram of the Graveney boat   229
156 Oselver   230
157 Nordlands boat   231
158 A keel/stem scarf   235

159 Log conversion   241
160 The structure of wood   242
161 Wood splitting techniques   244
162 Viking Age tools   246
163 Bayeux Tapestry   247
164 The Seal of Paris   251
165 The second Seal of Winchelsea   251
166 *Holrikjekta*   252
167 *Jekt* at Bergen   253
168 Coble   254
169 Cornish gig   254
170 The *Peggy*   254
171 Gaspé schooners   256
172 Prince Edward Island shallop   256
173 Block Island boat   257
174 Beach boat *Boy Albert*   258
175 Seal of Keil   260
176 Seal of Elbing   260
177 Bremen cog   261
178 Rother barge   262
179 *Schokker*   262
180 *Pavilionpoon*   263
181 *Botter*   263
182 11th century wreck of cog type   264
183 Bridgwater flatner   266
184 Bridgwater boat   267
185 Boat from Uttar Pradesh   268
186 Dory building shop   269
187 Dories on deck   270
188 The Continental gunboat *Philadelphia*   271
189 Lumberman's *bateau*   271
190 Sharpie   273
191 Skiff from Georgia   274
192 Skiff from Maine   275
193 Weston-super-Mare flatner   276
194 Chesapeake skiff   277
195 Gaspé skiff   277
196 St Lawrence *goelette*   278
197 V-bottomed lobster boat   279
198 Dugout to scow   280
199 *Owhtı*   281
200 *Alma*   282
201 Seal of New Shoreham   284
202 Hulk on a coin   284

203 Mataro ship   290
204 Three-masted ship   291
205 Caulking   293
206 Intermediate construction, Sweden   295
207 Intermediate construction, Japan   295
208 Intermediate construction, Pakistan   296
209 *Shamrock*   297
210 Planking-up   299
211 *Jessie A Bishop*   299
212 *Savannah*   300
213 *Theoline*   301

Author's note

THIS BOOK IS intended as a simple guide, to outline aspects of the present state of the study of boats and boat building development. As soon becomes clear, however, this study is still in a very early stage, although now rapidly advancing. This may well be the last occasion on which a layman without professional qualifications as an archaeologist, ethnographer or naval architect, will be able to venture into the subject on this scale in the hope of providing fellow laymen with a general guide. At the same time perhaps a small contribution will be made, by suggesting some new ideas and some new solutions to old problems, not in the belief that these original ideas are in themselves very significant, but that the suggestions, and indeed the book itself, will stimulate interest and controversy and thereby advance the study.

The obvious necessity of so advancing the study of the development of boats as one of man's principal tools led to the initiation of archaeological and anthropological work at the National Maritime Museum in 1971. The preliminaries to the establishment of the new Department and Research Centre involved close contact with several people with very original minds whose subsequent friendship has proved immensely stimulating. Ole Crumlin Pedersen of the Danish National Museum, Eric McKee, at the time of writing a Caird Research Fellow of the National Maritime Museum, Arne Emil Christensen, Junior, of the University Museum of National Antiquities in Oslo, and Olof Hasslöf of Malmö in Sweden, formerly of Copenhagen University, have each in their very different ways advanced the study of the development of boats most substantially in recent years and I am very grateful to them, and in particular to the two first-named, for their continual inspiration, encouragement and help. It was also a delight to make the close acquaintance of the late Howard I. Chapelle and to get to know John Gardner who has done so much to record the history of the boats of North America. As always where United States maritime history is concerned my principal guide has been

Captain W. J. Lewis Parker, United States Coastguard, retired, who has also been my companion on visits during the last twenty-one years to numerous small harbours between Georgia and the Magdalene Islands, Quebec. He and I also travelled together in Japan and watched boatbuilders at work, using the 'intermediate' methods of construction described in this book, at many places between Tokyo and Inatori.

The first of the two central themes of this book, that the broadest classification of boat structures in history is into boats of which the planks comprising the outer skin are joined to one another at the edges and boats the planks of which are not joined edge to edge, is one which I formulated very early in my own field observations in Bangladesh in 1950. I subsequently tested the idea in observation of boats all over the world, and in wide reading. It held up well enough to be published, firstly as a footnote to one of the introductory labels to the permanent display on the development of boats which was opened at the National Maritime Museum in 1972. In this book I have examined the idea rather more extensively, but it still needs much further development. I have, of course, devoted much the greater part of the relevant text of this book to the examination of the long and complex history of edge joined boats and devoted relatively little space to non-edge joined structures. The methods of construction of these are on the whole less varied and the basic principles have been described in a number of books. As explained in the text, relatively little is known still of the origins of this complex of building traditions.

The second theme is that of the basic nature of the problems the boatbuilder meets—those of shaping the strakes; what to do with the plank ends; joining the strakes; or building a simple boat with the minimum of skilled work. The same problems have occured whenever and wherever men have built boats of wood. On the whole, similar solutions tend to recur, especially in the western world. The broad characteristics of the boats which are built are governed by the solutions adopted to these basic problems. Thus the builders of the medieval hulk and of the river cargo boats of Bangladesh today adopted similar solutions to problems of strake shape and plank ends.

Of course in a book of this kind at this early stage in the development of the study the opinions expressed are essentially personal. This is one man's view of the archaeology of boats. Certainly this book must not be taken to represent the 'official thinking' of the National Maritime Museum on this subject at this stage. It would be quite inappropriate for a great national museum to have institutional views on the detail of a new subject the study of which it is seeking to advance.

The people who have helped in one way or another with this book, other than the contributors and those already named above, are too numerous to mention. I would however like to thank particularly the Trustees of the National Maritime Museum for making it possible to write it at all, and my wife and Mrs Hitchcock, whose highly efficient, and frequently equally highly critical, production of numerous drafts has left me much indebted.

London and Boetheric 1970–1975   Basil Greenhill

Introduction

BOATS AND SHIPS have long occupied an important place in human affairs. At their lowliest over some 12,000 years they have been the means of earning a livelihood for countless generations of fishermen. As transport, growing in size and complexity, they have played a crucial part in the spread of new things and new ideas, linking islands and continents, opening up waterways and overcoming obstacles to communication: forests, mountains and marsh. Other considerations apart, they deserve study for their own sake. Their relevance is not confined to those who actually live by water.

To a landsman like this writer the difference between a boat and a ship is one of size. 'Boats are things that are carried on ships', as a naval acquaintance once put it, no doubt over simplifying the matter. In the nature of the case, boats belong to relatively simple people with limited resources in techniques and materials and since the materials are usually organic and perishable the study of ancient boats is by that fact the more difficult. The problem is one with which students of other aspects of material culture are familiar: one result is that actual examples of early boats are hard to come by. Contemporary records where they exist are inexact and leave important questions unanswered. If, as correspondence in *The Times* has shown, there are basic uncertainties regarding the functioning of the Greek trireme, relatively well documented as it is (a ship, of course; not a boat), what of the boats of the Scandinavian rock-carvings? Simpler and smaller they may have been; but their significance and that of others like them must have been incalculable in their time.

Whatever the difficulties, the history of boats acquires a new stimulus from the development of nautical archaeology, which with the invention of the aqualung might well in the jargon of today be described as a growth activity. It has led—or is leading—to commercially—or curio-minded treasure-hunting gradually giving way to a more scholarly approach. Sites and objects thus become important for the

15

light that they shed upon one another and for the contribution that they jointly make to knowledge of their time. A distinguished practitioner in this work has emphasised that land archaeology and underwater archaeology are one in both methods and objectives. The widespread acceptance of this attitude will not of course be achieved without the introduction of the same kind of constraints as were necessary for the older branch of the subject. There are those who do not recognise the highest when they see it—who may need to be persuaded that the unregarded timbers of the ship may be even more important than its brass cannon, and that the wrecked vessel, literally the container of valued objects, is significant on its own account. And what goes for ships goes also for boats.

It is labouring the obvious to say that Basil Greenhill's book has value in its own right; its appearance at this time and in these circumstances is particularly opportune. It focuses attention on an aspect of marine archaeology which will not presumably involve the big ships, though even for them it may not be entirely without value. Boats, after all, are the craft from which (however distantly) the big ships grew. The *Archaeology of the Boat* will form a starting-point for further studies, defining objectives for those who undertake them, suggesting what to look for. It is also a model of method. Its treatment of the subject argues inescapably for the total approach in which ancient and modern, primitive and advanced all have their contribution to make. For boats are at once universal and timeless; and boat-building traditions are long lived.

W. F. Grimes

PART ONE

The General Theory

Chapter I

A New Study

WHY IS IT especially necessary now to write a new short, simple, popular, introductory handbook on the history of boats and boat-building?

There are several good reasons for doing so. One is that the study of the development of boats in history and prehistory, which until recently lacked intensive specialist attention, has now undergone a change. Other artefacts of man—pottery, houses, temples and churches, fortifications, tools, jewelry, metal work—had all developed their own disciplines, but the boat had not. This was partly because wooden boats do not survive the centuries as well as pottery and stone. There were few scientific excavations and a poor record of publication of discoveries. There had been no specialists in the field, partly perhaps because of the classic alienation of the seafarer from the rest of society, and to a lesser extent by association, the alienation also of those who follow trades closely allied to seafaring.

As Campbell MacMurray's recent investigation (on behalf of the National Maritime Museum) of social and working conditions in merchant ships in the early years of this century has demonstrated, the two separate worlds of the seaman and the landsman must have developed very early in the course of mankind's encounter with the sea, and they persist as separate entities to the present day. The seaman's world is alien to the landsman unless he makes a lifetime study of part or all of it, the more so since the seaman's very alienation makes him difficult to communicate with, makes his world not only other, but also closed. Consequently scholars whose lives have been involved with the history of the landsman have rightly been inclined to avoid the otherness of the world of seamen and boatmen. When they have ventured into it they have frequently gone rapidly adrift and lost their bearings for lack of intense study of sufficient examples and of knowledge of the background of the artefacts. Their conclusions have in consequence sometimes been superficial, occasionally even quite inaccurate.

19

Boats were developed where there was a need for them, and were almost invariably built for basic utilitarian requirements—they were either necessary, beneficial, essential or important to help people live. Time, work and scarce raw materials were not put into boats for reasons of romance or normally of aesthetics. Men and women did not take to the water unless the benefits were considerable. They exploited their environment and since the land alone could not support them, they took to the sea, river or estuary to fish for food, or to travel to new hunting grounds; to earn money by carrying other people's goods; or by stealing in acts of piracy—or any combination of these.

People take to the sea when the land alone is not enough. The ownership or occupation of land has been so important that it is still very widely regarded as a status symbol. For this reason, among others, inside a society, those who have been forced completely off the edge, full time fishermen, seamen, boat people—have often been lowly rated by their contemporaries; and their settlements if such they have, regarded as poor, outlandish, even lawless places. The inhabitants of these settlements tend to become people apart. From the nature of their occupations, if they are full time specialists, and the fact that their menfolk are cut off from ordinary human intercourse, even with other members of their own group, for much of their working lives, the communities become more and more separated from the landsman's life of the members of most societies. But materially these communities developed their own status symbols and the boat, like the horse among landsmen, was probably very early an important status symbol itself.

It is only since the early 1960s that intensive professional study of the development of boat structures has begun to evolve as a subject in its own right. Almost a new profession was needed to make this development possible. The men and women who follow it must have a deep feeling for boats and knowledge of boatmanship, a practical commitment over and above the requirements of a normal academic study. As Arne Emil Christensen of the University Museum of National Antiquities in Oslo, one of the pioneers of the new study, has said, 'the archaeologist may theorise as much as he wants, but boatbuilders will be able to give him definite answers, if he takes the trouble to ask them, and watch them at work'. The archaeologist must have the practical approach which enables him to appreciate the problems faced by boatbuilders working in wood and the way they solved them, for here lies the solution to many problems presented by other evidence from the past. This is no desk bound study, but one requiring extensive field work. He must acquire professional knowledge of boat structures and considerable archaeological experience and ethnographic knowledge. The process of generating such skills and interests is lengthy and experimental, but in a number of countries this is now happening.

The present students of the development of boats have had their great forebears. For generations people have been examining occasional boat finds more or less rigorously and a few people have been studying the structures of boats around the world. In Britain the most significant contributor in ethnographic field studies was James Hornell, Director of Fisheries in the service of the Provincial Government of Madras in the old Imperial India. Hornell was of a type of professional expert now virtually extinct; without degrees or formal training he successfully filled a professional role. After his retirement he published in 1946 a book which remains unique, the only attempt in the author's own words 'to marshal in due order the major part of the knowledge . . . concerning the origins of the many devices upon which men . . . launched themselves upon river, lake and sea'. Because of its structure—it is mostly an assembly of previously published academic papers—it is not an easy book to follow and in some fundamental aspects Hornell's general conceptions have been overtaken by the new study, but nevertheless the book remains perhaps the most comprehensive single source of descriptions of boats all over the world.

The serious archaeology of the boat in this country perhaps began with Edward and C. W. Wright's first excavation of the Ferriby boats in 1937 and the first excavation of the Sutton Hoo ship two years later. Now the subject of renewed intensive study by Edward Wright himself and others at the National Maritime Museum, the Ferriby boats of the second millennium BC are among the oldest, if not the oldest, plank-built boats found anywhere in the world outside Egypt.

In recent years, especially since the development of modern diving equipment, invaluable work has been done in the Mediterranean by G. F. Bass, Honor Frost, S. Dumas and many others, and in British waters especially by Colin Martin. In Britain there has been the further examination by Rupert Bruce-Mitford of the evidence for the structure of the boat in which the great Sutton Hoo burial was made, and the examination by Marsden of the Museum of London (then the Guildhall Museum) of the remains of boats buried in the old foreshore revealed by improvement work to the Thames embankment in the Blackfriars area. In the United States John Gardner of Mystic Seaport has published very valuable detailed descriptions of the structure of a great many East Coast boat types, and the late Marion Brewington published detailed accounts of local vessels of Chesapeake Bay. The late Howard I. Chapelle of the Museum of History and Technology in Washington cast his net wider and published general studies of the development of boats in North America.

There have been a number of very interesting studies in recent years of the possible strands in the development of the boat on the basis of evidence so far available, notably by Lionel Casson in New York, Lucien Basch, Arne Emil Christensen Jnr, and Olof Hasslöf. In the Netherlands there has been the unique massive excavation and study by G. D. van der Heide of some two hundred vessels of various periods revealed by the reclaiming of the lands of the Zuyder Zee.

But the birth of this new full time study of the development of the boat as a specialism in its own right can perhaps be considered really to have taken place with the discovery and examination of the series of five boats or ships of the Viking Age, the Skuldelev finds, in Roskilde fjord in Denmark in the late 1950s and their excavation, recovery and continuing study by Olaf Olsen, Ole Crumlin Pedersen and others of the Danish National Museum. In Britain it really began with the excavation and recovery of the Graveney boat of c. 950 AD by the National Maritime Museum and the British Museum late in 1970, and the subsequent establishment of the Archaeological Research Centre at Greenwich. Since its first beginnings as the Graveney Boat Unit this new Department has already to its credit, among many other things, the detailed study and publication of the Graveney boat herself by Valerie Fenwick, Eric McKee and others, the location and excavation of the Brigg boat of c. 600 BC by Sean McGrail and the development of the study of this boat and of the Ferriby boats.

All this work has perhaps begun to point the way towards the development of a new sub-branch of archaeology in Britain. But it is not archaeology in a narrow sense, for the study of the development of boat structures involves not only the study of ancient boats but also of boats today. This is for the very good reason that in the other world of the seafarer the ancient and the modern co-exist side by side to a degree perhaps unusual with the artefacts of man. Not only does the dugout canoe still greet the steel diesel container ship in some Asian and African ports, the same dugout lies on the river bank alongside highly sophisticated wooden boats which have developed from dugout origins and less sophisticated boats which represent intermediate stages in the development. There is a great deal to be learned about the development of boats from the detailed study of modern examples, providing that we do not assume that things were necessarily the same in the past as they are now, but use the study as a source of ideas and an indication of what is possible. So the new discipline involves ethnography as well as archaeology, and since each boat was made for a utilitarian purpose and the nature of the environment in which they work does not change, the naval architect plays a large part in the team working in the new discipline.

It has become indisputably clear though, for all the work that has been done, that we are still in the early stages of the study of the history of boat structures. For example, the detailed study of the Graveney boat and the Ferriby/Brigg finds is not only deriving the maximum possible knowledge from these particular finds, it is generating new methods and techniques for the future. Recent work in Denmark and Norway has revealed a great deal about Viking Age shipbuilding within 250 miles of the Skaw, and there are a number of other fields which are proving very profitable of study. But when all is added up these are only fragments, and every find, every new idea and every hypothesis, underlines the fact that we are right at the very beginning of the study of a new branch of the history of man's activities. The confident statements of the writers of only a generation ago, who had, for instance, worked out an evolution for the 'Viking ship' on the basis of the then known finds of remains of vessels in North West Europe, have been undermined and it will be a long time before they will be replaced. In this regard the study of boats parallels a process going on in the rest of archaeology generally, where the development of scientific method is leading to the questioning of many ideas.

Two examples perhaps illustrate the present state of the study. In a western world in which the sailing of boats and ships rigged only with one squaresail on a mast more or less amidships has not been regularly practised for three-quarters of a century, and only in a few backward pockets for half a century before that, many interpretations have been put on the fragmentary evidence that exists for the form, rigging and handling of this sail as used during the centuries of Scandinavian expansion—the Viking Age. In fact, we know almost nothing about the sails and rigging of Viking ships, or of contemporary vessels in this country and elsewhere in Europe, or how they were handled. Preliminary experimental work going on at the time of writing at the Danish National Museum and in our National Maritime Museum has already shown that a great deal more practical work must be done, before we are really in a position to begin to interpret the surviving evidence for the way in which the Vikings and their contemporaries rigged and sailed their boats and ships. First the problems of sailing with one type of single squaresail, about which we know more than most because it was the last in regular use (only seventy years ago in northern Norway) must be mastered, then we can work outwards to see how this sail might be varied to match the evidence about sails a thousand years ago, and thus empirically begin to build up at least a minimum body of knowledge about what the various ancient sails cannot have been, and what some of them may have been. This will involve not only trials in the rigging and sailing of replicas of such boats, it will also involve the weaving of hypothetical fabrics of the period and their processing—shrinking, bleaching, etc—as they may have been processed before or after they were made up into sails.

The second example concerns the shape and structure of hulls. Of the very numerous finds of remains of ancient boats in Northern Europe and elsewhere the great majority have never been properly published.[1] Only a very few finds have been subjected to the rigorous examination now demanded as necessary before serious conclusions can be drawn from wreckage. Indeed the very questions this examination should seek to answer are only just beginning to become clear. In the absence of these questions, and of agreed general methods for seeking the answers, very different interpretations have in the past been put on surviving evidence. The Äskekärr ship is an important Swedish find of the period of the Scandinavian expansion. Two hypothetical reconstructions of the remains have been published,[2] very different from one another in major features of hull form. Neither appears to be supported by the sort of detailed analysis of structure, hydrostatic characteristics and probable performance at sea which should now be demanded of full reports on all such finds.

For the development of a new study to be possible, especially one which is by definition international, an agreed terminology is needed, and such terms should necessarily be comprehensible for ease of reporting and discussion. Terminology presents far greater difficulties than might at first appear, because in the English language there never has been any standard nomenclature for the parts of

---

[1] Detlev Ellmers, *Frühmittelalterliche Handelsschiffahrt in Mittel-und Nordeuropa*, Neumünster, 1972, lists 211 finds, some containing the remains of several boats, from Norway, Denmark and Greenland, Sweden, Finland, East Germany, USSR, Poland, West Germany, Holland, Belgium, France, Britain and Ireland, which have been published in greater or, more frequently, lesser degree and he excludes boats found in graves from his list.

[2] Sibylla Haasum, 'Vikingatidens Segling och Navigation', *Theses and Papers in Northern European Archaeology*, The Institute of Archaeology at the University of Stockholm, 1974.

traditional boats or the processes of boatbuilding. Just as boats and building methods varied greatly from area to area, even between adjoining counties or the opposite banks of the River Thames, so did the terms used to describe the constituent parts of the boats. Purely for the purposes of communication and in no sense to imply what is, or was, right or wrong in usage, the National Maritime Museum is seeking to build up a standard terminology.[3] This is a major undertaking, on which work has really only just begun, but it is hoped that the suggestions will be improved upon and in due course widely adopted.

The time is right, therefore, to make a short review of parts of the field of knowledge in this new study as it now is. To a degree this has already been done in the display on the Development of the Boat in the New Neptune Hall at Greenwich. This book draws on the same sources as this display and uses largely the same examples and illustrations, mainly from the Museum's own collections, and some from the splendid collection of boats at the Mariners' Museum at Newport News in Virginia. It shows much the same unevenness of emphasis, the same inadequacies, because it is a book about a subject on which our knowledge is at present uneven and inadequate and it draws for illustrations on arbitrarily assembled collections. Its emphasis and structure is derived from existing knowledge, and is concerned essentially to present in simple terms some of what we know at present. Like the display at Greenwich it is mainly about the development of the boat in Northern Europe, Britain and North America, where the great majority of boat types probably evolved from dugouts – hollowed logs – in different and devious ways, perhaps with influence in some areas from boats made by covering skeletons of wood with skins and maybe a little influence from boats developed from rafts with sides built on to them. But there is enough about the development of boats generally to help to set that of the boat in Britain and Northern Europe into its world context.

There are other reasons why it is particularly necessary at the present moment to write a book on the history of boat building. Boats have developed all over the world in different ways and at different speeds. Their development has been conditioned by the geography of the local waters; climate; purposes for which the boat was needed; availability of materials for their construction; tradition of craftsmanship which grew up among the boatbuilders and the general state and nature of the culture of the people building them. Different types of boat developed in different environments. To give a few simple examples: if a lot of timber grew close to the water in the territory of a people and there were enough of them to provide labour, then—if the timber was small, the climate beneficent and particularly if the waters to be navigated were sheltered, rafts would probably be developed; if the timber was big and the climate colder we might expect to find single and double logs shaped into boats—dugouts. If the timber was very small and there were skin bearing animals which could be hunted then skin boats made by stitching skins over frameworks of

---

[3] Some ideas have been published in the glossaries to two pamphlets: McKee, *Clenched Lap or Clinker* and McGrail and McKee, *The Building and Trials of the Replica of an Ancient Boat: The Gokstad Faering, Part I, Building the Replica*, Maritime Monographs and Reports No. 11, The National Maritime Museum, London, 1974.

light branches would probably be built. In the few parts of the world where some of the trees have bark of the right properties, bark canoes developed. Indeed when a people have a need to build boats, that need is often so great that they will build them even though the choice of material available contains nothing that other and better endowed peoples would ever think of using for the purpose. It is only in sophisticated societies which are rich enough to have a considerable degree of choice that ideal boatbuilding timbers, and even ideal timber for particular types of boat, begin to be regarded. Thus, builders of Bridgwater River flatners in Somerset in the last century made the sides of the flatners of elm, because it was cheap and readily available in the sizes needed for the work. But boatbuilders in areas with a wide choice and where people were ready to put more money into their boats, would never have used elm in this way.

From time to time in many parts of the world sophisticated techniques of boatbuilding have evolved and the end products have become highly efficient vessels for their area and purpose, often beautiful to look at and frequently the products of very skilled craftmanship. For example the very developed and very different edge-joined overlapping plank building techniques of Northern Europe and of Bangladesh, have resulted in the construction of many boats which are so well designed for their purpose and so pleasing in form that they are almost works of art in their own right. The complex structures of the Viking ships found in Norway and Denmark, the high degree of technical sophistication which marks the design of the Graveney Boat, the beauty of form of these and many other boat finds of the 9th and 10th centuries justify the description of the clinker boatbuilding of that period as one of the greatest technical achievements of North European society before the building of the early cathedrals.

The method of building in modern Bangladesh, and as used by many of the builders of clinker-built boats in Northern Europe as long as such boats were built, involves the construction of a hull shell without any frames or moulds, by the shaping and joining of planks into strakes which are added to one another edge to edge. It has been compared at its best to an act of sculpture.

These are perhaps extreme examples, but until a few years ago the world was full of beautiful boats built by men who constructed them within the disciplines of a strong local building tradition conveyed from generation to generation only by example and therefore strongly protected against hasty innovation. To take examples illustrated by actual boats on display in the National Maritime Museum alone—the raft boats of the south west coast of Africa, the dugout fishing boats of the coasts of Brazil around Rio, the smooth-skinned fishing boats of Clovelly in south west England, the dory from Portugal and north eastern North America—were all products of different environments, societies, technologies and requirements, yet all highly developed, efficient and beautiful, each in its different way.

But a boat should be judged only, and I repeat only, in the light of the requirements for which she was built and the resources of the society which built her. She should never be judged by comparison with other boats built for different purposes of different materials in different circumstances. The basic question is one of fitness of purpose in relation to broad local circumstance. To appreciate a boat one must be aware of the factors that gave rise to her building, the timber available, the general environment, the building traditions of the society which produced her and, above all, the purpose for which she was built.

Most boats since men began building them have been the products, not of an organised industry with full-time craftsmen specialised to their trades, but of the part-time work of men who also had other trades and who had learned local boatbuilding traditions as part of their preparation for life. It was in such circumstances that the oldest elements in local traditions lasted longest, so that boats built in recent years even showed evidence of their origins in the gouging and hollowing techniques of dugout building, or the techniques of the extension with planks of an expanded dugout's sides to make a boat.

Now, quite suddenly, all these traditions and skills are in grave danger of being lost within a very short time. The reason, of course is simple. It is one of the many cumulative effects of the development of the world we live in, seen most obviously in the introduction of glass-reinforced plastic, plywood, and resin glues for boatbuilding; less directly in the development of highly commercialised, centralised production of boats in factories; in the introduction by such bodies as the Food and Agriculture Organisation of the United Nations of standard designs using standard materials and parts, to be built with the minimum of labour; in the widespread adoption of power in the form of small outboard motors even in the most remote areas of the world, with consequent changes of the boats' shapes and structures. All these developments mean the early end of the widespread use of boatbuilding traditions which, in some local areas in some countries, go back more than one thousand years.

This great change, from the traditional disciplines of the local boatbuilder using simple readily and locally available materials to the techniques of the factory using exotic and largely artificial materials, is a second reason why it is now especially necessary to write a new basic book on the history of boats and boatbuilding. Soon popular awareness of one of the oldest technologies is going to be lost altogether.

Of course, the new materials, glass-reinforced plastic and glued plywood, and sometimes the two used together in the form called wood-reinforced plastic, have many and great advantages. In a world where labour is everywhere becoming the largest component in costs they save labour time spent in boatbuilding. They are relatively cheap and readily obtainable in standard sizes and qualities. Above all, once the boat is built, they are strong, stable materials which will not change in shape and size with variations in humidity and temperature. The boat, therefore, does not have to be nursed like the relatively delicate, flexible structure of even the most massively built traditional wooden vessel. The materials will not dry out and leave gaping seams to 'take up' when she is put in the water, so that in the end the boat is destroyed if she is allowed to dry out too completely too often. They will not be destroyed by marine borers—commonly and generally known as 'worm'. A working boat leads a very hard life and the plastic, or partly plastic, boat can lead it with less trouble and much less maintenance than a traditionally built wooden boat of any form. The factor of time in building is also very important in the modern world. Traditional boatbuilding was a slow business and the maintenance of the tools alone occupied a good deal of the boatbuilder's time.

The skills of traditional boatbuilders all over the world were often fascinating examples of mankind's resource in adapting locally available materials in relation to environment and purpose. The boat has been an extremely important tool in the ascent of man. The boats of a society have occasionally—as with the Vikings in Europe and the Polynesians in the Pacific—represented not only the supreme technical achievement of the society, but more than that, perhaps its principal aesthetic and social achievement as well.

We have unfortunately no detailed professional description of the building of a Viking or Saxon ship, but Sir Joseph Banks (as he later became) was in modern terms the chief of scientific staff on the first of Captain James Cook's three great voyages of Pacific exploration two hundred years ago, and this is how he described the building of a boat on the Island of Raiatea in the Society Islands in a society in which there had been no recent technical innovations from outside:[4]

> '... the inhabitants were at work makeing and repairing the large Canoes called by them Pahee, at which business they worked with incredible cleverness tho their tools were certainly as bad as possible. I will first give the dimensions and description of one of their boats and then their method of building. Its extreme length from stem to stern not reckoning the bending up of both those parts 51 feet; breadth in the clear at the top forward 14 inches, midships 18, aft 15; in the bilge forward 32 inches, midships 35, aft 33; depth midships 3 ft 4; hight from the ground she stood on 3 ft 6; her head raisd without the figure 4 ft 4 from the ground, the figure 11 inches; her stern 8 ft 9, the figure 2 feet. Alongside of her was lashd another like her in all parts but less in proportion being only 33 feet in her extreme length. The form of these Canoes is better to be expressed by a drawing than by any description. This annexd may serve to give some idea of a section: aa is the first seam, bb the second, cc the third. The first stage or keel under aa is made of trees hollowd out like a trough for which purpose they chuse the longest trees they can get, so that 2 or three make the bottom of their largest boats (some of which are much larger than that described here as I make a rule to describe everything of this kind from the common size); the next stage under bb is formd of streght plank about 4 feet long and 15 inches broad and 2 inches thick; the next stage under cc is made like the bottom of trunks of trees hollowd into its bilging form; the last or that above cc is formd also out of trunks of trees so that the moulding is of one peice with the plank. This work difficult as it would be to an European with his Iron tools they perform without Iron and with amazing dexterity; they hollow with their stone axes as fast at least as our Carpenters could do and dubb

[4] Beaglehole (ed), *The Endeavour Journal of Joseph Banks 1760–1771*, Sydney, 1962.

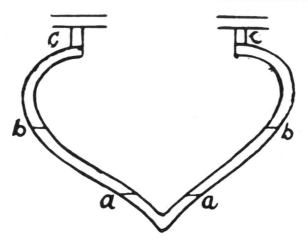

National Maritime Museum

Figure 1   Joseph Banks' diagram of a section of
a canoe from the Island of Raiatea.

tho slowly with prodigious nicety; I have seen them take off a skin of an angular plank without missing a stroke, the skin itself scarce $\frac{1}{16}$ part of an inch in thickness. Boring the holes throug which their sewing is to pass seems to be their greatest difficulty. Their tools are made of the bones of men, generaly the thin bone of the upper arm; these they grind very sharp and fix to a handle of wood, making the instrument serve the purpose of a gouge by striking it with a mallet made of a hard black wood, and with them would do as much work as with Iron tools was it not that the brittle Edge of the tool is very liable to be broke.'

The boat as man's tool and toy has had very special significance in many societies; not only has it been essential to mankind's encounter with water, especially with the sea and to the development of the world as we know it, it is also so fundamental that despite the low status in most societies of its professional users and their alienation from the majority of their fellow men, it has acquired significance—aesthetic, religious and sexual—beyond its great utilitarian importance. To take a very immediate and relevant modern example, the cult of the small yacht could not have been pushed, for commercial ends, to the degree that has been achieved in Europe and North America in the late 20th century if the boat herself, and the simple fact of ownership of her, had not had a significance even beyond the return in leisure and pleasure her use gives.

On what materials can the professional boat archaeologist draw for his work? As I have said already the account of the development of the boat available to us at present is essentially fragmentary and we have as yet little real knowledge of the history of that development. The subject has been studied and recorded only here and there as chance has brought informed observers into circumstances in which they could record in some degree the details of the structures of boats. Sometimes chance has brought about the survival of actual remains of ancient boats and their discovery and, much more rarely, proper excavation; even more rarely still, adequate recording and publication. There are illustrations or representations in one form or another of some ancient boats and there are a very few written accounts of them. It is from these sources, much more rigorously examined, sometimes, than they have been in the past, that the study can be developed.

As a result of archaeological work there is now quite a considerable body of evidence about the development of Scandinavian boats and ships between AD 800 and about AD 1200, but there is not yet sufficient evidence to reach any conclusions about much else, not even the development of other European boatbuilding traditions. There are very many areas of the world where there exist all the geographical features and historic social conditions necessary for the fostering of boatbuilding traditions which have been studied relatively little, or not at all. To take only a few examples—there are the Slav areas fronting on the eastern Baltic, the boats of which may well have had a great influence on developments elsewhere in Northern Europe; the Biscay coasts of France and Spain; the coasts of Portugal; many areas of the Mediterranean; the whole area of Arab influence; South America and Indonesia. The boats and their archaeology in these areas have been studied and published in English only in a fragmentary way, and often very little in other languages. Soon the old traditions of boatbuilding will be absorbed by technological change. The simple boats which satisfied simple needs, which told in their own building so much about their ancestry and about how boats in general could be and were developed from logs, skins and reeds, will have gone with the traditions and cultures of which they were part.

There have been descriptions of ancient boats in literature from time to time since Homer. Some of them are relatively clear, like the famous passage in *De Bello Gallico, Book III*, in which Julius Caesar describes the boats of the Veneti. This is so detailed it might be a contemporary description of the building of a 19th century vessel. Of course, a lot is still missing, and there has been a great deal of discussion of the description, but we can scarcely hope for anything better. Most descriptions are oblique and brief, but nevertheless much can be learned from them, as for instance from the references to boats in the Icelandic sagas. And the written descriptions are virtually all we have to go on for a number of 19th and 20th century boat finds which are not adequately recorded in drawings or photographs and are not conserved.

Works of art provide some evidence about the history of boats, and can be of several kinds. There are actual models of boats, like the model of a Viking cargo ship found while excavating a Scandinavian settlement in Greenland, that is, models made at the time the boats depicted were actually in use and which were, therefore, subject to contemporary criticism. There are carvings on rock, engravings on coins, images on seals and in later years, of course, there are actual paintings. There is a great deal of evidence about the development of boats and ships in and after the 15th century locked away in the art galleries of the world and in carvings, frescoes and decorations, which has never yet been adequately examined.

Of course this evidence can be very controversial and difficult to interpret. Right down to the present day when considering any painting or drawing representing a ship or a boat it has to be asked 'was the artist trying to make an authentic representation of a boat or vessel, or was he giving an impression'? In other words, was the result primarily a work of art or primarily an illustration and if the latter, how valuable is the illustration? Was the artist limited by the materials with which he had to work or the tools he had to use? Was he strongly influenced by contemporary conventions in drawing, carving or engraving, so that he was not able for reasons practical or psychological to make an accurate picture of a boat? If his picture is not accurate are there still things which can be learned from it? Almost always there is something to be learned, some elements which convey accurate information.

Neither written evidence nor the evidence provided by works of art of different kinds provide information of the degree of detail and reliability to be gained from the actual remains of ancient boats. The remains of a boat are a first class primary source, since no longer are there authors and artists between the archaeologist and the reality. But although this sounds very splendid, in fact the problems posed are still enormous because boat finds are never complete. Almost always the upper parts have been destroyed, quite often the boat is in a shattered state and has to be rebuilt and the wood from which it must be reassembled is often distorted, possibly even broken into fragments besides being water-logged and probably badly decayed, so that there are many problems in determining the original shape. Indeed, as part of the new approach to the study of the history of boats a new technical discipline is now growing up in this country and in Denmark and Norway, a system of methods for hypothesising the form and structure of an entire boat from remains which may resemble those of a crashed aeroplane and which may be a thousand years old or more, even, as in the case of the Brigg boat, two and a half thousand years old.

The most important source of information other than major finds of ancient boats is that provided by the boats of the ancient building traditions which still exist today. These are to be found all over the world and they vary from the simplest dugouts and skin boats to the most sophisticated plank-built constructions. They require detailed study by people knowledgeable in the history of boat structures and the mechanics and methods of boat building. There are still great opportunities to do this even in Great Britain and North America. But there will not be for very much longer. Every opportunity should therefore be taken to record in detail not only the structures of old boats, but as far as possible the methods, processes and order by which they are still built and the materials used, and the way they were rowed, sailed, poled or paddled.

There is one other source of information about ancient boats, a source not yet properly explored, but which is beginning to be in the 1970s. This is the construction of full-sized replicas of boat structures. A number of these have been made in recent years, but a proper discipline and philosophy for this type of archaeological model making are only now beginning to be developed. As Sean McGrail has pointed out,[5] this method, straight forward as it seems, is full of pitfalls. He has gone on to indicate a number of requirements which must be satisfied if replica building is to make a serious and successful contribution to research. The subject must be very carefully chosen. The boat must be sufficiently documented or have sufficient remains so that there is a reasonable probability of being able to deduce both the methods of building and the probable shape of missing parts, and indeed the probable shape of the boat herself as a whole. The boat must be sufficiently representative to make the information and experience gained a significant advance in knowledge of boat archaeology generally. The builder or builders of a replica must be chosen very carefully because they must be able to make themselves think in terms of the boat building techniques of the time and place of the original boat and must not impose their own professional solutions from their own experience and training. They must not seek to improve on the original, but must limit themselves to the form and structure of the original, and the materials and methods of the original builders.

Experience has already shown that boatbuilders trained in the modern West European traditions have great difficulty in adapting themselves to the use of solutions to which they themselves were not brought up, but unless they do this the experiment is rendered at least in part invalid. The environment in which the experiment is carried out is very important. The modern boatbuilders must work in circumstances in which they can appreciate some of the problems faced by their predecessors long ago. It is unlikely for instance that a successful experiment can be carried out in a modern boat yard and in a modern industrial environment. In a rural environment which at least approximates the sort of surroundings in which the original boat was built, the various aspects of the experiment will interact naturally and authentically over time. The building techniques to be used should be determined only after exhaustive study of all available evidence. Where there are conscious deviations from what are known to be original methods, the decision to make them and the reasoning behind the decision must be fully recorded. The experimenters must be very clear in their minds as to how far they are seeking an exact replica, how far a boat with the general characteristics of an original, and how the decision as to what to build is likely to affect the value of the whole experiment. Lastly, the trials programme should be carried out rigorously and should be designed preferably on lines which enable the results to be matched with those of other experiments to answer specific questions asked in advance.

Any book such as this, which seeks to present a brief account of aspects of our present knowledge of boat development history, inevitably over simplifies. The development of the boat has a vastly complex history. I have already pointed out that in the modern world very primitive boats which have changed little if at all in thousands of years co-exist with sophisticated structures which have developed much later. Boats which represent both the most basic and the most complex type of floating structure of the age continue to stand side by side on the same beach in

---

[5] *The Building and Trials of the Replica of an Ancient Boat.*

China or Bangladesh, or indeed on the fashionable foreshore at Rio de Janeiro. This was probably as true of 12th century Britain as it was of the mid-20th century before the plastic age began. There has been a constant interplay throughout the history of man's encounter with the sea between different types of boat and between boats in different stages of development, and an almost endless variety of local variations have developed wherever boats have been built in any numbers. This fact will undoubtedly become more apparent as the number of finds of ancient boats increases. The various types of boat in use on one river in Britain provide enough material for a small book, the boats in use on a major river in a heavily populated part of Asia enough for several volumes. A book such as this can do no more than indicate the general nature of a few trends, the general shape of developments in a few areas.

We are at the beginning of the study of boat structure development, and for a long time we shall be at the information gathering stage. Too much time has perhaps been spent in the past in building hypotheses on too slight a basis of evidence, on imposing on the study a premature rigidity when it has scarcely been born.

The next chapter describes a few examples of boats of the old building traditions in Britain, Western Europe and North America which still exist in the modern world, though they are unlikely to do so for very much longer.

Bibliography

BASCH, L.   'Ancient Wrecks and the Archaeology of Ships', 1972

BASS, G. F.   'Cape Gelydonia, a Bronze Age Shipwreck', 1967

BASS, G. F.   *Archaeology Under Water*, 1970

BASS, G. F. (ed)   *A History of Seafaring based on Underwater Archaeology*, 1972

BEAGLEHOLE, J. C. (ed)   *The Endeavour Journal of Joseph Banks, 1760–1771*, 1962

BRUCE-MITFORD, R. L. S.   *Sutton Hoo Ship Burial*, 1968

CARPENTER, A. C. et al   *The Cattewater Wreck*, 1974

CASSON, L.   *Ships and Seamanship in the Ancient World*, 1971

CHAPELLE, H. I.   *American Small Sailing Craft*, 1951

CHRISTENSEN, A. E.   'Boatbuilding Tools and the Process of Learning', 1972

CHRISTENSEN, A. E.   'Lucien Basch: Ancient Wrecks and the Archaeology of Ships. A comment', 1973

CRUMLIN-PEDERSEN, O.   'Skin or Wood', 1972

ELLMERS, D.   *Frühmittelalterliche Handelsschiffahrt in Mittel-und Nordeuropa*, 1972

EVANS, A. C.   'The Sutton Hoo Ship', 1972

FENWICK, V. H. (ed)   *The Graveney Boat*, (in press)

FROST, H.   'The Third Campaign of Excavation of the Punic Ship, Marsala, Sicily', 1974B

GREENHILL, B.   *Boats and Boatmen of Pakistan*, 1971

HAASUM, S.   *Vikingatidens segling och navigation*, 1974

HASSLÖF, O.   'Main Principles in the Technology of Shipbuilding', 1972

HORNELL, J.   *Water Transport*, 1970

LANDSTRÖM, B.   *The Ship*, 1961

MCGRAIL, S.   'Models, Replicas and Experiments in Nautical Archaeology', 1975A

MCGRAIL, S.   'The Brigg Raft Re-excavated', 1975B

MCGRAIL, S., and GREGSON, C.   'Archaeology of Wooden Boats', 1975

MCGRAIL, S. and MCKEE, J. E. G.   *Building and Trials of the Replica of an Ancient Boat: The Gokstad Faering*, 1974

MCKEE, J. E. G.   *Clenched Lap or Clinker*, 1972

MCKEE, J. E. G.   'Flatners', 1970

MARSDEN, P. R. V.   *A Ship of the Roman Period from Blackfriars in the City of London*, undated

MARTIN, C. J. M.   'The Spanish Armada Expedition 1968–70', 1973

NICOLAYSEN, N.   *Viking Ship discovered at Gokstad in Norway*, 1882

OLSEN, O. and CRUMLIM-PEDERSEN, O.   'Skuldelev Ships', 1967

SJØVOLD, T.   *Oseberg Find*, 1969

van der HEIDE, G. D.   'Ship Archaeological Investigations in the Netherlands', 1970

WRIGHT, E. V.   'The Boats of North Ferriby', 1972

Chapter 2

Six Boats and their Builders

Carolina skiff

GEORGE ADAMS LIVES near the little old town of Bath, North Carolina, on a tributary of the Pamlico River which flows into Pamlico Sound, inside the Outer Banks. He works at a filling station for several hours a day. He has a patch of ground where he can grow vegetables. He helps with odd building and carpentry jobs and he fishes, for the family pot mostly. Besides these occupations he builds the simplest kind of boats, flat bottomed boats—skiffs as they are locally known—and George's skiffs were the sweetest little rowing skiffs built for miles around. Nowadays there is no demand for rowing skiffs and he has to build them for outboard motors, which means the sterns are broader and they have a trunk to take the outboard.

The whole tradition of George's skiffs lies in the shaping of the lower edges of the sides. He always builds the same skiff, with some variation of the size, because he always begins with the same side shape. The side shape is the whole secret of his skill as a boatbuilder transmitted to him by his father and his grandfather. In his youth, George could use a single piece of fine white cedar for the side of a 14 ft skiff, that is the side was 14 ft (4·27 m) and the finished skiff was about 12 ft 6 ins (3·81 m). For a long time however such pieces of timber have not been obtainable at the price George's customers can possibly pay, so he now has to use plywood.

He begins building his skiff by cutting out the sides, two identical pieces, straight on top where the curves of the sloping sides will give a natural sheer, subtly shaped in a very elongated and flattened S on the lower edge, so that the bottom of the boat will be slightly raised forward—the heel of the stem just touching the water, the line of the bottom running straight and sloping downwards to just forward of amidships. Here the bottom is gently curved and then it rises in a long straight line to the transom. This fore and aft rocker to the bottom gives a boat which will row well and perform well with a low powered outboard. There is no rocker athwartships; the bottom is flat at its lowest point, just forward of amidships.

34

The whole secret of George's boats is in the bottom curve of the sides, for there is no other cut curve to speak of in these boats, and this bottom curve and the maximum beam between them absolutely determine the whole form of the finished boat. If the sides are not made in one piece each from plywood, apart from the bottom planks of the sides she can be built from stock timber, that is straight planks bought from a timber dealer, without another curve to be cut. Occasionally, although there is more work involved, George builds a skiff with two or three planks, instead of a single sheet of plywood, on each side. It is cheaper in timber, but not in labour, to do this. When he does so he has to shape only two planks, the lowest on each side, and these only on the bottom edges. He fastens cleats across the planks to hold them together and thus act as the skiff's only frames.

A completely flat-bottomed boat with no fore and aft rocker is even simpler to build. The outboard powered skiffs built for the oyster fishery in the creeks in the New Bideford area at the west end of Richmond Bay, Prince Edward Island, Eastern Canada are an interesting example of a boat which has been developed locally in recent years by part-time builders, for a specific commercial purpose. Here the bottom edge of the plywood sides has only to be slightly arched to produce a boat otherwise comprised of straight lines except for the shape of the bottom in plan. This is the simplest of all boats to build.

When he has made up the sides, however he does it, George makes up a solitary mould by tacking together some laths. This mould gives him the beam of the boat and the flare of the sides and, of course, this flare must exactly match the sides he has

Figure 2   An outboard skiff from the Pamlico river area of North Carolina. Note the kitchen chair used by the driver.

Basil Greenhill

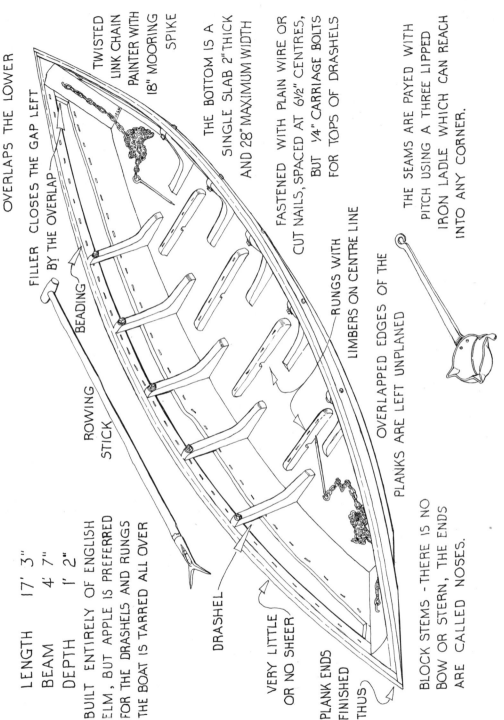

TURF BOAT FROM WESTHAY MOOR
NORTH SOMERSET

LENGTH   17' 3"
BEAM   4' 7"
DEPTH   1' 2"

BUILT ENTIRELY OF ENGLISH
ELM, BUT APPLE IS PREFERRED
FOR THE DRASHELS AND RUNGS
THE BOAT IS TARRED ALL OVER

UPPER STRAKE
OVERLAPS THE LOWER

FILLER CLOSES THE GAP LEFT
BY THE OVERLAP

BEADING

ROWING
STICK

DRASHEL

VERY LITTLE
OR NO SHEER

PLANK ENDS
FINISHED
THUS

BLOCK STEMS – THERE IS NO
BOW OR STERN, THE ENDS
ARE CALLED NOSES.

TWISTED
LINK CHAIN
PAINTER WITH
18" MOORING
SPIKE

THE BOTTOM IS A
SINGLE SLAB 2"THICK
AND 28" MAXIMUM WIDTH

FASTENED WITH PLAIN WIRE OR
CUT NAILS, SPACED AT 6½" CENTRES,
BUT ¼" CARRIAGE BOLTS
FOR TOPS OF DRASHELS

RUNGS WITH
LIMBERS ON CENTRE LINE

OVERLAPPED EDGES OF THE
PLANKS ARE LEFT UNPLANED

THE SEAMS ARE PAYED WITH
PITCH USING A THREE LIPPED
IRON LADLE WHICH CAN REACH
INTO ANY CORNER.

Eric McKee

Figure 3   A Somerset turf boat.

made to give the right rocker to the bottom. Then he fastens the front ends of the sides to the sides of the stem piece of the skiff, and places the mould in such a position that when the sides are wrapped round it the curve of the bottom will give the skiff shape; that is long and sharp in front in plan, the maximum beam aft of amidships. With her flat bottom shaped in this way the skiff is less likely to pound when being rowed or driven in a lop of water, and skiffs do pound if they are not properly shaped.

George draws the ends of his sides together with a Spanish windlass made of rope and a stick twisted in the rope. The straight upper edges of the sides then assume a curve in profile, which gives the boat a graceful sheer. He cuts the transom and fits it to the ends of the sides. When he has done this he turns the half-built skiff over and nails a chine beam along inside each side at the bottom and then cuts off the projecting corners of the chine beams and the sides to form a bed for the boat's bottom. Then he planks the bottom by laying on planks athwartships taking great care to set the annual rings curve down on the chine, and that each plank is wedged in close against its neighbour before it is fastened to the chine beam and the sides. When planking is finished he saws off the ends of the planks. Thus the bottom of the boat never exists at all as a separate unit. It is something the shape of which emerges from the bottom curve of the sides and the beam measurement. A few thwarts and some red paint, and the skiff is finished and George goes and gives a hand in building a frame house or barn. Probably the skiff's owner will give her a name, certainly she will be required by North Carolina State legislation to carry a number on her bows.

George with his two secrets of side shape and cross section amidships is a very long way from the world of full-time professional boatbuilders of the last years of wooden boatbuilding, and from the working world of urban boatyards using building techniques and terminology which, though they vary greatly locally, are comprehensible throughout the trade.

Somerset turf boat

Like the housebuilder with his use of stock timber (straight cut planks from a lumber yard), George is still essentially of the industrial world in which such material is commercially available. His British near equivalent of the first half of the 20th century built double-ended, flat-bottomed boats for carrying cut turf or peat down the canals or over the floods from the peat beds of the Somerset Levels around Shapwick and Mere to the roadsides where it was collected for sale. They were used for general farm transport purposes, like carts or pick-up trucks, as well.

This man was a small farmer or a village carpenter who might also be the undertaker and coffin maker. He scarcely thought in terms of plank-built boats at all, and the boats he built were probably the oldest in design and structure of any in use in 20th century Britain. He used simple natural shapes, grown curved timbers and forked branches as they came to hand. He built clinker, clenched lap, because it was easier to build in this way, rather than a boat with a smooth skin, and he clearly revealed one of the factors in the origin of clinker construction in that he did not bother to smooth off the upper edges of his lower strakes, which is not necessary, but left them rough and with the bark still on them. Technically, of course he need not

Figure 4   This turf boat, the *Peat Princess,* was built for the National Maritime Museum in 1970 by Stanley Baker of West Hay, who had built a number of the boats in former years. He has roughly finished off the upper edge of the lower strake. The piece cut off to give the arch of the lower edge is resting on the trestles. The bottom is made of two broad planks glued together because timber wide enough for a single piece is no longer available.

National Maritime Museum

have smoothed off the lower edges either, except for the bottom strake, but he did, for appearance's sake. In the massive stem and stern post of his boat he gave evidence of its probably remote past as a dugout, as did the bottom, made from a single piece of wood from a very large tree. He was not concerned with stock timber bought from a merchant but with what could be made out of a suitable tree. The smooth lines in his boat were cut in the rough boards only when and where necessary and he never worked with a straight-sided plank at all. In reverse of George Adam's building process he began with the bottom, added the 'noses' or stem and stern post, then the first strake. The knees were then cut from grown crooks and fitted and the second strake added. This strake was cut down at either end, so as to keep the sheer as low as possible to minimise the effect of wind on the boat and make it easy to pole. His tarred boat might be used for any farm purpose when the floods came, as they used to before the big drainage ditches were dug, the last of them in the 1960s. His boat had no name, but the parts of it were named in strictly local terminology, quite unrecognisable to other boatmen—*hrung* for a floor timber, *drashels* for the side frames.

Cornish clinker-built working boat

These two men, George Adams and the undertaker/turf boat builder of the Somerset levels of the 1920s, both built boats very old in form but of simple construction, boats which served their purposes well but which were not amenable to much development. There are structural parallels between a turf boat and a medieval cog, between a Carolina skiff and some boats of the Netherlands in the first millennium AD, and flat bottomed boats are used today, and have been used widely across the world for many centuries. But an ordinary clinker-built working boat of the late 19th century is much more part of the mainstream of North European boat building traditions.

A boat of this kind spends the winter in a barn by a farmhouse in southern England. The farmhouse was built in the early 1880s when trade on the tidal river, which runs half a mile away down across the fields in clear view of the front windows, was booming. The local copper mines were still prosperous, as were the brickworks, quarries and blacksmiths, the arsenic works and the riverside dealers in coal and fertilisers. In a local shipyard, some years before the house was built, a trading smack was launched. This smack's principal employment was to bring the groceries from the town on the sea coast up the river on the flood tide and land them at the quay on the river bank down below the farmhouse. Pack donkeys and carts pulled by horses took the groceries to the shops in the villages up the valley which ran down to the river at the quay. The coal for the villages came to the quay from South Wales in schooners, whose crews were among the best customers of the little beer shop in the cottage by the limekilns at the back of the quay. For manure on the farm they often used a load of horse dung, fermenting and stinking, from the streets of the town on the sea coast, brought up on the flood tide in sailing barges whose crews never seemed to notice the stench, though they slept in the little hutch-like cuddies while the barges lay in the creek by the quay.

When the house was built the estate specified that the dairy and the kitchen should have floors of blue stone slate from the Delabole Quarries in North Cornwall. The slates, each about 3 ft square and $1\frac{1}{2}$ in thick were brought down from the quarries in wagons drawn by oxen to Porth Gaverne on the coast, and loaded into smacks which lay aground on the beach. They were loaded by women who wore long aprons of white leather and broad brimmed hats. The cargoes were taken by a builder's merchant in a village on the river bank a mile above the quay below the farmhouse. Often a smack from Porth Gaverne would take on board a boat built at a yard in the village to take back home for the local fishery, for the village had a great name for its boats, which were exported in visiting vessels all around the west coast of Britain.

It is not too much to say that the whole life of the valley depended upon the tidal river, and had done so for a thousand years or more. Scandinavian raiders came up on the tide in great clinker-built boats and landed in a creek which still bears their name. Everything for the big house of the estate, all the furniture and tapestries, the kitchen and dairy equipment, the gardener's tools, all the foods which were not available locally, came up the river in smacks and barges.

The river was alive with boats, ferries, salmon-fishing boats, boats used to collect seaweed from the beaches at the mouth of the river for use as fertilisers, farm boats used for family and working transport up and down.

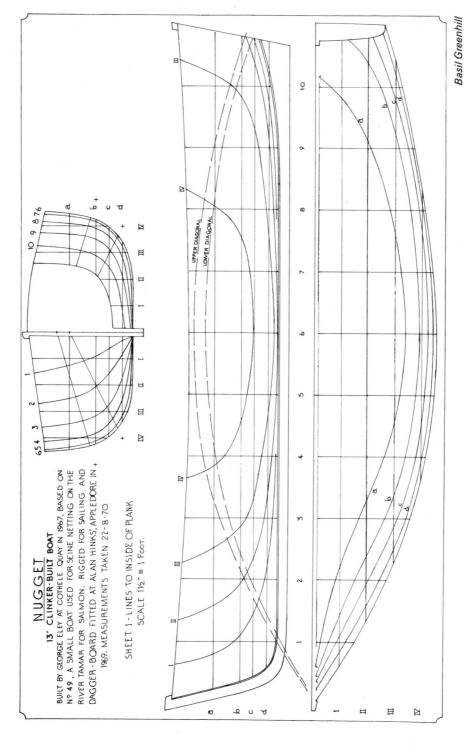

NUGGET

13' CLINKER-BUILT BOAT

BUILT BY GEORGE ELEY AT COTHELE QUAY IN 1967, BASED ON
N° 49, A SMALL BOAT USED FOR SEINE NETTING ON THE
RIVER TAMAR FOR SALMON. RIGGED FOR SAILING AND
DAGGER-BOARD FITTED AT ALAN HINKS, APPLEDORE IN +
1969. MEASUREMENTS TAKEN 22·8·70

SHEET 1 – LINES TO INSIDE OF PLANK

SCALE 1½" ≡ 1 FOOT.

UPPER DIAGONAL
LOWER DIAGONAL

Basil Greenhill

Figure 5   Lines of the 13 ft (3·96 m) ketches' boat *Nugget*, drawn by Eric McKee from measurements taken from the
boat.

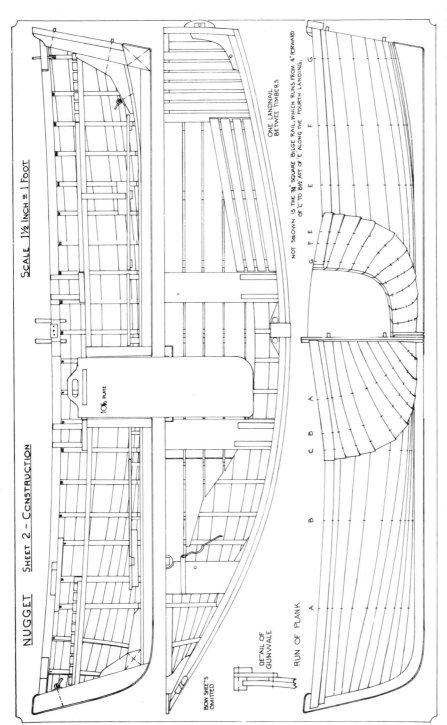

Figure 6   Structural drawing of *Nugget*, drawn by Eric McKee from the boat.

Basil Greenhill

The farmhouse was built in the yard in front of a much older building, a cottage which was demoted to become the dairy. The old barns which were around the old farm cottage still stand and in one of them each winter lies the 13 ft (3.96 m) clinker-built wooden pulling and sailing boat. She was built on the quay of larch from a local wood lot, with local oak for the ribs and knees, elm for the transom and imported pine for the thwarts and gunwales. She was built as a copy of an old boat which worked off the quay in the net-fishing for salmon on the bend just below, by a skilled craftsman in wood, who built boats from time to time. The original boat had been built seventy years before on the river bank half a mile upstream, by a housebuilder who turned out a few boats, as one to be sold to a small smack or ketch as its working boat. So her shape, and the shape of her copy which lies in the barn each winter, was the one traditional in the late 19th century in this part of Britain for the work, very full in the stern so that she could carry weights like a kedge anchor and chain without sinking herself to an unreasonable depth or becoming unstable, sharp and narrow forward so that she could be pulled easily, Figures 5 and 6.

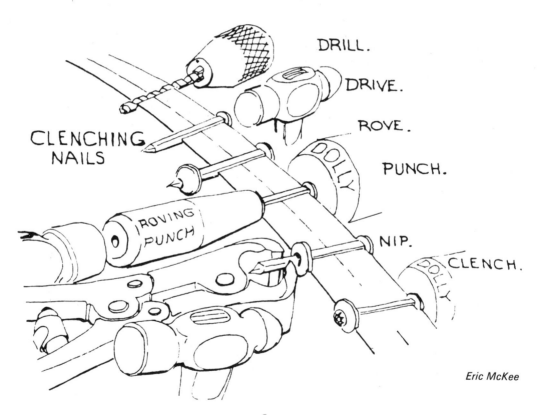

Eric McKee

Figure 7   Fastening strakes in clinker building—a common method—and the tools used.

Figure 8   A clinker-built boat under construction. The display in the National Maritime Museum illustrating methods traditionally used at Charlton on the south bank of the Thames near Greenwich. Half moulds are used as guides for the setting of the planking. These are guides to shape, playing no active role; the strakes are not wrapped around them and indeed in this photograph the midships mould, lightly placed in position, has fallen down.

The men who built her worked in a tradition as old, or older, originally than that of George Adams and the Somerset turf boat builders, but developed into something infinitely more complex to become the main tradition of Northern European boatbuilding. A clenched lap or clinker-built wooden boat at its best, which is by no means its most expensive or sophisticated, is a work of craftsmanship so developed as to verge upon art. Bob May, who built the original smack's boat, did not think in terms of an ideal boat he would set out and build, but rather of something of roughly the right shape he could put together from available timber, a gale-felled larch tree, some oak posts, some deals. Apart from the keel every line in the boat is shaped and curved. The planks, scarfed together to make the strakes, are all curved and recurved, high in the centre, dipping towards the ends and turning up again as may be necessary to take their place in the shell which they comprise when joined together. The strakes were fastened together with copper rivets, driven through from the outside and mushroomed out over round copper washers called roves, on the inside, see Figure 7. The curves were developed as the boat was made, strake added to strake, by a process called spiling.[1] This shell, formed with a few moulds, became the boat when the stiffening ribs and the gunwale had been added. Bob May used one or possibly two moulds to help him develop the shape of his boat, but half a century before she would have been built by eye, with struts and guys, if they were necessary, and clamps and wedges to hold the planks while they were joined to make the shell of the boat, Figure 8.

There is nothing in the boat in the barn which would not have been in her model, that is, nothing which could not have been made locally and cheaply, except the copper rivets with which she is fastened, for the owners of the original smack's boat, like almost all old style boatmen throughout the world, were poor, and they could not afford to buy anything they could not at a pinch make themselves, even if it were available. They scraped up a living, or more likely part of a living, from the water.

The boat in the barn has thole pins in place of imported iron crutches; the mast is a single piece of solid wood, short enough to be stowed in the boat when not in use; there is no rigging. The mast is kept up by a crutch of iron made years ago in a local blacksmith's shop, attached to the after side of the fore girt. The sails, either a spritsail or a lug, depending on the circumstances of the boat's use, are of heavy brown proofed natural fibre canvas. She is usually sailed in the river without the drop keel, but if sustained sailing to windward is needed she has a single dagger plate of sheet iron.

Each summer the boat is carried down the road to the quay on a pair of wheels and she is used off the quay for pleasuring up and down the river. Expeditions are arranged to suit the tide. She is pulled and sailed upstream to the tide head on the afternoon flood and back on the evening ebb, six hours of pulling and sailing on the puffs that come down out of the side valleys, downstream on the ebb beyond the bend where the river opens into the mile-wide estuary and into the creeks that lie beyond on the early flood, and then back when the evening flood has grown strong. For this sort of work, with five minutes of fast sailing on a puff, five minutes of pulling and then another puff, the spritsail, so quickly brailed up and set again, and the simple lug are ideal, with a mast which will stow in the boat to reduce windage when the breeze sets in contrary in the narrow river.

The boat is a family boat of the farm, an object held in some affection as a favourite pony or dog might be. But rather more than that, there is something of an overlay of respect for the craftsman's skill of a very special type.

In only one respect does the farm boat differ from her ancestors. Because there are two boats at the farm and it is often necessary to distinguish them in conversation, she has a name, as a big ship must have under the successive Merchant Shipping Acts since 1786. She is not, like the farm boats when the house was built, simply 'the boat' as it might be 'the cart', 'the wagon', 'the barn' or other items of essential every day equipment which it would never occur to anyone to name.

[1] McKee, *Clenched Lap or Clinker*, available from the National Maritime Museum, Greenwich and International Marine Publishing Company, Camden, Maine. The most complete description of clinker boatbuilding yet published.

She is called *Nugget*, a round brown object which is worth much more than might at first appear.

North American lobster boat

The river runs out into the Atlantic. Two thousand five hundred miles away to the west is the coast of Nova Scotia. West of Cape Breton Island is the Gulf of St Lawrence and lying something like a foetus in the womb of the Gulf is Prince Edward Island, once a British colony, now for more than a century a Province of the Canadian Confederation. At the west end of the Island is Port Hill, a great centre of the Island's 19th century shipbuilding industry, which, in the 1880s when the farmhouse was being built, still provided a great many ships, barques, brigs, brigantines and schooners for the expanding British merchant shipping industry. Like the valley upstream of the farmhouse the area was industrialised then but now, like the valley, it has reverted to a deeply rural state. It lies at the back of the great Richmond Bay and off the Bay shallow creeks reach far into the land, carrying with them the smell of the tide and evening light of a peculiar clarity.

In one of the creeks Bob Strongman kept his 45 ft (13.72 m) lobster boat in the summer. In the winter when the snow blizzards sweep over the Island and the sea freezes solid in every bay and creek, the boat is hauled out and propped up high above the tide line, Figure 9.

The boat is narrow for her length and open for the greater part of it, with a short cuddy forward and a steering shelter. Her bows flam out, that is, they flare so that a choppy sea is thrown back on itself as her 70 hp converted Chevrolet automobile engine drives her into it. There are a couple of bunks, a cedar bucket as a seat of ease and a stove in the cuddy, but Bob Strongman rarely spent a night on board. Most of his days in the short two months of the lobster season were spent in the boat on the water, but he slept at home. He drove down the red dirt road to Brown's Creek in the big pickup in the early light each morning, pushed the high-sided, flat-bottomed oyster boat which he used as a tender to the big Cape Islander off the red beach into

Figure 9   A lobster boat, of similar design to Bob Strongman's, hauled out at the beginning of winter in Prince Edward Island. The pickup and the hut for the gear are part of the equipment of every lobsterman.   *Basil Greenhill*

the water and pulled himself out to the white-painted Cape Islander. He left the dory, as he called the oyster boat without respect for the formal use of terms, on the mooring, and motored out across the bay in the Cape Islander to the narrows of the entrance, where the sand is yellow instead of red, and then out into the Atlantic. Here he hauled his fleet of pots, the long flat-bottomed pots of the North American lobster fishery, a fleet of two hundred or more and baited and set them again as necessary. It was a hard life but in a good season he could make enough to live comfortably, with a big late model car as well as the pickup and a nicely heated modern house, with the aid of the oyster fishery in the shallow waters of the bay in season and some long-lining for cod out in the Atlantic in the summer.

The Cape Islander is lightly built of cedar. She is quite unlike any of the boats so far described. She is a smooth-skinned boat built partly on a skeleton of pre-erected frames. As such she represents an entirely different kind of thinking about boatbuilding from the Carolina skiff, or the peat boat or the clinker-built smack's boat. We do not yet know enough about the origin of this kind of thinking about boats. It may have existed in different degrees and forms in different places in history. As far as Northern Europe is concerned it seems to have come into general fashion only in the 1400s and developed very gradually. Briefly, the men who built the lobster boat thought of her, not as a shell of timber strengthened as may be necessary after completion with internal stiffening, but as a skeleton of ribs covered with a fabric of planks to keep the water out. They decided her shape from the shape of her skeleton, rather than making the skeleton to fit the boat.

She was conceived, not as a complete shell of planks but as a shape indicated by a series of rib-like formers, frames and moulds, the beginnings of the skeleton of a boat. She was thought of from inside out. Some of these shapes were actual timbers which later were to comprise some of the frames of the boat. Some of them were floors, the lower part of these timbers, which lie across the keel. Some were temporary patterns, moulds as they are called in boatbuilding, shapes made from light timber which were removed before the boat was finished. Many of the lobster boat's frames were not made until after some of the planking had been erected around the first frames, floors and moulds, and these later frames were shaped to fit the planks as they had formed up on the basic skeleton. Indeed the majority of the frames in the boat were, in fact, literally pressed into shape inside the planking, because they were made of light flexible timber, softened by steam so that they could be bent into shape inside the planks. But this does not alter the fundamental difference between the lobster boat and the other boats described.

She was built on the mainland of New Brunswick by a full-time boatbuilder whose big shed usually has a Cape Islander under construction for the local lobster fishery of the Gulf. Besides the big boats he makes smaller ones, dories and punts; he makes furniture and turns out the local road signs, builds wooden sheds and repairs decaying wharves. His approach is thoroughly modern. He uses power tools, orders his timber in bulk, uses glues and laminates and is part of a complex industrial society which interlocks over half the earth.

The boat was brought to Port Hill not by water but on a low-loader across the

Basil Greenhill

Figure 10   A lobster boat building on Beals Island, off Jonesport, Maine. The wooden trough alongside is the steam box. Filled with steam from a simple boiler the planks are softened in it, if necessary, to make it possible to wrap them around the frames. The 16 ft (4·88 m) boat in the foreground is a miniature of the big vessel.

ferry from Cape Tormentine to Borden and launched into the water for the first time in Brown's Creek. Because of her light construction her working life will be limited—ten or fifteen years may see her through. Her shape is very characteristic and is a local variation on one common all the way from Connecticut to Cape Breton. The long narrow Cape Islanders began in southern Nova Scotia at Cape Sable and at Jonesport in Maine when motor engines were first used in the lobster fishery. The long narrow shape was meant to give speed to low-powered boats. Now the stern has been widened out and in some versions, like those built in the Island and in northern New Brunswick with their flaring bows, a considerable degree of refinement of design has been achieved. To Bob Strongman his boat was strictly a tool, a part of earning his living. He did not regard her as anything special at all. As far as he was concerned her status was pretty well the same as that of his big Chevrolet pickup which he changed every four or five years. He would no more think of giving her a name than he did the pickup. So, like the great majority of the world's working boats, she has not got one. She is simply 'the boat' and he would never have used her for pleasure. In fact, he did not like driving her very much.

Bob's grandfather came to the Island to be one of the sailmakers for the wooden sailing ships which were built in the next creek to the west. His family came from north Devon and one way or another have been people of the sea for many generations.

Norwegian clinker-built pram

The winters in Prince Edward Island are no more rugged than those of Norway and the winter days are longer in the Gulf of St Lawrence. Neils Andersen has a boat he keeps on an almost tideless inlet off a fjord to the south of Oslo in Norway. She is a pram, a clinker-built boat whose basic structure is quite different from that of either of the other two clinker-built boats described in this chapter.

Neils is a small farmer whose holding is in a valley which runs down to the inlets from the mountains. He does some fishing with the pram, largely for the family's own cooking pot. The boat is built with only nine strakes, three in the flat bottom, three in each of the curved sides. She is long and narrow and her cross section amidships is like a half circle with the bottom cut off, but despite this shape she is very stable, especially when she has been ballasted down with the weight of two people and their gear. She is also extremely seaworthy and because she has a long skeg aft and a shorter one forward she can be rowed easily. Not all prams have these skegs and those which do not have them are extremely difficult to steer when rowing in a breeze or a rough sea.

The pram has a transom at each end and her planks are brought up in the bow tapering to the bow transom above the water instead of to a stem like all the other boats described in this chapter. She was built in a shed belonging to a pram-builder higher up the fjord. This pram-builder was also a part-time farmer like Neils and supplied nets and gear to fishermen and bought fish from them. When he built the

Figure 11   Building a small pram in Blagdon's boatyard at Plymouth, England, on one mould, in 1973. In pram building at this yard the moulds are often used only as guides. The clutter is typical of boatbuilding shops the world over.   *Basil Greenhill*

pram he followed a tradition which his father taught him by example and by a few words of explanation. The boatbuilder's father did not believe it was possible to communicate the ancient mystery of this specialised form of clinker boatbuilding in words, but only by example and trial and error, and then by trial and error again until it was right. Such a method of training, the lack of challenge in the tradition, the unquestioned following of what had been painfully learned before, led not only to a complete absence of innovation but in due course to a positive inability to innovate. The pram was almost exactly like every other pram built in the neighbourhood in the last five generations, and differed from prams built by other neighbouring pram-builders only in a few small details which were always the same. She was built purely as a shell with no moulds, not even the transoms were fitted until the shell of planks was complete. The curves of the planks were obtained and held with struts from the floor and from the roof beam of the shed in which she was built. Some local pram-builders used one mould amidships as a guide to the creation of the shape as they planked up. Like the farm boat in England she was fastened with rivets mushroomed over roves.

National Maritime Museum

Figure 12   This pram in the National Maritime Museum was built in Knivsvik, Holmsbu, Norway, about 1910 by Kristian Johansen and was used in the herring fishery in the Oslo fjord.

It has not yet been possible to find positive evidence for the existence of prams before the second half of the 18th century, but it is very probable that the type is much older. It may, in fact, represent a strand in European clinker boatbuilding tradition which goes back to the Utrecht ship of AD 800 or even earlier—see page 190. There is some evidence in graves excavated near the site of the Norwegian Viking trading town of Kaupang that some people may have been buried in boats which had the basic characteristics of prams in the 9th and 10th centuries AD. The use of transoms at both ends of a boat seems to represent a logical and sound way of solving the problem of the plank ends—simply by having them all out of the water—and one which has similarities with the medieval hulk—see page 85.

Prams are easier to build than almost any other kind of clinker-built boat. The shed in which the pram was built measured 25 ft by 26 ft (7·62 m by 7·92 m). It had an earth floor so as to keep the atmosphere permanently damp and prevent the timber of the prams drying out in warm summers and splitting and spoiling. The pram was built of unseasoned wood, a single tree of pine which was felled by the boatbuilder and sawn up tangentially to give ten planks, enough for the pram and one to spare. Crook-grown timber was used for the frames and knees, but nowadays prams are built with glued laminated frames. Because the building of a pram is less complicated than other kinds of clinker-built boat, builders in the pram tradition were looked down upon somewhat by the neighbours who built the various types of keel boats traditional on the Oslo fjord.

But for all her apparent simplicity, Neils Andersen's pram is, in fact, a highly sophisticated work of engineering in wood. She has the very minimum of frames, made from crooks of branches or visible roots chosen from the tree before it was felled. There is nothing wasted in her. The frames were of course shaped and trimmed to fit the planking after the shell was complete. She too is a work of art as well as a work of engineering.

Neils Andersen occasionally sails the pram under a small spritsail. She has no centre board but she has an outboard motor under which she handles extremely well. She has no name. She is just 'the boat' and the family all regard her as they do the dog, and the pony that lives in the paddock behind the house.

Bangladesh boat

Lal Mian lives in Bangladesh. His home is a hut of woven bamboo with a corrugated iron roof and a floor of hard dry mud. It stands under betel nut palms on the corner of a little flat topped hill about twenty feet high. All round is a great plain stretching as far as can be seen in every direction. This plain is dotted with little wooded hills, like the one on which Lal Mian lives, each with its cluster of bamboo huts. The plain laps at the foot of the hills like a placid sea, and the analogy is more apposite than it might at first seem, because for four or five months of the year, from June to November, during and after the south west monsoon, the plain is under water, perhaps six or more feet under water, and the small wooded hills become islands.

Lal Mian lives in what in Europe and America we should consider to be intolerable poverty. His total income is about £50 or $125 a year. His assets comprise the right to cultivate a bit of land around his mud and thatched hut on another man's wooded island, the use of another tiny piece of land in the flood area near the island, his cooking pots and his hookah pipe and some tiny pieces of jewellery his wife wears, their clothes and the rags the children wear—and his boat.

Most of his money comes through his boat. He operates it rather like a country hire car, taking people to and from the big river where the motor launches run to the district town thirty miles away, carrying small cargoes of rice, jute and pots. The boat was built on the river bank on the outskirts of the district town—on *char*, a stretch of land which exists as dry land for a few months in winter and is submerged for the rest of the year under the flood. The boat is about 30 ft (9·14 m) long, narrow, round-bottomed, shaped like a slice of melon, but with the raised pointed bow stretching low over the water and the stern curved up higher and more steeply. Her greatest beam is in the stern. Here she can carry weights and here Lal Mian lives under a woven bamboo cover called a *chauni* with one of his sons for the six months of the year the boat operates, when the north west storms of May and the south west monsoon in June have drowned the greater part of the countryside.

The boat was built of planks joined edge to edge, half overlapping, with the edges of the planks rabbeted so that the outer skin of the boat is smooth, to make a great shell which was almost completed before the first floor timbers were shaped to match and fit it. Her conception was the laying of the keel plank along a row of small hardwood logs lying like railway sleepers, side by side at regular intervals. This keel plank was a little thicker than the other planks in the boat were going to be. It was held firm with bamboo pegs and with short lengths of jute cord passed through paired holes drilled in at intervals of about 1½ ft and pegged into the ground at either end. The keel plank was shored up at either end with baulks of timber to make a low curve where the bows of the boat were to be and a much steeper higher curve in the stern. To each end of the keel plank *golois*, that is shaped solid blocks of wood which mark the extremities of one of these Bangladesh boats, were fastened. They were roughly hewn to shape at this stage with adzes and only later cut to their final form.

Basil Greenhill

Figure 13   Fitting a plank at the bow of a big motor cargo boat under construction in Bangladesh.

The shell of the boat was then built up plank by plank. First the garboards, the planks next to the keel, were shaped and fitted and held into place with ropes and wedges and shores. Some of the hardwood planks which were to lie in parts of the boat where they were steeply curved had to be softened so that they could be forced into position. In Europe or America they would have been softened with steam in a rough steam chest like that in Figure 10. In Bangladesh they were charred on the side of the plank which was to be the inside of the curve in a shallow trough of glowing shavings.

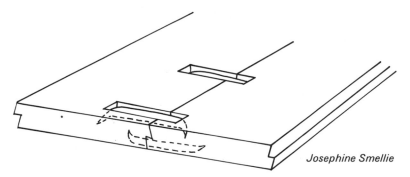

Josephine Smellie

Figure 14 The system principally used in joining the edges of the strakes in boatbuilding in Bangladesh.

At the first fitting a plank might show need of a good deal of reshaping. It was then scored with a sharp nail to mark the necessary alterations, removed, cut again, presented again to the boat, removed and shaped again and finally the edges rabbeted with a fine chisel. Then it was fitted again and a difficult curve might call for levers, clamps, guide lines and wedges and the combined strength of all the labourers and *mistris* at work on the boat before it was finally secured in position, Figure 13. Once in position it was held there by a system of guys and wedges and clamps and struts, while shallow slots about $\frac{1}{8}$ in (.32 cms) deep, 2 ins (5.1 cms) long and $\frac{1}{4}$ in (.64 cms) wide, were cut across the seam at intervals of about every 2 ins (5.1 cms). Into these slots staples were driven to hold the planks together, edge to edge, Figure 14. As soon as a plank had been joined to its neighbour the clamps were removed and the struts and guy lines kept in position while the next plank was fitted and shaped and fastened. The planks were added in pairs, one on each side. This helped to produce the symmetrical hull. A constant check was kept on the hull shape by measuring with a stick from a thin line suspended from the stern *goloi* to the bow *goloi*. The planking was so developed that by the measure of this stick the distance from the centre line to the planking at the same distance from the keel plank at either side was the same. No moulds of any kind were used. The shell of the boat was shaped by eye and the swinging stick, which was in fact a stalk of jute, and as she was built she was surrounded by a forest of struts and guy lines holding the planks in tension. Only when the shell was almost complete were the frames shaped and

Alan Villiers

Figure 15   As a Bangladesh boat is built she is surrounded by struts and guylines holding the planks in tension.

inserted. Their function was to strengthen the boat and to hold the shell of planks in shape. They were in three separate pieces, not a continuous 'U' shape, but a floor piece to stretch across the keel and join up the planks at the bottom of the boat, a corner piece at the turn of the bilge where the boat's sides turned upward and a rib to strengthen her side. Far from being joined together into a continuous frame, they did not even touch one another, but overlapped with their ends several inches apart.

The building of this Bangladesh boat represented perhaps the purest form of 'shell construction', that is the building of the outside skin of the boat first, which can readily be seen in the modern world. The purity of the form is all the more apparent in that although Lal Mian's boat had strengthening frames in three parts, if such they can be called, many big Bangladesh cargo boats, 50 ft (15·24 m) long or more, have no frames at all. Some have a few floor timbers. As they grow older and weaker they may be framed up with bilge pieces and side pieces but they are not only conceived as shells, they are used and sailed as shells with minimal strengthening frames, if any above the floors, for years on end. Some of them never have any frames at all although they spend years earning their living on the great rivers.

The men who built Lal Mian's boat were *mistris*, itinerant boatbuilders, very simple men, skilled in a trade which they had learned from their fathers and grandfathers. They had learned by copying, by holding the tools and using them in the way their fathers did, with almost no explanation, trying and trying again until, as the years passed, they mastered the complex process of judging and shaping the

Basil Greenhill

Figure 16   In a common boatbuilding tradition in Bangladesh the frames are shaped and inserted only when the shell of planks is almost complete. The vessel shown is designed to be fitted with a motor.

Basil Greenhill

Figure 17   The staples joining the planks together; the separate floor timber and ribs, linked only by the planking; and the tools used by boatbuilders are all shown in this photograph of a small boat under construction in Bangladesh.

Basil Greenhill

Figure 18 Bows of a frameless cargo boat photographed near Narayanganj, Bangladesh.

planks to make the strakes of the boats. Such a method of teaching made for extreme conservatism. Although other methods are used in building boats in Bangladesh, there was little or no innovation in the lives of these men, nor in the lives of the smiths who accompanied them, and who made all the fastenings for the boat from iron rod and strip in the little smithy they built from woven bamboo under shade trees on a wooded island adjacent to the *char*.

This conservatism among boatbuilders, shown at its extreme among the illiterate and very simple men who build boats in Bangladesh, but paralleled in Norway and Britain and the United States, is extremely important in the history of boats. Because of the methods of communicating the secrets of the trade to future generations, boats have been very slow indeed to change. In many parts of the world, they are still being built today much as they were many hundreds of years ago, sometimes more than one thousand years ago. This means that the evidence presented by boats built in the last years of wooden boatbuilding is relevant to the problems of the evolution of boats, moreover the small boats of recent years often show some of the basic characteristics of the great ships of the period in which they first evolved. A number of examples of this kind of survival will be investigated as the argument in this book develops.

Of course, Lal Mian was not the first owner of the boat. He had found her more or less abandoned, and paid forty or fifty hard-earned rupees to the man who said he owned her and who allowed him to take her away. Lal Mian himself has to have the boat because without her he could not live. He has not enough land to feed himself, his wife and his sons and daughters. If he had he would not go away in the boat, but be a cultivator and stay at home. To be a cultivator on your own land is considered good. Boats are for those who have not got enough land, and to be a boatman is to be a low man on the totem pole.

When he is away in the boat Lal Mian has with him a pot for cooking rice, a small earthenware stove, a frying pan, a plate or two, some bottles and a tin mug. He has one blanket but no change of clothes. He has one hurricane lamp and oil in a bottle and a fishing net. His diet is enriched by fish he catches as he goes along and by wild vegetables, growing out on the *char* land at some places during certain seasons of the year. The secret of Lal Mian's existence lies in an understanding he has with a merchant in the district town who gives him regular cargoes of pots for the homesteads in the area around Lal Mian's own tiny strip of land on someone else's island. Lal Mian delivers the cargoes relatively intact and undamaged and the merchant, to whom Lal Mian is in debt as a result of money needed to marry off a daughter (which took more than a whole year's income) and to finance a small law case both in the same year, is lucky to have this regular work.

Lal Mian's world comprises the rivers spread over about three thousand square miles of country. He has an intimate acquaintance with almost every yard of the main routes, so that he can find his way along them even at night. He learned the ways and the channels partly when he was working with his father, as his own son is now working with him, and partly by experience since. This world is one of high colour, the continually changing shades of the rivers, the dramatic pageantry of the clouds, the incredible sunsets during the south west monsoon. It is a very hot and humid world, when at times every living thing seems to gasp for air and the heat strikes at the back of the very eye balls. It is a world of toil at the oar, at the tow rope, at the bamboo pole. It is a noisy shouting sort of a world, with busy waterside markets where boats lie in their dozens, half beached, the crews hawking their wares in strident variations of basic Bengali. But it is also a quiet world of still evenings by lonely islands in great rivers and a leisurely world with little to do sometimes except trim the great bellying squaresail of the boat and to steer her. Lal Mian's boat has no name. It would never occur to him that it was right to give a boat a name. Some of the motor launches which come near his home have names painted on them in garish colours, but this practice is an innovation from another world and has nothing to do with the peasant boatman living on the border-line of existence who will cease to work only because he cannot work any more and so must die. In his way of life Lal Mian is much more typical of the boatman in the history of the world than are prosperous Bob Strongman and Neils Anderson.

The six boats described in this chapter have one thing in common—they were built as tools of work, used to earn all or part of a living. They are not playthings, luxury items, articles of conspicuous expenditure or social prestige. The boat in the barn no longer has to earn her living, though she was built to do so and she lives as if she still

Basil Greenhill

Figure 19   A boat similar to Lal Mian's vessel. She is carrying cattle and their fodder. The single mast is lowered in its tabernacle. Note the flat-bottomed boat, see Chapter 12, she is also carrying as cargo, not as her own boat.

had to earn her living. Bob Strongman with his television and his pickup and his warm house, and Lal Mian with his diet of wild vegetables and fish he has caught himself, and his one set of clothes, both look on their boats in the same way, as a means to a living, not in any way endowed with personalities or to be named or otherwise specially regarded among possessions.

All these boats were built with local materials readily available, by men with highly developed special skills which they had learned by example and practice. They were built to be tools and servants, like carts, sheds and trucks, tractors and ploughs. In the history of man as a boatbuilder, most boats have been built in the way that Lal Mian's was, as a job done by very simple men who moved from place to place always doing the same work, always building the same type of boat or group of boats. No element of rent or capital investment was involved, except that made by the future owner in the raw materials of the boat's construction.

These men had something else in common too. They did not use drawings. Nowadays, of course, we think on paper, all planning begins on the drawing board and any big building project, be it a ship, house or factory, requires literally dozens, perhaps hundreds of drawings, which no-one will act without. So prevalent has this method of communication of ideas become that even in simple small scale craftsman's work, drawings are regarded as essential.

The drawings of course must be accompanied by written instructions, and again so prevalent has communication and training by writing become that, as with drawings, we have forgotten that there are other means of conveying information. I have touched once or twice on the significance of the apprenticeship system in its various forms, training without drawings, writing, perhaps even speech, for the development of the boat. We must remember that writing particularly, and to a lesser extent drawing, as a means of universal communication is a very modern phenomenon and it has been largely confined to Northern Europe, North America and their spheres of influence. But even there until very recently only a fraction of the population has been able to use these methods of communication. Universal adult literacy is really a product of the 20th century.

Moreover the construction of boats by the development of a shell fabric is a building method which does not lend itself to communication by drawing, or indeed by anything except example; it does not lend itself to innovation. It is only with the development of the skeleton building technique, the lobster boat technique in its various forms, when the shape of the finished boat is dependent on the shape of a skeleton of frames and therefore upon the shape of each individual frame, that innovation becomes readily possible and thinking on the drawing board a practical method of developing design. As far as Britain is concerned it was after the almost universal adoption of this method of construction for big vessels in the late 1500s that drawings on paper of ships' hull shapes first begin to appear and probably to have been used.

The examples I have given in this chapter are all except one from the western world. The greater part of this book, because it deals particularly with the development of the boat in Northern Europe, Britain and North America, is concerned with the boatbuilding traditions of the western world, and those of the great majority of the rest of the world, including Japan, which are full of parallels and similarities with the traditions of the west.

The boatbuilding traditions of China, however, are substantially different. It has been suggested that the differences may arise in the main from the possibility that a principal influence in the development of boats in China may have been the raft (see Chapters 4 and 5), while in the western world the principal influence very probably was the hollowed-out and shaped log, the dugout. Rafts cannot be used in northern climates at sea because people cannot survive on them; they die of exposure. Rafts can be and are used in tropical seas and they can be and have been used on big rivers in temperate zones. Whatever the reasons the main issues described in the next Chapter—shell construction, skeleton construction, edge-joined boats and non edge-joined boats—do not arise in the same way in the Chinese traditions as in the western. These traditions are not therefore discussed in the first part of this book, where we are concerned with general matters, but they are described in some detail in the second part, where we are dealing with some of the evidence in more detail.

Bibliography

CHAPELLE, H. I. *American Small Sailing Craft*, 1951

CHAPELLE, H. I. 'The Migrations of an American boat-type', 1961

CHRISTENSEN, A. E. *Boats of the North*, 1968

GILLMER, T. C. *Working Watercraft*, 1972

GREENHILL, B. *Boats and Boatmen of Pakistan*, 1971

McKEE, J. E. G. *Clenched Lap or Clinker*, 1972

WEIBUST, K. 'Holmsbuprammen', 1964

Chapter 3

Shells, Skeletons and Things-in-Between

ALL BUT ONE of the plank-built wooden boats so far described in this book have been conceived, designed and built from the outside in. Their builders have thought of and constructed them as continuous watertight envelopes of wooden planks, shaped so that the submerged parts will pass through the water as easily as possible in relation to the other things required of the boat—its ability to carry goods and people; to provide a stable platform for fishing; to be built cheaply and easily from readily available materials; to meet local requirements for operation—that is draft, ability to sail or be pulled, seaworthiness in local conditions, and so on. They have built them as a shell of wooden planks, of one shape or another, and then, perhaps as the building has gone forward, or in the case of the Bangladesh boat and the pram at the end, have added the minimum internal strengthening necessary to keep them permanently in that shape, bearing in mind whatever normal stresses they may have to undergo. These shell-built boats all have one fundamental characteristic in common—their strakes are joined together edge to edge, in one way or another.

One boat, the North American lobster boat, is fundamentally different. She was conceived as a framework around which a watertight skin of planks was to be wrapped, while the other boats were conceived as watertight shells into which strengthening members were to be inserted to fit. The basic difference is that the planks of the lobster boat are not joined to one another edge to edge; the common uniting structure is the skeleton, the framework. There is no physical bond between the planks themselves.

The Carolina skiff, the turf boat, the British trading smack's boat, the pram and the Bangladesh river boat, for all their very different shapes, ancestry, purpose and environment have a common link. Their shape was first thought of and visualised as a shell of wooden planks, even though in the case of the skiff the shell began with its sides. The shape of the lobster boat was first thought of and visualised as a skeleton which gave shape to planks secured to it, but not to each other, to make a waterproof covering.

Thus it can be said that there are two great general classes of boat in the world. There are boats built of planks joined edge to edge and also usually, but not always, joined to strengthening frames, and boats build of planks which are not joined edge to edge, but only to the supporting framework inside the boat.

In the history of boatbuilding in different parts of the world the great majority of boats in the first category have probably been built as pure shells, their building an act akin to sculpture. Their shaping and symmetry have been made by the simplest of measuring devices, such as the Bangladesh jute stick swung from side to side of a line from the inside of the stem to the inside of the stern to give a very rough symmetry in athwartships section, or by the use of the 'building level', or something comparable to one of the other devices described by Arne Emil Christensen Jr,[1] or they may have been built by eye alone.

But many boats built as shells in the last century or two at least have been shaped around one or two temporary frames, called moulds in 20th century British boatbuilding practice. Their shape was then basically conditioned by these moulds, though if only one was used, as was the normal practice in boatbuilding in this country in the late 19th century, the mould did no more than give the basic athwartships limits of the vessel in the way that her length and the rake of her stem and stern post gave the limits overall. Such boats were built as shells, and their permanent frames cut, or latterly steamed and bent, to fit the shell once it was complete, or nearly complete. Sometimes these moulds were not in position all the time but presented and periodically used in order to check the development of the shape. On occasions they were only half moulds which were swung from side to side and were no more than a general guide to shape and an important aid to symmetry—a development of the basic jute stick of Bangladesh, Figure 8. Certainly they were not often points of stress around which the planks were bent, 'active moulds', the curvature was usually still obtained by struts from floor and roof if such support was needed. Sometimes, even, the moulds were a general guide to the shape of a vessel actually bigger than that for which they were designed and gave only a general indication to the boatbuilder in developing the shape of the larger boat. At times they played a more active role and the planks of the strakes were bent around them so that they acted as internal props. But the role of the mould was rarely as simple as that. Its assistance might sometimes be needed in the first setting of a plank, but once the plank was fastened to its lower neighbour the shell structure acted as its own prop; and the mould relinquished its active role. Now and then the same mould would have an active role for some strakes, act purely as a guide or have nothing but a checking role—the jute stick role—for others. On the whole the mould was a guide rather than an internal prop, its role was passive rather than active. One of the very

---

[1] Hasslöf (ed), *Ships and Shipyards, Sailors and Fishermen*, Copenhagen, Rosenkilde & Bagger, Copenhagen University Press, 1972. Obtainable from the National Maritime Museum Bookshops.

STRENGTH OF PLANKING WHICH IS NOT EDGE-FASTENED

A SOFT BACKED BOOK LIKE A TELEPHONE DIRECTORY
CAN SHOW HOW A ROW OF PLANKS BEHAVE WHEN BENT

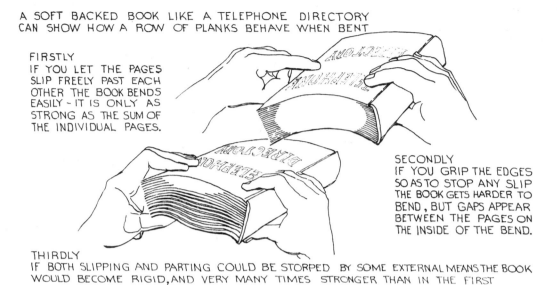

FIRSTLY
IF YOU LET THE PAGES
SLIP FREELY PAST EACH
OTHER THE BOOK BENDS
EASILY ~ IT IS ONLY AS
STRONG AS THE SUM OF
THE INDIVIDUAL PAGES.

SECONDLY
IF YOU GRIP THE EDGES
SO AS TO STOP ANY SLIP
THE BOOK GETS HARDER TO
BEND, BUT GAPS APPEAR
BETWEEN THE PAGES ON
THE INSIDE OF THE BEND.

THIRDLY
IF BOTH SLIPPING AND PARTING COULD BE STORPED BY SOME EXTERNAL MEANS THE BOOK
WOULD BECOME RIGID, AND VERY MANY TIMES STRONGER THAN IN THE FIRST

USING SEA TERMS- SEAMS IN PLANKING TRY TO-

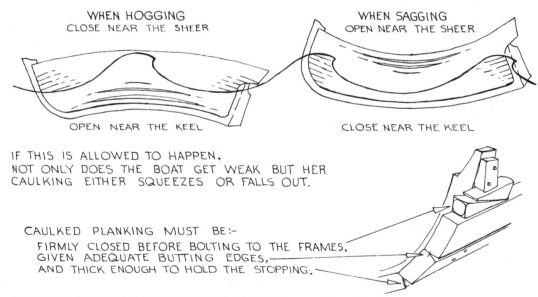

WHEN HOGGING
CLOSE NEAR THE SHEER

WHEN SAGGING
OPEN NEAR THE SHEER

OPEN NEAR THE KEEL

CLOSE NEAR THE KEEL

IF THIS IS ALLOWED TO HAPPEN,
NOT ONLY DOES THE BOAT GET WEAK BUT HER
CAULKING EITHER SQUEEZES OR FALLS OUT.

CAULKED PLANKING MUST BE:-
FIRMLY CLOSED BEFORE BOLTING TO THE FRAMES,
GIVEN ADEQUATE BUTTING EDGES,
AND THICK ENOUGH TO HOLD THE STOPPING.

TO ENSURE THE EFFECTIVENESS OF THESE MEASURES A STRONG FRAMEWORK IS ESSENTIAL, BUT ONCE
PROVIDED, WILL MEAN THAT THE SHELL CAN BE UP TO HALF AS STRONG AS IF IT HAD BEEN EDGE-FASTENED.

Figure 20   Stresses and strains.   *Eric McKee*

few contemporary writers with direct personal knowledge of boatbuilding techniques in the 19th century summed up:

> 'working clinch boatbuilders use few moulds or patterns beyond one midship section, to verify the required width of each plank, and the equal curve of the sides as the boat unfolds herself, plank after plank, from the keel trusting rather for the general contour and model of the boat to a practised eye, and the bend of clean grained wood.'[2]

Boats have been built for centuries in some parts of the world by planking up to the turn of the bilge as a shell and then inserting a few frames to fit, then planking up to these frames and then adding more frames made to fit. Sometimes vessels have been built by adding non edge-joined topsides fastened to the upper parts of frames inserted into an edge-joined lower hull. One very early wreck, discovered at Yassi Adda off the south coast of Turkey and dating from the 7th century AD may have been built in this way. And boats have been built in other hybrid ways too numerous to describe here in detail. But always the greater part of their planks have been joined together edge to edge and they have derived a great part of their structural strength from this fact, though in being built they may have derived their shape in greater or lesser degree from the shape of moulds or part frames.

The nature of that structural strength requires some clarification. When a boat or vessel is pulled ashore, or takes the ground in a tidal berth, or is afloat in waves, she is subjected to certain stresses. When she is pulled ashore or takes the ground these can be very complex, especially if she has a heavy cargo in her. In such conditions even a strong wooden ship built specifically for trades involving these stresses creaks and groans and cracks in a manner alarming to the uninitiated.

A boat or vessel afloat in waves is continuously flexing as she moves through the waves or they move past her. To take two extreme cases, when she is balanced with a single wave amidships her ends are unsupported and they will tend to drop. In this situation the upper strakes are under tension and the seams will be pulled tighter, while the lower strakes will be under compression and the seams will be pushed open. When the wave has reached the stern and the next one the bow, the boat is suspended by her ends with her middle unsupported and the reverse condition occurs, Figure 20. And, of course, rarely is the vessel subject to such simple stresses. Normally, they are much more complex and are continually changing. So as the vessel moves along forces are at work which are continually trying to tear her to pieces. Up to a certain size lightly built, strongly edge-joined structures could deal with this situation very well indeed, and on these grounds alone it is easy to see why edge-joining remained such a universal practice as long as wooden boats and small vessels were built anywhere in the world.

I have spelled out the nature, very simply, of some of the stresses to which a vessel is subject because they were a very important factor and at the same time a great

[2] Robert C. Leslie, *The Sea Boat, How to build, rig and sail her*, London, 1892.

Figure 21 The ultimate development of non edge-joined fully skeleton-built construction. The four-masted schooners *Charles A. Dean*, left, and *Helen Barnet Gring*, right, building at the R. L. Dean shipyard at Camden, Maine, in 1919. They were two of the 135 or so four-masted schooners launched on the East Coast of the United States between 1917 and 1921, the last big wooden merchant sailing ships ever to be launched in such numbers.

problem in the development of non edge-joined construction. I shall be coming back to them from time to time and particularly in the last chapter of this book.

For lack of evidence the whole subject of how different boatbuilding traditions developed and in what order in different parts of the world is still very controversial. There is evidence that the use of moulds, half frames, and part shell/part skeleton construction, all developed only after skeleton construction itself had separately developed and are in fact borrowings from skeleton construction into shell construction. In other words it seems likely that in most places pure shell construction came first. Much historical research still needs to be done, and it is here that the finds of remains of ancient boats, perhaps particularly in the Mediterranean and Southern Europe, and the recognition and more intensive study of illustrative material, may make it possible one day to hypothesise and argue on a basis of real evidence. Until then prolonged discussion of what came before which and when and where it came from is unproductive, particularly as it is at least arguable that the development of the boat happened many times over in different parts of the world. But if it is true that the various hybrid building techniques follow upon, and are borrowings and adaptations from skeleton building techniques, then the origins of boats in the second category, non edge-joined skeleton built boats, are indeed obscure.

Boats in the second category have been built in a variety of ways. In the relatively sophisticated big shipbuilding yards of the late 19th century and for a good deal earlier, vessels were built by shaping every frame from full-sized plans drawn out on a scrieve board, or a mould loft floor, Figure 21. But at the same period, small vessels, coasting smacks and small schooners were built, for instance in Cornwall in the 1870s, by setting up a few frames or even one frame only, approximately amidships, running battens from them fore and aft and deriving the shapes of the remaining frames from the curves of the battens—a halfway house between shell and the skeleton approaches to building. But, of course, the planks of the finished vessel were not edge-joined.

Between these two extremes many methods were used—but always the planks of the finished boat or vessel were not joined edge to edge, but only to the frames, which, because of the stresses already referred to, had to be either much stronger or more numerous, or both, than the frames of an edge-joined boat or vessel. Strength in a vessel the planks of which were not joined edge to edge was derived also from two other sources. Caulking was driven hard between the edges of the planks into the seams and this driving put the planks under tension which made the whole body of the vessel stronger. Ceiling, a lining of planks, was fitted inside the frames and greatly increased the strength of the whole vessel. More will be said about these strengthening methods in the last chapter of this book. But always the planks were not joined edge to edge, even though in some cases the shapes of some of the frames were derived from the shape assumed by the inside of the planking fastened to frames already erected on the keel.

Among big wooden ships there were some exceptions to this general rule of shell conceived edge-joined and skeleton conceived non edge-joined. For instance, some barquentines built of spruce wood in the late 19th century at New Bideford and Summerside in Prince Edward Island, Canada, had some of their planks bolted across to one another, edge to edge, to give them greater strength. The same thing was done in some big United States schooners, and in history there have certainly been other vessels built in greater or lesser degree in the same way in other parts of the world. But in modern times these Prince Edward Island vessels were exceptions, built for a special reason by men who were trained in traditions which did not include the edge to edge joining of planks in wooden ships. They were basically skeleton-built vessels. The records show that both the men who built them and organisations which classified the vessels for insurance purposes had to be convinced of the soundness of such a novel method of construction before it was accepted and used.

We can now refine somewhat the descriptions of the two great categories of plank-built boats and ships in western history, those which are built of planks joined edge to edge and usually, but not always, to strengthening frame timbers inside the shell of planks, and those which are built of planks not joined edge to edge but only to frames. We can say that boats in the former category have tended mostly in history to be shell-constructed, that is, to be conceived as a whole as a watertight envelope of planks into which a strengthening framework deriving its shape from the shell is inserted after the completion of part or the whole of the shell. The majority of such boats and vessels in history have probably been completed as shells before frames were inserted, but there are many other ways of building them. The latter category tended to be skeleton-constructed, that is to be conceived as a skeleton of frames around which is wrapped a watertight skin of planks, but again there are many ways of developing the shape, using partly the skeleton of frames and partly the growth of the skin of planks itself. But however blurred the middle ground of building methods may be, the fundamental distinction remains between boats the planks of which are edge-joined and those the planks of which are not edge-joined. As to the order and system of building there may well often be dispute in the cases of individual boats, but as to whether the planks were joined together edge to edge by one method or another there can be no dispute. As we see shortly, there are a few types of boat in the world which combine the two categories, the strakes are edge-joined for a distinct part of the structure, not edge-joined over the rest. Such hybrids are rare and each one has to be considered and examined separately. It is possible that hybrids may provide useful evidence as to the origins of non edge-joined construction.

This basic division of boats into edge-joined and non edge-joined is a new kind of fundamental categorisation, but the evidence of history and the evidence of surviving boats of the old building traditions in the world today strongly suggest its validity. The history of attempts at similar broad classification is interesting. Because most writing on the history of boats has been North European, for a long time there was a widespread tendency to be confused by the clearly defined principal late 19th century methods of building boats in Northern Europe. Put very simply, these were that boats built with overlapping planks were edge-joined, boats with planks lying flush to one another were not edge-joined. Therefore, the train of thought runs, explicit or implicit, through much writing about the history of boats, all boats throughout the world and history with planks lying flush were not edge-joined, and only boats with overlapping planks were edge-joined. Even James Hornell, the great British pioneer in the study of the development of boats, was liable to slip into this trap at times, despite his world wide observation and experience, and in places his thoughts and writing become very confused by it.

A valuable classification put forward very clearly by Olof Hasslöf[3] which remains a most useful working tool is that which divides boats into those which are shell-constructed and those which are skeleton-constructed. But for reasons given above this cannot be accepted as defining the fundamental differences between the two great categories of boats, because the difference does not at all times and at all places rest in the order and method of construction. It rests in the simple fact of whether the planks of the boat's shell are joined together at the edges or not.

For lack of evidence there is still considerable controversy as to where, when and

---

[3] Conveniently and accessibly in *Ships and Shipyards, Sailors and Fishermen*.

Figure 22   Flat-bottomed river cargo boat under construction on the river Indus at Sukkur in Pakistan.

Figure 23   A completed flat-bottomed river cargo boat on the Indus at Sukkur. One of the advantages of the type is shown by the fact that, although quite a large vessel, she draws so little water that she can discharge her cargo straight on to the gently shelving river shore.

how building without edge-joining began, and this situation is likely to continue for many years as the new more rigorous study of the development of the boat progresses.

The question is not even as simple as it seems, for, just as edge-joining and pure shell-construction are not necessarily synonymous, so the absence of edge-joining cannot be taken as evidence for skeleton-construction as it has widely developed in the western world in the last four hundred years. Here, too, there are intermediate forms. On the banks of the Indus at Sukkur in Pakistan some years ago I watched the construction of a large flat-bottomed river boat. First her two sides were assembled. They were made of planks joined edge to edge with wooden pins driven in holes drilled diagonally across the seams from plank face outside to plank face inside. The vertical columns of cut off pin-heads are clearly visible in Figure 22. The heads are of oval shape because of the angle at which the pins emerge from the plank face. Behind the complete sides the bottom is being made and is clearly visible in the photograph. A row of floor timbers, like railway sleepers across the dry mud of the river bank, has the planks fastened across it, outside ones first working inwards. The finished bottom is then turned over and the sides fastened to the beam ends. The ends of the bottom are forced up at either end to follow the shape of the sides. Side frames or timbers are then added and then deck beams and decks, the whole making a strong box-like boat Figure 23, admirably suited to her environment and purpose, which is to be the great cargo carrier on the River Indus.

Such a form of construction is a mixture both of edge-joining and non edge-joining, of skeleton and shell construction, since the finished boat derives its ultimate shape partly from the shape of shell components and partly from the shape of part of a skeleton. It is interesting to imagine some future archaeologist discovering the bottom structure of such a boat and hailing it as evidence of non edge-joined pure skeleton construction in the 19th century European sense of the term on the Indus in the mid-20th century.

In the Peshawar Valley in northern Pakistan a boatbuilder described to me another method of building flat-bottomed river boats which appears to represent a strand in the world's boatbuilding traditions, which may have existed in one form or another for some two thousand years in Northern Europe as well.

To build a flat-bottomed double-ended river boat Figure 24, first the floor timbers are laid out upside down on a stretch of flat river bank. At either end of the boat-to-be the timbers are small, perhaps 6 in (15 cms) deep, amidships half a dozen timbers may be twice as thick. The keel, a plank of timber 3 in (7·6 cms) thick, is then fastened over the middles of the floor timbers and then, working outwards from the keel plank the progressively shorter planks of the bottom, each 2 in (5·1 cms) thick, are fastened on and cut to shape at both ends. The planks of the bottom are laid flat edge to edge without edge-joining and without rabbeting, and a caulking of locally-grown cotton is driven between them.

Then the whole bottom of the boat is turned over and the centre part held down by weights, lumps of rock, while the bow and stern are forced up with poles used as levers to give a slightly increased rocker, over and above that given by the shaping of

Basil Greenhill

Figure 24   Flat-bottomed cargo boat on the Kabul river in the Peshawar valley, Pakistan.

the floor timbers to the bottom of the boat. Then the stem and stern posts are fitted and the side frames, quite straight timbers with no attempt at any kind of shaping are added, then the beam shelf and deck beams, so that in its next stage of construction the boat is an angular skeleton built up on the finished bottom. Last of all she is planked up in the sides and the decks are laid. This whole process took my informant and his few assistants about twelve days for a large cargo boat and between them he and his family had built forty-four boats in the year before I discussed his trade with him. Despite their apparent weakness these boats wore well in the limited conditions of the river trade. It is fun occasionally to speculate on very little evidence, providing one does not take the results too seriously, and I suppose it is just possible that the methods of construction could indicate that both the Indus River boat and the Peshawar Valley boat have descended ultimately from rafts, rather than from the dugouts and to a lesser extent skin boats which appear to have provided the origins of most North European building traditions.

There would appear to be some evidence for a similar tradition of rather specialised building at least in part without edge-joining provided by some wrecks of the 17th–19th centuries found in the draining of the Zuyder Zee.[4] The bottom

[4] Wrecks R43, B6 and the wreck of a Tjalk lost about 1815 illustrated in van der Heide, *Zuyder Zee Archaeology*, reprinted from *Antiquity and Survival*, *No. 3*. This evidence was pointed out by Basch, *Nautical Archaeology*, Volume 1, p. 43.

planks of these are not edge-joined and their side frames are not joined to the floor timbers. They, too, may well have been built by laying down the floor timbers up-side down, fastening the bottom planking to them, turning the whole over, erecting the side timbers secured to the outermost bottom plank only, and then perhaps fitting such beams as there were and then planking up to the side timbers with or without edge-joining. One of the vessels of which fragments were found during the construction work at Blackfriars (see page 21) and which dates from the first centuries AD, would appear to be of somewhat similar construction. The planks found were apparently not edge-joined and practical reasons would suggest that she may well have been built in the same way and represent another and earlier manifestation of what may well be very old traditions of boatbuilding existing in several parts of the world, just possibly derived ultimately from rafts (see Chapter 5) and usually associated with big rivers. This kind of construction is not really suited to withstand the stresses, already described, of prolonged seafaring.

In the last seven or eight years excavations have revealed more evidence for this type of construction. Preliminary reports have been published on a boat find from Kapel Avezaath in the Netherlands; boats 2 and 4 from Zwammerdam also in the Netherlands; and the Bevaix and Yverdon boats from Lake Neuchatel in Switzerland. These are all flat-bottomed boats dated to the 1st and 3rd centuries AD. Their bottom planks are not edge-joined but are secured by trenails and iron nails to the floor timbers, which are often arranged in pairs. The iron nails may be driven from above or below and they are clenched by turning the point back into the wood. The outer bottom planks have an 'L'-shaped cross section, and the floor timbers are continued up the sides either as natural crooks, or as side frames morticed to the floor timbers. Side strakes have not always survived, and reports on those that have are not detailed, but it appears that those on Zwammerdam boat 4 were edge-joined.

A pattern of trenails through the bottom planks of the Bevaix boat, which must have been there before the floor timbers were fitted, has been interpreted by the excavators as evidence for the temporary lashing together of the bottom planks at a very early stage in the construction.

Medieval boats, having many of the characteristics of these 1st–3rd century vessels, have recently been excavated at Krefeld on the Rhine in West Germany, and at Utrecht in the Netherlands. The latter is provisionally dated to the 12th century, whilst the Krefeld boat is 13th–14th century. Dr Detlev Ellmers tells me in a personal communication that the Bremen cog's (page 261) flat bottom strakes are not edge-joined, but fastened only with trenails to the floor timbers, while her sides from the fourth strake upwards are fastened in normal clinker fashion.

But these apart from the cog appear to be all local intermediate forms, co-existing and even sharing with widespread edge-joined techniques. Many such variations may have existed at different times in history and pre-history. How, when and where the great step to the erection of a skeleton and the wrapping around it of a skin of planks, not joined to one another edge to edge, took place, remains for the time being a mystery which is likely to continue to provide healthy, if not very productive,

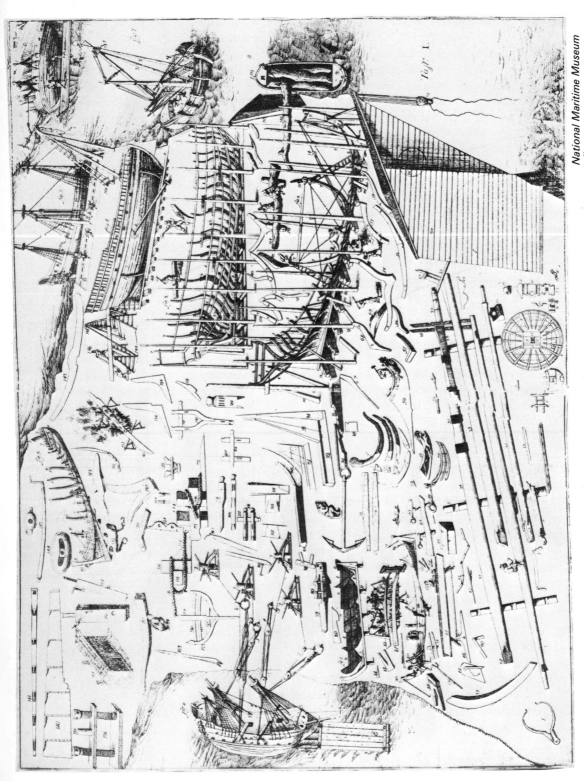

Figure 25   A 17th century Scandinavian dockyard from Rålamb, *Skeps Byggerij eller Adelig Öfnings Tionde Tom,* Stockholm, 1691. The drawing clearly illustrates different building traditions. Note the deliberately-drawn partly hulk style planking of the vessel in the top right-hand corner.

academic controversy. Rather than to speculate it is more important to collect evidence. If the idea dates from antiquity, sooner or later proof will turn up in the form of archaeological remains. The important thing is that they should be recognised when they do appear. At present, as I have said repeatedly, we are at the very beginning of this study. We know very little and every opportunity should be taken to observe, examine and record not only the remains of ancient vessels but of those in use today, and the methods of wooden boat and shipbuilding recently in use.

The great development is very clearly illustrated in Figure 25 of a Scandinavian dockyard of the 1600s when both traditional and transitional methods, as well as the relatively new non edge-joined construction, were in use. The vessel number *fig. 9* is edge-joined below with upperworks of planks not edge-joined on a skeleton of upper frames, which derive their shape in part from the edge-joined lower body of the vessel. *Fig. 4* has a planked-up hull while *fig. 3* is being built on a skeleton, the planks not joined at the edges. *Fig 2* shows building from a single midships frame, with ribbands from which the shape of the rest of the vessel is basically developed. Of the two boats shown at *fig. 1*, one is an edge-joined clinker-built boat built to moulds, while the other shows the classic 'act of sculpture' mouldless clinker shell construction.

The basic reason for the success and general adoption of the greatly changed method of building was very probably economic. Very simply, western man required bigger ships to carry more goods and more people for longer distances. Ships were required which could carry heavy guns to defend themselves and to establish control over the regions with which western man was establishing trade. The skeleton technique of non edge-joined construction is susceptible to far greater development than edge-joined construction can ever be. Vessels can be bigger and new shapes and forms can be readily initiated. Once the problem of providing sufficient strength to withstand seagoing stresses was understood vessels could be built which were large enough and strong enough to make possible the great European expansion of the 1400s and 1500s. The development of the non edge-joined, skeleton-built ship is one of the technical factors which made possible the exploration of the world by western European man and the development of the commerce which gave him predominance. So this highly complex change in shipbuilding methods is one of the key points in our history.

In the Mediterranean great maritime civilizations developed and died away and the successive generations of Egyptians, Phoenicians, Greeks and Romans ranged far and wide in trading and raiding voyages which played their significant part in setting the pattern of western civilization for thousands of years. Archaeological and literary evidence suggests that they did so in boats and vessels, the planks of which were joined together at the edges by one means or another. In recent years much further evidence has been obtained from underwater excavations which suggests that Mediterranean vessels of the classical traditions were edge-joined, often by some variations of tenons, mortices, dovetails and so on. John Morrison deals with this subject in detail in Chapter 9 of this book.

The different techniques of building non-edge-joined boats and vessels developed probably at different times and in different parts of the world. As far as Northern Europe and Britain are concerned, it may have grown up from the 13th century and it seems to have been widely adopted in the late 1400s and early 1500s, spreading outwards through the Middle East to India, see Chapter 19. But it never supplanted edge-joining for the building of boats and small vessels, even in Northern Europe, and in the rest of the world thousands of large vessels continued to be built with edge-joined planking, and will continue to be as long as wooden vessels are constructed—which in most places will not be for very many years more.

Intermediate forms in which the boat was started with edge-joined planking as far as the turn of the bilge or even above the waterline may possibly sometimes have preceded fully non edge-joined construction, though, as I have already said, this is disputable. Certainly intermediate forms lingered on in some areas until the late 19th century. But gradually in Northern Europe smooth-skinned boats and ships became synonymous with boats and ships the planks of which were not joined together at the edges, and before very long construction without edge-joining became the standard procedure for nearly all big vessels.

The builder who works in the skeleton tradition works very differently from one who does so in the shell tradition. In shell construction the builder can constantly check and alter his work. If he begins to go wrong he can correct his mistakes. He can take out the plank, change its shape, change the angle at which it is joined to its neighbour. He has plenty of opportunity in fitting and re-fitting the planks to re-work his theme.

A Swedish master shipwright described working in the edge-joined tradition to Olof Hasslöf in 1930. A *mistri* in Bangladesh used almost the same phrases to me twenty years later, though he was from a society culturally and geographically utterly remote from Sweden:

> 'When you build clinker, the ship takes shape under your very hands: if it doesn't turn out so well, you can finish it as you want it. Once you get over the bilge the thing is practically done.'

But the skeleton builder has to make up his frames and put his skeleton together before he can see what his ship is going to look like and, although he can do some correcting by padding out frames and so forth, unless it is going to be the very expensive matter of making new frames, always several at a time, the possibility of changing shapes is very limited. It is not surprising that new methods involving the making of half models of various kinds and later the making of scale drawings on paper, then drawing out the frames full scale on a mould loft floor, began to develop. Nor is it surprising that intermediate methods owing something to older and well understood shell-building traditions were adopted by simple men faced with the very difficult challenge of skeleton-building.

It follows from this categorisation of boats and ships into two groups, one old and very big and the other newer and much smaller, the one built of planks joined at the edges, the other of planks not so joined, that some standard definitions which have been widely used are no longer appropriate. As has already been said, because in the

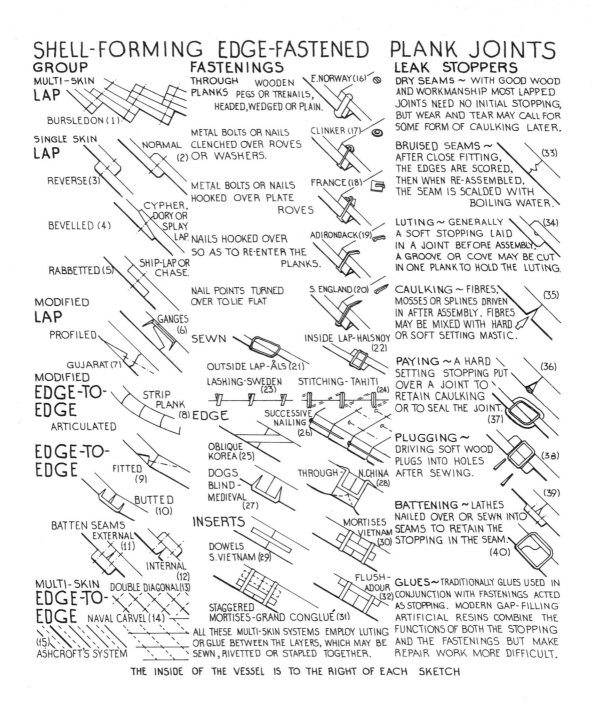

Figure 26 Some different kinds of edge-joining.

Eric McKee

late 19th century two basic ways of building a wooden boat were predominant in Britain, edge-joined with overlapping planks, and non edge-joined with the planks lying edge to edge so that the outside of the boat was smooth, it was, and still is today, often assumed that only boats built of overlapping planks were edge-joined and that all boats built with smooth skins were and are not edge-joined. For these two types of construction respectively the terms clinker, clenched lap or lapstrake, and the term carvel were generally used, though there never seems to have been general agreement on the definition of carvel. The first of these terms we can still retain, closely defined. The second, carvel, is now meaningless and must be dispensed with altogether.

Clinker or lapstrake construction we can define, in the words of Eric McKee, as the method of arranging the strakes of a vessel so that they overlap and are fastened together through the overlap. The term is really appropriate only to boats built in the North European traditions of clinker building in which the planks usually fully overlap for the greater part of their length without substantial thinning of the overlapping parts, though there may be considerable local fairing of the overlap in places, for example to produce watertight joints where the ends of the planks are fastened to the stem and stern posts of the vessel. It could be added that the overlap is with the lower edge of the upper plank outside the upper edge of the lower plank. The unqualified term will be used in this book only to mean building in this main North European tradition.

But boats are built in different parts of the world with planks which overlap in other ways and are joined to one another at the edges. A number of these methods will be described later in this book. It may be useful here to mention three methods of building with overlapping planks other than the method of the main European tradition, by way of example.

As has already been said the smooth-skinned boats of Bangladesh are built of planks which are cut to a half rabbet at each edge so that they overlap, but the thickness of the skin at the overlap is rarely greater than that of one plank. They are then joined edge to edge with metal lugs. Some Swedish lake boats are built in a very similar way and fastened in a very similar way, but with the plank edges, like those of the dory, faired rather than rabbeted and there is archaeological evidence that this method of fastening has been in use since Viking times. Both of these methods of fastening, so widely separated geographically, are so reminiscent of the sewing methods used in extending some dugouts (see Chapter 8) that it is difficult not to believe that the one is a development from the other. The middle West European and north east North American dory of which a detailed account is given later in this book, has planks which overlap and which are joined edge to edge, but they are so faired away at the edges as to produce sometimes almost a smooth skin. The term clinker cannot perhaps properly be applied to any of these construction methods. They can only be described in detail as specific building traditions.

The drawing in Figure 26 shows a series of examples of different kinds of edge-joining and it will be seen that for obvious reasons of strength many systems involve some degree of overlap, whether this is visible on the outside of the finished hull or not. Despite the apparent weakness consequent upon the lack of adequate bearing edges, which might be considered likely to make the vessels less able to withstand the normal working stresses already described, there were many different ways of joining planks lying square edge to square edge. Figure 27 shows a vessel built in this way, the shell of a Pakistani *hora* just at the stage when the first floor timbers were being inserted.

Figure 27 The almost complete shell of a *hora* fishing boat at Ibrahim Hyderi in Pakistan. The next stage in construction is the insertion of floor timbers.

Basil Greenhill

The term carvel has been given many meanings. It is acceptable for it to be used to signify a building method which involves the use of a single layer of fore and aft strakes closely fitted and fastened to a pre-erected frame work and not joined to one another at the edges. But in this book I shall not use the term at all. It has too unfortunate a history of confusion behind it. The various building traditions which have from time to time been covered by this term will be described separately as they arise.

It follows from the preceeding paragraphs of this chapter that a boat has been thought of by most boatbuilders in pre-history and history as a reasonably watertight shell of strakes made up from planks joined at the edges and held in shape by such minimal internal reinforcement as may be necessary, given her environment and the work she is to do. It follows also that, since wooden planks are flat, the builders of most boats in history have been successful in part to the degree in which they have been able to acquire the skill to convert flat material into shapes which, when joined together at the edges, will make a hollow object. The shape of that object will depend on the shaping of the flat parts, more than on any other single factor. Men building boats of planks have therefore been concerned more than anything else with the shaping of those planks. To understand the significance of this I can do no better than to recommend *Clenched Lap or Clinker* by Eric McKee to which I have already referred, see page 24. This book not only explains the process of deriving the shapes of the planks, it demonstrates it very clearly, by giving the reader a small cardboard half model of a 10 ft (3·04 m) clinker-built working boat to make up for himself. By doing this one can learn more quickly about the real nature of the problems of wooden boatbuilders and the structure of boats built in the main North European tradition than perhaps by any other means.

The success of boatbuilders in their trade has depended on their ability to foresee the flat shapes which will make up into the three-dimensional curved shapes they want. This is a very difficult and sophisticated skill to acquire, and this difficulty is very clearly demonstrated by the regularity and lack of innovation in the shape traditions that developed in different societies and provided solutions to this problem, and the incredible longevity of some of the successful solutions once firmly established. Thus the Oselver boat, still built to order near Bergen in Norway today, is only slightly developed from the four-oared boat found inside the Gokstad ship and dating from approximately AD 850. It is no wonder that, from time to time in different places, intermediate methods may have developed, designed to simplify the feat of predicting the necessary curves to be given to flat shapes so that they make up into an extremely complex curved three-dimensional object. Yet the art and skill have perhaps been best developed by the least schooled of men, Scandinavians of a thousand years ago, illiterate, itinerant craftsmen in Bangladesh today, who used and use no structural aids to building, but create shells of great efficiency for purpose by eye and swinging stick, or its equivalent, alone.

Since it is the shape of the edges of the planks that principally determines the shape of the boat it follows that the best way of recording the boat is to record these shapes. This fact has fundamental implications, because it is now becoming recognised that one of the most important tools of the boat archaeologist in recording a boat find, and then studying and comparing it with other finds, is the strake diagram, that is the drawing of the curved shapes of the planks in the flat. The strakes are the joined-up planks making, in most cases, a complete run from one end of the boat to the other. This tool is proving especially valuable for studying boats in the North European clinker tradition, but it can probably be adapted for use with boats of other traditions with equal success.

The simple examples given in Figures 28, 29 and 30 illustrate the point very well indeed. Figure 28 is a photograph of the four-oared boat, the *faering,* found inside the Gokstad ship burial of AD 850 in Norway. She is a very beautiful Viking boat and is described at length in Chapter 13. Figure 29 is the strake diagram of this boat. These strakes joined together at the edges and to the keel, stem and stern post will make up in only one way, that is into the shape of one half of this boat. With a little practice it is possible to read straight off from this drawing the characteristics of a complete boat and by comparing the drawing with strake diagrams of other boats to compare the boats also. It is probably also possible to examine and analyse the structural details and characteristics of the boat herself more easily in the strake diagram than by any other method. Thus the strake diagram has many advantages over conventional naval architects' drawings with all their difficulties in interpretation, their unreality and their over simplification.

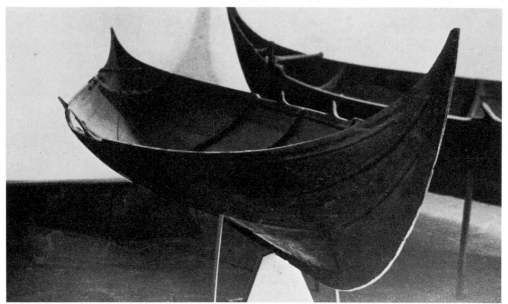

Figure 28   The four-oared boat found inside the Gokstad ship of about 850 AD, as she is displayed today at Bygdøy near Oslo.

Figure 30 shows an excellent, conventional drawing of the *faering*, within standard conventions, made several years ago by Arne Emil Christensen Jnr. As a means of recording, comparing and analysing boats, the strake diagram is likely to be used more and more as a principal tool as the study develops, although its current use is very new. It was developed in this country by Eric McKee and in Denmark by Ole Crumlin-Pedersen.[5] The reality behind the strake diagram is clearly demonstrated by Figure 31. This shows the thirty-six constituent parts of a small dory built in the Lawrence Allen Dory Shop in Lunenburg, Nova Scotia and it is obvious that they can make up in only one way. The strakes themselves are slightly shaped to fit at the bevels, but in a classic flat-bottomed boat of this kind only the bottom edge of the lowest strake need in fact be curved, the rest can be parallel-sided stock timber; a single very wide board, perhaps made from two pieces joined end to end as in the Bridgwater flatner; or a sheet of plywood—see Chapter 17.

There is, of course, another relevant factor which worries the boatbuilder. The strakes, be they overlapping or fitting edge to edge must be bevelled to fit one

[5] It is important to emphasise that in recording and reporting a boat find, it is not adequate to publish only the strake diagram which, when it is derived from incomplete remains, must inevitably be partly hypothetical. Besides the diagram, representing as it will one carefully considered solution to the problem of what was the shape of the whole boat, scale drawings of the strakes and fragments of structure actually found must be published, in order that the reader can apprise for himself the evidence on which the hypothetical solution is based, and form his own conclusions. This has been done in the report on the Graveney boat—see Bibliography.

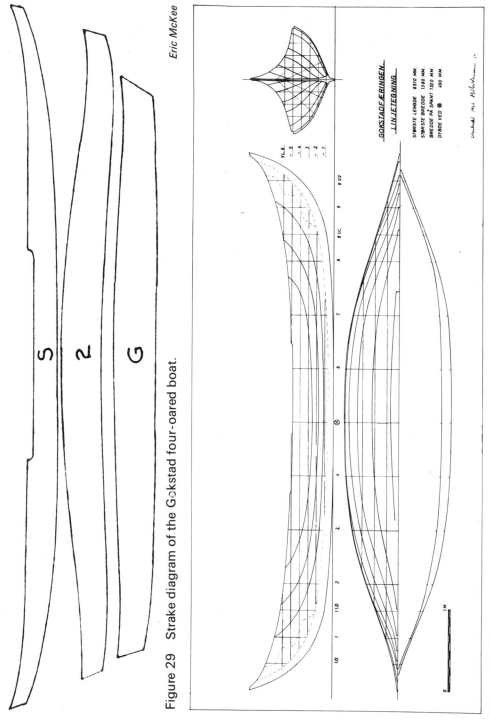

Figure 29 Strake diagram of the Gokstad four-oared boat.

Eric McKee

Figure 30 Naval architect's drawing of the Gokstad four-oared boat.

Universitetets Oldsaksamling

another. To the boatbuilder working in an edge-joined pure shell tradition this bevel is fundamental, since he works with stock of indeterminate length, cut to fit at stem and stern only after it has been joined to its neighbour; the angle at which it joins its neighbour, the bevel, is crucial to the shaping of the shell. Thus his tradition may be embodied partly in a series of figures for the bevels of different strakes. But once the strake has been shaped and cut to length it will only fit one way and to one angle of bevel to make one shape of shell. The archaeologist dealing with the finished product, should record both the strake shape and the bevel, though the latter is not essential.

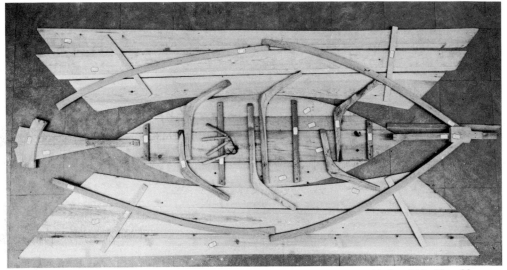

National Maritime Museum

Figure 31   The 36 constituent shaped timbers of a small dory from Lunenberg, Nova Scotia.

There is one further fundamental problem which faces the builder of a plank-built boat, and the solution he adopts is one more detail which does not appear in the strake diagram and which must be recorded to make it possible to assess, appreciate and compare the full boat. This is the problem of the plank ends.

Once the builder has determined the shapes of the edges of the planks which make up his strakes, he has to determine the ways in which he is going to bring these strakes to a conclusion at either end to make his hollow vessel watertight. The shapes of the edges of the strakes determine the general form of his boat; the shapes of the ends and the way they are brought to a watertight conclusion determine the remaining characteristics of the boat. Now, although the problem may at first sight seem obvious and simple, it is in fact very difficult to decide what to do with the plank ends to produce a watertight vessel, and many solutions have been tried in history. Eric McKee has prepared a series of drawings illustrating some of the classic solutions.

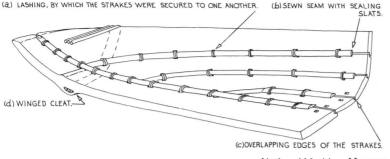

(a) LASHING, BY WHICH THE STRAKES WERE SECURED TO ONE ANOTHER.   (b) SEWN SEAM WITH SEALING SLATS.

(d) WINGED CLEAT.

(c) OVERLAPPING EDGES OF THE STRAKES.

Figure 32 The plank ends of the first Ferriby boat — one hypothetical solution.

National Maritime Museum

The first, Figure 32, is a possible solution of the problem of ending one of the oldest boats—if not the oldest—of which remains have been found anywhere in the world outside Egypt, Ferriby 1, see Chapter 5. Here all the parts are shaped from the solid:

(a)   is the lashing by which the strakes were secured to one another.
(b)   the sewn seams with sealing slats.
(c)   the overlapping edges of the strakes.
(d)   the winged cleats.

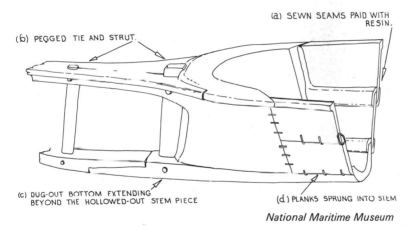

(a) SEWN SEAMS PAID WITH RESIN.

(b) PEGGED TIE AND STRUT.

(c) DUG-OUT BOTTOM EXTENDING BEYOND THE HOLLOWED-OUT STEM PIECE

(d) PLANKS SPRUNG INTO STEM

Figure 33 The plank ends of the Als or Hjortspring boat.

National Maritime Museum

The next drawing, Figure 33, shows the Als boat of about 300 BC, see Chapter 6. Here is shown:

(a)   the sewn seams paid with resin.
(b)   the peg tie and strut.
(c)   the dugout bottom, extending beyond the hollowed-out stem piece.
The Als boat was probably built by wooden boatbuilders familiar with contemporary skin boatbuilding practice.

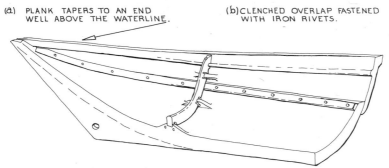

(a) PLANK TAPERS TO AN END
     WELL ABOVE THE WATERLINE.

(b) CLENCHED OVERLAP FASTENED
     WITH IRON RIVETS.

(c) THE DUG-OUT BOTTOM PROVIDING MOST OF THE STRENGTH AND WATERTIGHTNESS
                                OF THIS HULL.

National Maritime Museum

Figure 34 The
plank ends of
the Björke boat.

In the Björke boat, see Chapter 10, shown in Figure 34:

(a)   the plank tapers to an end well above the waterline.
(b)   shows the clench overlap fastened with iron rivets.
(c)   the dugout bottom providing most of the strength and watertightness of the
      hull.

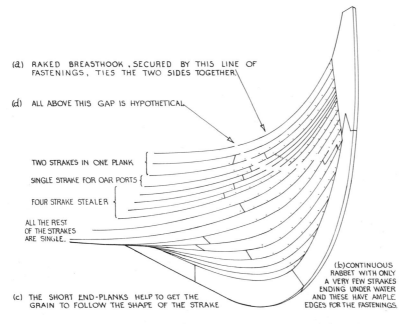

(a) RAKED BREASTHOOK , SECURED BY THIS LINE OF
     FASTENINGS , TIES THE TWO SIDES TOGETHER.

(d) ALL ABOVE THIS GAP IS HYPOTHETICAL.

TWO STRAKES IN ONE PLANK

SINGLE STRAKE FOR OAR PORTS

FOUR STRAKE STEALER

ALL THE REST
OF THE STRAKES
ARE SINGLE.

(b) CONTINUOUS
RABBET WITH ONLY
A VERY FEW STRAKES
ENDING UNDER WATER
AND THESE HAVE AMPLE
EDGES FOR THE FASTENINGS.

(c) THE SHORT END-PLANKS HELP TO GET THE
     GRAIN TO FOLLOW THE SHAPE OF THE STRAKE

National Maritime Museum

Figure 35 The
plank ends of
the   Gokstad
ship.

The next diagram, Figure 35, shows the Gokstad ship, see Chapter 14. This is engineering in wood; massive strength with minimum weight.

(a) shows the raked breastbook, secured by a row of fastenings and which ties the two sides together.
(b) the continuous rabbet with only a few strakes terminating underwater, but these have plenty of edge for fastenings.
(c) the short end planks allow grain to follow the shape of the strake.
(d) the line above which, because of the destruction of that part of the original boat, the drawing is hypothetical.

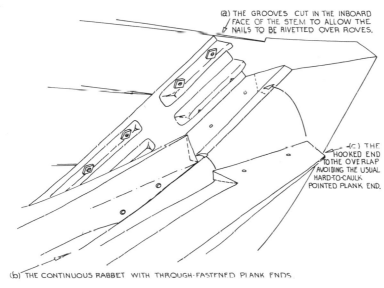

(a) THE GROOVES CUT IN THE INBOARD FACE OF THE STEM TO ALLOW THE NAILS TO BE RIVETTED OVER ROVES.

(c) THE HOOKED END TO THE OVERLAP AVOIDING THE USUAL HARD-TO-CAULK POINTED PLANK END.

(b) THE CONTINUOUS RABBET WITH THROUGH-FASTENED PLANK ENDS.

National Maritime Museum

Figure 36 The plank ends of the Graveney boat.

The Graveney boat, see Chapter 14, shown in Figure 36, dates from about AD 950 and is a cargo vessel, found in Britain, a near contemporary of the Gokstad ship.

(a) shows the grooves cut in the inboard face of the stem post to allow nails to be rivetted over roves.
(b) the continuous rabbet with through-fastened plank ends.
(c) the hooked end to overlap, avoiding the usual weak and hard to caulk pointed plank ends.

A century later, Skuldelev Wreck 1, see Chapter 14—Figure 37 shows three solutions in one vessel. This is master craftsmanship.

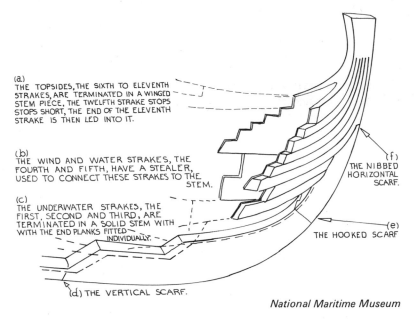

Figure 37 The plank ends of S k u l d e l e v Wreck 1.

(a)   the topside, the sixth to eleventh strakes, are terminated in a winged stem piece, the twelfth strake stops short, the end of the eleventh strake is then lead into it.

(b)   the wind and water strakes, the fourth and fifth, have a stealer, used to connect these strakes to the stem.

(c)   the underwater strakes, the first, second and third, are terminated in a solid stem with the end planks individually fitted. These show:

(d)   the vertical scarf.

(e)   a hooked scarf.

(f)   the nibbed horizontal scarf.

The Norwegian pram, see Chapters 3 and 18— Figure 38 represents simple efficiency, jogged transom at each end, the central plank is also the keel.

(a)   shows the bow narrow with forward overhang, all plank ends are well clear of the water.

(b)   iron bands add strength to narrow plank ends which can have only a few fastenings.

(c)   the stern is strong, beamy and buoyant.

The next drawing, Figure 39, shows a hypothetical reconstruction of the strake ends of a medieval hulk. The hulk is described at some length later in this book—see Chapter 18. No archaeological remains have yet been identified as those of a hulk. Like the pram, all plank ends finish above the waterline, but these are cut off on a

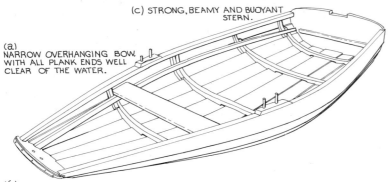

(c) STRONG, BEAMY AND BUOYANT STERN.

(a)
NARROW OVERHANGING BOW,
WITH ALL PLANK ENDS WELL
CLEAR OF THE WATER.

(b)
IRON BANDS ADD STRENGTH TO NARROW PLANK ENDS WHICH CAN NOT TAKE
MANY FASTENINGS.

National Maritime Museum

Figure 38 The Norwegian pram.

(a) NO STRAKE ENDS ON THE PLANK KEEL.

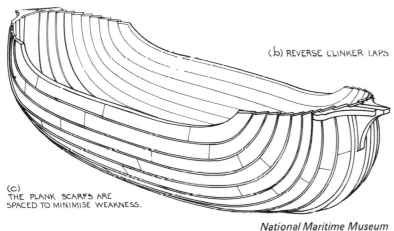

(b) REVERSE CLINKER LAPS.

(c)
THE PLANK SCARFS ARE
SPACED TO MINIMISE WEAKNESS.

National Maritime Museum

Figure 39 Plank ends of a hulk.

level plane and not on transoms. This drawing shows a 'reversed clinker' hulk and is based on the evidence provided by the carving on the font of Winchester Cathedral dating from about AD 1180, illustrated in Figure 40, and the ship on the seal of Poole from one hundred and fifty years later.

Once again there is a remarkable parallel in Bangladesh. As Figure 41 shows, a very common solution to the planking problem adopted by boatbuilders there is that all but the uppermost plank ends are cut off on a level plane and not on transoms, but this level plane is topped with strakes laid almost horizontally with very little shaping, thus the solution is almost identical to that adopted by the medieval builders of the hulk. The similarity of construction between the Bangladesh tradition and the hulk is even more clearly illustrated in Figure 15.

Figure 40   The hulk on the font of Winchester Cathedral.   *Albert W. Kerr*

Figure 39 shows a hulk built in 'reversed clinker', that is, of planks overlapping and fastened together through the overlaps, but with the upper edges of the lower planks outside the lower edges of the upper planks, in reverse of the main Northern European tradition defined on page 75. It is extremely interesting to find in Bangladesh today exactly the same construction. Figure 42 shows a 'reversed clinker'-built hull virtually indistinguishable from the medieval hulk, except for the horizontal strakes above the level plane of the plank ends at the bow.

A moment's thought will show that it is very difficult to build in reversed clinker if the plank ends are terminated in any way but those adopted by the hulk, the Bangladesh boat, or the Norwegian pram, for the simple reason that planks brought up to and secured to stems of any kind are very difficult to fasten if the upper plank lies inside the lower, simply because the lower planks are positioned first in virtually all building traditions. It has been done. Some medieval cogs (page 260) were apparently built in this way, although they had the plank ends fastened to straight stem and stern post and in this century some stem boats have been built in 'reversed clinker' in Sweden. But with the hulk solution to the plank ends it does not matter which way you build your boat of overlapping edge-joined planks and the one tradition is as likely to develop as the other. Indeed in Bangladesh both traditions have developed. The reverse clinker construction occurs in the Sylhet district in the East; in the middle of the country, in the Mymensingh district, ordinary clinker-style is used. It is difficult to imagine more range and variety, more different ways of making the ends of a wooden plank-built boat than these drawings and photographs illustrate and they do not include the solution latterly most common, the familiar solution of the everyday wooden boat, one of the most difficult, yet one of the most

Basil Greenhill

Figure 41   Small Bangladesh river cargo boat under repair on the bank of the river below Dacca, in 1951.

Basil Greenhill

Figure 42   A 'reversed clinker'-built boat from the Sylhet area of Bangladesh.

efficient, the straight or curved rabbeted stem with the plank ends nailed, bolted or pegged to it, see Figure 6.

Bibliography

ABELL, W.   *Shipwright's trade*, 1948

ARNOLD, B.   'Gallo-Roman boat from the Bay of Bevaix, Lake Neuchatel, Switzerland', 1975

BASCH, L.   'Ancient Wrecks and the Archaeology of Ships', 1972

BASS, G. F.   'Byzantine Trading Venture', 1971

BRØNDSTED, J.   'Oldtidsbaden fra Als', 1925

CHAPELLE, H. I.   *Boatbuilding*, 1947

CHAPELLE, H. I.   *American Small Sailing Craft*, 1951

CHRISTENSEN, A. E.   *Boats of the North*, 1968

CHRISTENSEN, A. E.   'Boatbuilding Tools and the Process of Learning', 1972

CHRISTENSEN, A. E.   'Lucien Basch: Ancient Wrecks and the Archaeology of Ships. A comment', 1973

CRUMLIN-PEDERSEN, O.   'Cog-Kogge-Kaage', 1965

de WEERD, M. D. and HAALEBOS, J. K.   'Schepen voor het Opscheppen', 1973

ELLMERS, D.   'Keltischer Schiffbau', 1969

ELLMERS, D. and PIRLING, R.   'Ein mittelalterliches Schiff ans dem Rhein', 1972

GJELLESTAD, A. J.   'Litt om Oselverbäter, 1969

GREENHILL, B.   *Merchant Schooners*, 1968

GREENHILL, B.   *Boats and Boatmen of Pakistan*, 1971

HASSLÖF, O.   'Main Principles in the Technology of Shipbuilding', 1972

HASSLÖF, O. (ed)   *Ships and Shipyards, Sailors and Fishermen*, 1972

HOEKSTRA, T. J.   'A note on the Utrecht boats', 1975

HORNELL, J.   'Fishing luggers of Hastings', 1938

HORNELL, J.   *Water Transport*, 1970

LESLIE, R. C.   *The Sea Boat. How to build, rig and sail her*, 1892

MCKEE, J. E. G.   *Clenched Lap or Clinker*, 1972

MCKEE, J. E. G.   Unpublished study of East Sussex and Chesil Bank beach boats, undated

MARSDEN P. R. V.   *A Ship of the Roman Period from Blackfriars in the City of London*, undated

NIELSEN, C.   *Danske bådtyper*, 1973

RÅLAMB, Å. C.   *Skeps Byggerij eller Adelig Öfnings Tionde Tom*, 1691

ROSENBERG, G.   'Hjortspringfundet', 1937

TORNROOS, B.   *Båtar och-båtbyggeri i Ålands östra skärgård 1850–1930*, 1968

TRAUNG, J–O (ed)   *Fishing Boats of the World*, 1955–67

van der HEIDE, G. D.   'Archaeological Investigations on New Lands', 1955

van der HEIDE, G. D.   'Ship Archaeological Investigations in the Netherlands', 1970

ZACKE, A. and HÄGG, M.   *Allmogebåtar*, 1973

PART TWO

The Roots of Boatbuilding

Chapter 4

The Four Roots of Boatbuilding

Besides the categorisation of boats into those which are built of planks joined together at the edges and those which are built of planks not so joined it would probably be possible, if we knew the line of development of each separate boat type, to categorise all boats from their origins into four general groups, because boats began in four principal ways. Boats from each of these four different roots developed independently, sometimes several times over in different parts of the world, and in places there was interaction between boatbuilding traditions of the

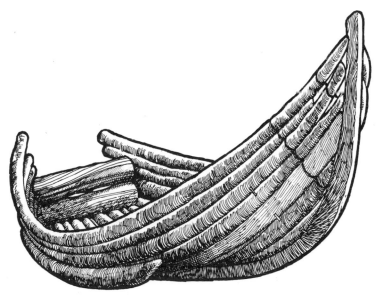

Figure 43
A raft boat.

National Maritime Museum

91

four different origins, so that influences from more than one group affected the shape and structure and development of later boats.

The basic types of boats are:

(1) The raft boat

The raft boat is made by securing logs or bundles of reeds together in a boat shape, Figure 43. Ordinary rafts, sometimes supported on floats of inflated skins, also performed some of the functions of boats, but always the raft boat and the raft gain their buoyancy, not from being watertight and thus enclosing air so that their total weight equals the weight of water they displace, but from the fact that the material from which they are made is lighter than water, so much lighter that they not only float themselves but have reserve buoyancy to carry people and goods.

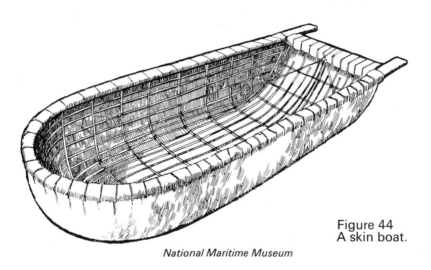

Figure 44
A skin boat.

National Maritime Museum

(2) The skin boat

The skin boat is made by sewing a covering of animal skin or fabric over a framework previously made of wood or bone, Figure 44. The framework can be long and narrow, like the Irish curragh, or round, like a floating bowl as in the Welsh coracle. A variation of this skin boat is the basket boat, where the difference is only in the framework. Instead of a skeleton, this boat, Figure 45 has a more complex and continuous frame made up like a basket, which is either covered by stretching cloth or skin over the wickerwork or by closing the holes with clay or tar.

(3) The bark boat

The bark boat is made by stripping a continuous cylinder of bark from a suitable tree

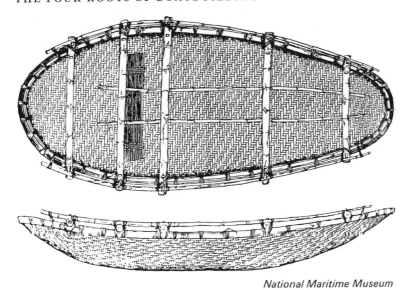

Figure 45
A basket boat.

National Maritime Museum

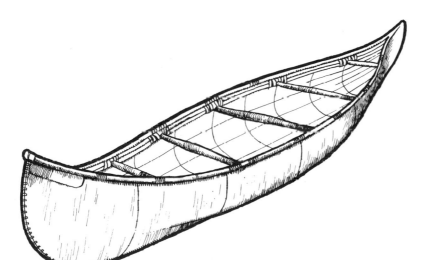

Figure 46
A bark boat.

National Maritime Museum

and then forming a boat shape out of the bark itself. The ends are sealed and the shape maintained by building a strengthening framework of wood, usually of twigs lashed together inside it, Figure 46.

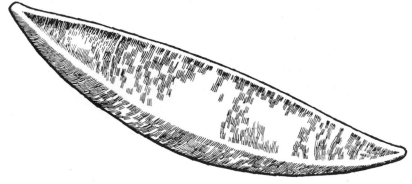

National Maritime Museum

Figure 47
A dugout.

(4)   The dugout

The dugout is made by hollowing out a log and thus producing a basic boat structure, that is, a watertight more or less boat shape which increases its power to carry burdens by an amount equal to the weight of wood cut out, Figure 47.

Hollowing out a log sounds a laborious and difficult process and it was, but in fact with primitive tools it was a great deal easier than producing planks and joining them together to make a watertight plank-built boat shape. As better tools became available and greater skills were developed planks were added to widen and deepen dugouts and thus the plank-built boat in most of its numerous varieties developed at different times in different societies in different parts of the world.

To make all four different kinds of boats the only tools needed were axes or adzes, chisels and needles, fire, water, rope and clamps, so all these basic types of boat could be built even by relatively primitive peoples.

Obviously the four roots of boatbuilding were each capable of different degrees of development, determined by the properties of the materials of which they were constructed. The bark boat was limited in size by the size and strength of the bark and in proportions by its shape. It could not develop far. The skin boat under ideal conditions of supply of good quality materials, skins, timber and fastenings, could go much further, but again was limited by inherent structural characteristics. The raft could be developed into a watertight vessel—a boat—but to do so meant a great change in the ideas of its builders. Once this barrier was crossed it could have many descendants. The dugout, however, was capable of almost limitless development and had the widest influence on boats in the long run. From this root the greatest variety of wooden boats evolved.

In the second part of this book we shall examine each of these basic types of boat in turn and some of the boat structures that have developed from them in different parts of the world, as illustrated principally by material in the National Maritime

Museum. We shall go on to consider the sorts of ships that developed from the boats that began in these four ways, and then finally examine briefly how the whole technique of shipbuilding changed in the 15th century to produce a different kind of structure for big vessels in the western world, and particularly in Britain and North America, which continued in use up to the end of the era of the wooden ship, approximately the middle of the 20th century.

Bibliography

GREENHILL, B. *Boats and Boatmen of Pakistan*, 1971
HORNELL, J. *Water Transport*, 1970

National Maritime Museum

Figure 48
A raft boat from Lobito Bay,
South West Africa.

Chapter 5

The First Root, the Raft Boat and the Raft

IN THIS AND the next three chapters I shall describe a few examples of boats representative of each of the four roots of boatbuilding traditions, some in use today, some found in archaeological excavations. Rafts and raft boats have been widely used in different parts of the world in warmer climates, but floating as they do partly under the water and with the seas continuously liable to break over them, they do not provide sufficient protection for human survival in cold seas, such as those of Northern Europe and northern North America, and so they have not evolved in these areas on any scale. They have, however, been used on big rivers in Europe as elsewhere in the world and from them, as I have already said, it is possible that a number of boatbuilding traditions may have developed. These building traditions tend to be associated with flat-bottomed boats and vessels.

Rafts and raft boats are still used in many parts of the world, especially in India, South East Asia and in Southern America where they have been very highly developed. The simplest rafts comprise a few logs or bundles of reeds, Figures 48 and 49, or inflated skins, Figure 50, joined together and paddled to a fishing ground. The most sophisticated comprise a complicated structure of beams and logs, equipped with sails and drop keels, Figure 51, like multiple versions of a sailing dinghy's centre plate and some of them, given crews of men and women brought up to them and their way of life, were capable of quite long ocean voyages under ideal conditions.

In many parts of the world the raft probably had only slight local influence on the development of boats. The step from a vessel which gained its buoyancy entirely from the nature of the raw material to a watertight vessel gaining its buoyancy from the enclosed air, was a very big one requiring an entirely different approach to the whole question of building a floating carrier of people and goods. Boats were much more likely to develop in a society building dugouts or one with the materials for skin boats than among raft users. But it has been argued by Hornell, Needham and others that the influence of the raft on the development of Chinese boats may have been wider and

Exeter Maritime Museum

Figure 49   A reed raft boat from Lake Titicaca.

Ann Bamford

Figure 50   An inflated skin raft from Swat State, northern Pakistan. The raft was in use as a ferry over the Swat river.

Basil Greenhill

Figure 51 A *jangada* sailing raft from Brazil. These rafts exist in several different forms and sizes. The base of logs of light wood is pinned together with strong transverse rods of hard wood. The single drop keel is clearly visible in this example photographed in the collection of boats at the Mariners' Museum at Newport News, Virginia.

stronger than its influence anywhere in the western world, and by others that the raft made of a bundle of reeds may have played a part in the development of the boat in ancient Egypt. In both cases the earliest boats were riverine.

The Lobito Bay raft boat illustrated here, Figure 48, with the accompanying photograph of the stern of a sampan from Bangladesh, Figure 52, a boat type certainly of Chinese origin, illustrates very clearly the way in which the raft may have played a part in the evolution of some Chinese boats and ships. The Lobito Bay raft boat is one of the relatively few examples of rafts found in Africa. She is built of poles of ambatch wood, arranged in a boat-like shape, but her buoyancy, as in all rafts and raft boats, is obtained from the sum total of the buoyancy of the individual poles and not from the buoyancy of the hull as a watertight whole. The use of tapering logs arranged in a boat shape with the thicker ends in the stern of the boat—as is obvious since only the thin end can be brought to a pointed stem—inevitably results in a distinctive stern shape clearly shown in the photograph

Basil Greenhill

Figure 52   Stern of a Chittagong *sampan* from Bangladesh.

of the Lobito Bay raft and to be compared with the stern of the Chittagong sampan, equally distinctive and generally very similar in shape. This characteristic stern shape, shared by many Chinese boats, has led to the theory that the raft played a larger part in the evolution of boats in China than perhaps elsewhere in the world.

An immense country with rivers thousands of miles long and a coastline of over two thousand miles, China is bisected by the great river Yangtze-Kiang. To the north of its mouth the coastline is low, the seas shallow; to the south the seas are deep, with a rugged coastline and many fjords.

The view has been expressed that many of the complex patterns of boats on the coasts and rivers of China may have evolved from plank-built copies of rafts of the Formosan type, formerly used on the southern coasts of China, and from where they were probably introduced into Formosa. This highly developed form of raft with its drop keels, rudder and sail was one of the most sophisticated in the world, Figure 53. It was built of bamboo poles lashed together and its shape shows in rudimentary form several characteristics of some Chinese boats and big plank-built Chinese vessels. The early 19th century drawing shown in Figure 54 of a small Chinese vessel,

Figure 53 The sailing rafts of Formosa were up to 35 ft (10·67 m) in length and 10 ft (3·05 m) across. This model in the National Maritime Museum shows the basic pa-limped shape, characteristic of all Chinese craft.

National Maritime Museum

National Maritime Museum

Figure 54 A small Chinese vessel. Detail from Paris, *Essai sur la Construction Navale des Peuples Extra-Européens.*

the lower hull of which is made up of half sawn logs arranged raft fashion, lends some weight to this theory.

The origins of Chinese boat types and structures generally still await thorough informed study by archaeologists specialising in comparative boat structures. At this stage the information available about the multifarious kinds of boat indigenous to China is really inadequate to generalise. It may well be that the raft boat played a larger part in the origin of some later Chinese boat types than it did in the origins of most of the world's boat types, but the flat-bottomed, expanded and extended dugout, which played such a large part in the development of boats elsewhere in the world, may have had a strong influence in China too, especially in the north, as it most certainly did in Japan. Thus on the navigable section of the upper region of the Hueng-ho or Yellow River near Shansi, to the north-west of the Wei River where Chinese civilisation first developed, a primitive three-plank boat is still used, though it is both curvaceous and sub-divided with bulkheads on the principle of cleft bamboo. The very word *sampan*, used for so many Chinese boats and small vessels, derives from *san* (in the Canton area *sam*) meaning three and *pan* meaning planks.

On the basis of information so far published, despite their variations in outward form the profusion of boat types which existed in China a few years ago all appear to have had certain common characteristics.

National Maritime Museum

Figure 55   Model of a 'duck' *sampan* from Wei Hai Wei, made in 1938.

Figure 56 Model of a 'chicken' *sampan,* also made in China in 1938.

National Maritime Museum

(1)   They were built without keel, stem or stern post. In the north of China generally speaking they were flat-bottomed with a sharp junction or chine between the sides and the bottom—the duck sampan, Figure 55. In southern China they tended to be deeper with more curves to them with a rounded turn of bilge where the sides met the bottom—the chicken sampan, figure 56. Almost all Chinese boats and vessels appear to be divisible into one or other of these two classic types.

(2)   Whether flat-bottomed or slightly rounded the bottom always has fore and aft rocker and the sides of the vessel do not close in towards the stern but end, leaving a space to be filled in with a transom of planks. In many classical Chinese types, especially in the south, the fore end is equally square ending in a smaller transom bow—the chicken type. In riverine and northern coastal types the ends are often filled in by carrying up the flat bottom structure in steep curves—the duck type. In some ways the general shape can be compared with that of a plywood-built pram dinghy, with its flat bottom, sides curved only in one direction at a time, broad transom stern and smaller transom bow.

(3)   In place of the various frames used in most of the world's boats and vessels, the classical Chinese vessels had solid transverse bulkheads of which both the bow and the stern transoms might be regarded as the terminating units. It has been pointed out especially by Needham that this structure resembles that of a bamboo stem made up, as it is, of separate cells joined end to end with cell walls between each.

(4)   Classical Chinese craft appear to have been built by laying bottom planks on baulks lying athwartships on the ground. These bottom planks were joined edge to edge and the bulkheads, prefabricated nearby, were then secured to the bottom planks and the side planking added, also joined edge to edge, using the bulkheads to give the shape of the final boat. The parallel with the method of construction of the *bohatja* of the Indus and with certain European types (pages 68 and 70), also possibly of raft origin, is obvious. With a few fairly easily identifiable exceptions the traditional rule of thumb designs and the method of construction of Chinese craft were not influenced by western practice as long as they continued to be built. Nor is this surprising, for until well after the development of the use of iron and steel for shipbuilding in the west, the interior of China and great stretches of the coast were unvisited by all but a handful of Europeans, and western craft were never seen.

A further characteristic of all Chinese craft is what has been described by David Waters[1] as their 'palmiped or water fowl shape' which gives them a greater breadth at the waterline aft than forward. In Yangtze and northern vessels, the bow is generally broad and flat. The wedge-shaped bow is more often found in southern vessels and can even develop into a stem post. Most river boats have balanced rudders—which appear to have been in use by the 2nd century AD. In most estuary and coastal vessels the rudder can be raised for beaching and lowered for work to windward, in which it is reported to act as an additional keel.

Figure 57, a model of a Pechili trading junk from North China, illustrates the traditional Chinese form of a large trading vessel very well. The Pechili junk is one of the two oldest types of Chinese sea-going vessel in recent use. She had a flat bottom and could carry up to 400 tons of cargo in numerous watertight compartments separated out by the bulkheads, each compartment a hold on its own, hired out to a different merchant. Big Pechili junks could run up to 140 ft or 180 ft (42·67 m to 54·86 m) in length with a beam of 20 ft to 30 ft (6·09 m to 9·14 m). The stepping of the masts was unusual, the foremast and the little mizzen were fixed on the port side and the main mizzen less to port of the central line. The general shape shows parallels with the duck sampan already illustrated.

Another big seagoing Chinese merchant sailing vessel was the Foochow pole junk, figure 58, which was also capable of long sea voyages, indeed one of them, the *Keying*, was sailed from Hong Kong to London in the middle of the 19th century. Big

---

[1] In his contributed labels to the Development of the Boat display at the National Maritime Museum from which I have drawn freely. He has rare extensive first-hand knowledge of Chinese vessels.

National Maritime Museum

Figure 57   When in Wei Hai Wei in 1938, David Waters had this model of a Pechili trading junk made as a copy of a vessel lying in the harbour discharging cargo.

National Maritime Museum

Figure 58 Similarly this model of a Foochow pole junk was made as a copy of a vessel lying in Wei Hai Wei harbour for David Waters in 1938.

Foochow pole junks could carry 400 tons, the huge rudder was lifted when in harbour or in shallow water by tilting it forward, when lowered it was held to the hull by lines running fore and aft and hauled taut by a windlass in the bows of the vessel. Here the general shape shows parallels with the chicken sampan.

It is convenient to deal with the boats of ancient Egypt in this chapter because it has been argued that they were ultimately derived, at least in part, from rafts made of stalks of the papyrus plant. The boats of ancient Egypt are, of course, except for one group of British vessels, described later in this chapter, the oldest boats about which we have any very extensive knowledge.

One authority, the Swedish writer Björn Landström, has suggested that the Egyptians may have developed simple flat-bottomed, plank-built wooden boats at a very early date. Such boats developed again in various parts of the world, and their evolution from dugouts is discussed in the appropriate chapter of this book.

Some flat-bottomed plank-built boats may have been built in a shape meant to imitate papyrus rafts and some authorities see a strong raft influence in the construction of one of the world's most exciting boat finds, the great river craft called the Royal Ship of Cheops, dating from about 2600 BC, which was found in 1952. She is flat-bottomed and sewn together with ropes. The planks are edge-joined in this way to make a great shell into which the shaped frames were inserted.

Models found in tombs, dated three hundred years later, show that the same basic hull form and probably the same construction were still in use. Some models can best be described as punt shaped, but with a marked sheer higher in the stern than in the bows. Vessels of somewhat similar form with the planks joined edge to edge are in use on the river Indus in Pakistan today. They share with some of the Egyptian ships a remarkable shape of hull in which the bottom turns upwards at a steep angle abaft of amidships.

The Indus punts are very graceful and attractive boats, seen under sail on the great river. They vary from the 16 ft (4·88 m) or so of a canal ferry or marsh fishing boat to the 50 ft (15·24 m) or so of large cargo-carrying vessels. The construction, however, appears to be always much the same. The punt is absolutely flat amidships and the planking of the bottom is bent up at a sharp angle at either end. This bottom planking is made up in one piece in the flat from a hotch-potch of planks of different lengths, re-using planks from old boats which have been broken up, joined together edge to edge with wooden dowels driven diagonally in holes already drilled and cut off at the ends flush with the plank face, so that the outside of the bottom is sprinkled with the oval shapes of the cut-off dowel ends. Across this bottom are laid light floor timbers at even distances, with more substantial timbers where the bottom planks are to be bent up to make the raised ends of the punt. These timbers, like the knees described below, are fastened with iron spikes.

The shaped side planks are then assembled in the same way as the bottom. The shape they are given determines that of the whole boat, where and how much the bottom planks suddenly turn up to make the raised ends and the curve of the sheer. To force the bottom planking up to the shape of the sides, levers are used while the flat midships section is weighted down with stones. The bottom planking is attached

Basil Greenhill

Figure 59   An Indus punt at Sukkur.

to the sides by sawn knees so cut as to give the sides a slight flare. The floor timbers are not shaped at the ends to fit this flare but are cut off square with the edges of the bottom planking, so that their ends do not come into contact with the side planking at all and, as they are laid quite separately from the side frames and are not only not joined to them but do not even touch them, they serve only as a means of holding the patchwork of the bottom planking together and in no sense as frames. There is no chine beam and the only caulking in the boats I examined in detail was one of mud applied to the outside of the join between the bottom and sides.

The upward sloping parts of the ends are decked with planks laid fore and aft on beams, the ends of the boat are finished off with bands of planks athwartships, laid across each deck for about one-quarter of its length. The open section of the boat amidships corresponds with the flat run of the bottom planks. There is a heavier beam where each deck ends and the open section begins. The tops of the knees are covered with a covering board and boards are nailed to them to act as a form of ceiling as far down as the beginning of the curved section of the knee.

The small boats of the canals and marshes, left unpainted and undecorated, are complete as I have described them. They are poled along from the foredeck. The larger, river cargo boats sometimes have a low wooden frame over the open centre section supported by turned posts and covered with bamboo mats. They have as well a long washboard perhaps 2 ft high along the outer edge of the hull to give further protection to the open section against spray and the river waves. This washboard is a fixture, and is supported by sawn knees. These big punts are steered by very narrow tall rudders and carved downward-pointing tillers. The rudders are hung from a massive framework built out from the bottom planking of the raised stern section. They are propelled with long sweeps pulled by men standing on the foredeck using single carved and turned thole pins to which the great sweeps are secured with ropes, with a massive sculling paddle made from a plank nailed and lashed to the end of a pole over the port quarter and, on occasion, by a settee sail set from a long light yard on a forward-raking mast. These big cargo punts are varnished and decorated with carvings, particularly on the planking at the underside of the raised stern and at the rudder head.

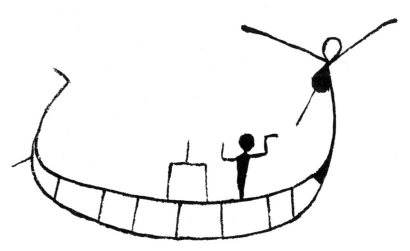

Figure 60   Papyrus raft.   *Landström,* Ships of the Pharaohs

The diagram in Figure 60 shows a pre-Dynastic Egyptian papyrus raft with a characteristic stem and stern. Papyrus rafts, of course, are still built in Africa and South America today. The model of a punt-shaped Egyptian boat, Figure 61, from the 6th Dynasty shows a shape startlingly paralleled by that of the Indus punt, photographed in Pakistan in the mid-1950s.

The surviving evidence suggests that Egyptian vessels were almost all flat-bottomed until the Middle Kingdom—roughly for the thousand years 3000–2000 BC. Towards the end of this period round-hulled boats begin to appear in surviving tomb models and drawings and soon after, in the period of the Middle Kingdom (c.2045–1780 BC), models of round-hulled boats begin to appear in profusion. The change seems to have been sudden and the flat-bottomed form may have persisted for large cargo vessels.

Figure 61   Tomb model of an Egyptian punt.   *Landström,* Ships of the Pharaohs

A new form of construction appears in about 1800 BC in the Dahshur boats, another tomb discovery. The planks were pegged together without sewing and made up from very small pieces of odd timber. They have no frames and again their shape appears to have imitated that naturally taken by papyrus rafts. Sewing persisted alongside the new form of fastening right through to the last millennium BC. There are interesting parallels between the Dahshur boats of the 18th century BC and the Nile *nuggar* of the present century. The drawing shown here, Figure 62, of a Dahshur boat compares with the photograph of the *nuggar*, Figure 63. The modern vessel was fastened with nails and not with pegs, but otherwise the construction was almost identical.

At this later period very large vessels were constructed for the transport of gigantic obelisks but their form of construction has been the subject of much discussion which has given rise to no general agreement.

There is a good deal of evidence about one type of boat which was in use in one local area of Britain at least from the middle of the second millennium BC to the middle of the first—during part of the North European Bronze Age. This evidence comprises the remains of four wooden boats which have been excavated from the area of the River Humber in the county of Humberside. These are probably the

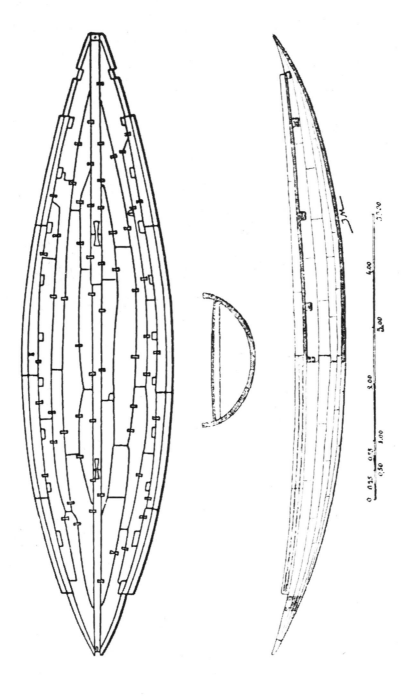

Figure 62   Drawing of one of the Dahshur boats.

National Maritime Museum

Figure 63   *Nuggar* on the Nile in the present century.

oldest remains of ancient plank-built boats found in Europe or indeed anywhere in the world outside Egypt. They show that very sophisticated wooden boats were also in use in Britain at this rather early period of North European civilisation. These remains are, at the time of writing, the subject of intensive study in the Archaeological Research Centre at the National Maritime Museum. A detailed report, or reports, on them will be published in due course. There are a great many questions still to be answered, but the evidence has lead to an opinion that the raft may possibly have been at least one of the influences in the origins of these vessels and, though ideas may well change as the current study of them develops, it is therefore not entirely inappropriate to consider them in this chapter.

The remains of three massive wooden boats were excavated from the mud at North Ferriby, then in Yorkshire, between 1946 and 1963 by Edward V. Wright. The fourth boat was excavated by a team organised by the National Maritime Museum under the direction of Sean McGrail, Chief Archaeologist, in 1974, from the banks of the river Ancholme at Brigg in what was formerly North Lincolnshire, Figure 64. It is only since this fourth boat has been recovered that full study of the evidence available has been possible.

Parts of the structure of the first of the boats excavated by Edward V. Wright have been dated by radio-carbon analysis at approximately the middle of the second millennium BC. The Brigg boat has been dated by the same process at approximately the middle of the first millennium BC.

Figure 64 The Brigg boat as revealed by the 1974 excavation by the National Maritime Museum.

National Maritime Museum

John Coates

Figure 65 Edward Wright's provisional hypothesis for a complete North Ferriby boat. Three strakes are joined to the projecting ends of the keel plank. Wright postulates the use of a pair of short strakes above the end of the keel plank. There is an inserted board and the final touch is the provision of props fore and aft further to shore up the board and butting against blocks on the keel plank. The hypothetical reconstruction is 54 ft (16½ m) long, 8 ft 6 ins (2·6 m) in the beam. Such a boat would have a carrying capacity of *c.* four tons provided that it was kept low.

Basil Greenhill

Figure 66   A *meia lua*, in the collection of boats at the Mariners' Museum, Newport News.

The remains are those of boats built with massive oak planks edge-joined by sewing together with yew or willow and caulked with moss. The Ferriby boats each had a flat keel plank. The boats were smooth skinned; there were no developed frames. Much study is being given to the possible form of the complete boats and the drawing shown here incorporates the latest provisional ideas based on the evidence of the Ferriby boats.

National Maritime Museum

Figure 67   A carving from Jonathan's Cave in East Wemyss, which the late T. C. Lethbridge suggested may represent a Bronze Age boat.

The parallels between the three Ferriby boats and the Brigg boat separated as they are by between five hundred and a thousand years is fascinating. Two of the Ferriby boats and the Brigg boat have cleats left standing on the surface of their massive planks through which pass transverse stiffening bars. In all four the planks were sewn together and the seams luted with moss capped with laths under the stitches. The boats were the products of a highly organised group working with great skill with very large supplies of timber readily available; the method of construction with the cleats left standing proud in the cut-down planks involved what seems now to have been prodigious waste both of timber and of labour. The boatbuilding tradition they represent however was strong and persistent, for it continued in the Humber valley apparently for something like a thousand years. The boats themselves are unlikely to have been ones in which sea-going voyages could be made. The most likely explanation of their use in the current state of knowledge is that the Ferriby boats were employed to connect north-south travel across the Humber and the Brigg boat east-west travel from the Lincolnshire wolds to the Lincolnshire limestone ridge across the shallow lake or creek which probably occupied the Ancholme region in the middle of the first millennium BC.

It has been suggested by Paul Johnstone that the *meia lua* (half moon), Figure 66, a large rowing fishing beach boat still in use in late 20th century Portugal, may stem remotely from the same roots as the Humber finds. It is possible that the bow and stern of the Ferriby boats were fashioned in a similar manner to that of the *meia lua*, while the general shape of the rock carving from Jonathan's Cave in East Weymss, Figure 67, which, it has been suggested, represents a Bronze Age boat, is not unlike that of the *meia lua* and another similar Portugese type surviving into the 20th century, the *saveiro*.

Bibliography

AUDEMARD, L.   *Les Jonques Chinoises*, 1957–69

LANDSTRÖM, B.   *Ships of the Pharaohs*, 1970

McGRAIL, S.   'The Brigg Raft Re-excavated', 1975B

McGRAIL, S. and SWITSUR, R.   'Early British Boats and their Chronology', 1975

NEEDHAM, J.   *Science and Civilisation in China*, 1971

WORCESTER, G. R. G.   *Sail and Sweep in China*, 1966

WRIGHT, E. V.   'The Boats of North Ferriby', 1972

WRIGHT, E. V.   *A Handbook on the Ferriby Boats*, in preparation

Chapter 6

The Second Root,
the Skin Boat

UNLIKE NEARLY EVERY other boat considered so far in detail in this book, the skin boat is of necessity of simple unqualified skeleton construction. She is made by wrapping a skin of animal hide or woven fabric around a pre-erected framework, and it is the shape of the pre-erected framework which determines the shape of the boat when she is complete.

A fundamental weakness of the skin boat is that she cannot cope with the stresses of seafaring as well as the wooden boat, be she a dugout or a plank-built boat, either edge-joined or non edge-joined. Although the skin or fabric covering can hold under the stretch imposed in the upper parts when the boat is balanced on a wave amidships, continuous stretching will wear it out very quickly and tear apart any stitches and it cannot resist the compression imposed on the lower parts in this situation, and *vice versa* a moment later. So the tendency of a boat in waves to be torn to pieces is very real with a skin boat, which must have a short, if merry, life under these conditions. An interesting and not too expensive piece of experimental archaeology would be the scientific sea trials of a big laden skin boat replica, to see just what would happen to her and how quickly, when subjected to the prolonged snap tight/concertina action to which she would be subjected.

The best known example of the skin boat in the modern world is the Eskimo kayak, frequently illustrated and described and widely used in modern Britain and North America by canoeists, Figure 76. Modern kayaks are made of synthetic fabric stretched over metal frames.

Skin boats have existed very widely and recently were still in use in various parts of the world. They are of two principal kinds, the round coracle type shaped like a floating bowl only slightly longer than she is broad and still used in Wales, Figure 68, Shropshire, and in other parts of the world and the curragh type, a long narrow structure, a boat form in its own right still in use today in Ireland and elsewhere, Figure 69.

116

National Maritime Museum

Figure 68   Coracle from the river Teifi in south-west Wales.

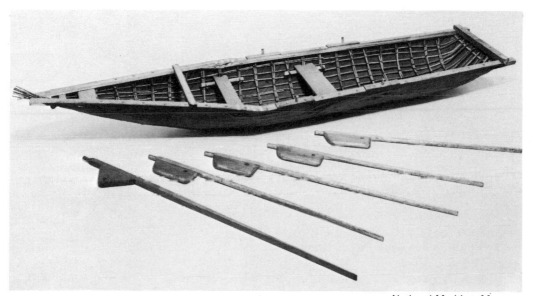

National Maritime Museum

Figure 69   A model of a curragh from Mulroy Bay in County Donegal in Ireland.

A variation on this skin boat is the basket boat. Here the framework is more complete, made of wicker like an old-fashioned basket of woven twigs, covered with a skin or fabric or merely made waterproof with clay or heavy tar.

It is likely that the skin boat was an important means of transport in Bronze Age Europe, and possibly later. There are fragments of evidence about the use of skin boats in Britain in pre-history, some of these have been gathered together here.

But, of course, by very definition, unlike dugouts and round-hulled plank-built boats like the massive structures which survived in the mud of Humberside for nearly three thousand years, skin boats with their short lived covering and light flimsy skeletons simply do not survive to provide archaeological evidence, though one piece of wood believed to be part of the gunwale of a skin boat has been discovered in a burial mound at Ballinderry in Ireland and dated from the 10th century AD. Archaeologists have long argued over the significance of the skin boat as a factor in the origins of wooden boat types. It is a simple and obvious basic boat form, but it could only develop in areas where a hunting people had both sufficient suitable skins and sufficient and suitable timber for the framework. It was unlikely to develop where people had both the available timber and the tools to make dugout boats, which in their extended forms are far more durable, of greater capacity and at their best more seaworthy than skin boats.

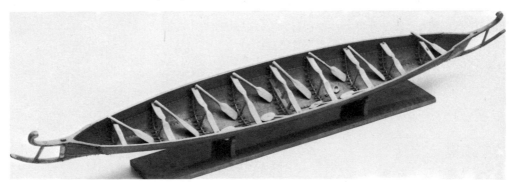

National Maritime Museum

Figure 70   Model of the Als or Hjortspring boat, the earliest known planked boat found in Scandinavia. Her planks are sewn together clinker-fashion with cord; her ribs are lashed to cleats cut out of the planks.

But, of course, tools of sufficient size and strength to cut out a dugout are a relatively modern development in the history of man. Dugout making can be easier than might at first seem. With the aid of fire a great deal can probably be done, given a good deal of time, with very simple tools. But there have to be tools of a reasonable size and archaeological evidence suggests that some peoples who do not appear to have had such tools nevertheless conducted maritime trade. Paul Johnstone has recently suggested that the maritime trade which appears to have existed in the Eastern Mediterranean as early as the later part of the seventh millennium BC may well have been conducted in, or on, reed-bundle raft boats, and there is good local evidence for this in some specific cases. But where the right conditions suited them, much later in the development of man, the skin boat probably played a large part in commerce over water in different societies at different periods and without necessarily

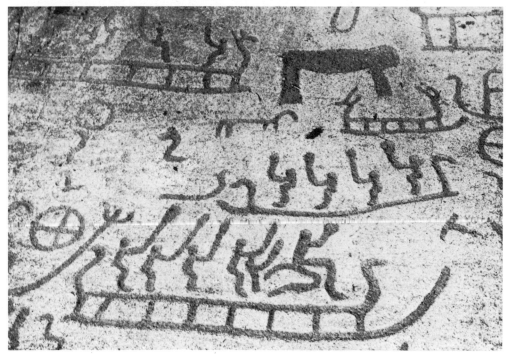

National Maritime Museum

Figure 71   Bronze Age rock carvings at Kalnes in Norway.

always influencing the development of local wooden boats later, when materials, tools and skills became available. It is likely though that the individual boats did not last very long.

For several reasons then, it seems likely that the skin boat played only a marginal role in the history of the development of most later wooden boat types, which, particularly in Northern Europe, appear to have evolved principally through that of the dugout—this argument is developed extensively in succeeding chapters of this book.

The skin boat probably particularly influenced the development of boats, in those areas where conditions were such that skin boatbuilding peoples and dugout boatbuilding peoples came together, as they may have done in parts of Scandinavia in pre-history. Indeed, it has been argued by Eric McKee that the skin boat, although not a main stream of development, had a vital part to play in the improvement of efficient internal stiffening of edge-joined plank-built boats and could account for the apparent superiority of Scandinavian framing in the Viking Age (see Chapter 14). It is argued by some archaeologists that the rock drawings found at many places in Norway and Sweden represent Stone Age and Bronze Age skin boats and that the Als or Hjortspring boat, Figure 70, a wooden boat dating from about 200 BC, is a wood-built imitation of a skin boat made by a wood

Paul Johnstone

Figure 72   Experimental skin boat built at Frederikstad, Norway in 1971.

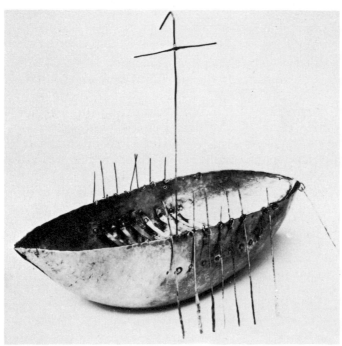

National Museum of Ireland

Figure 73   Gold boat model found near Broighter in Ireland.

boatbuilding people, already far advanced beyond the simple dugout, copying for some reason an earlier boat form or a boat form used perhaps by a conquered enemy, or for ceremonial purposes.

The rock carvings at Kalnes, Norway, illustrated here, Figure 71, have been dated to the Bronze Age and they are considered by some authorities to represent skin boats, in this case with six paddlers. In 1971 Professor Marstrander of Oslo University and Paul Johnstone organised the building of a hypothetical reconstruction of this boat by Mr. Odd Johnson of Frederikstad, also illustrated—Figure 72, and established that the boat was manoeuvrable, seaworthy and could carry a substantial load in calm water. The experiment did not prove that the Kalnes and other similar rock carvings represented skin boats, or even boats at all. But it did show that it was possible to build effective boats with the materials available in the Bronze Age and much earlier. The boat was not however subjected to prolonged trials, laden, in rough water.

The Als boat is the earliest known plank-built boat found in Scandinavia, indeed the earliest known plank-built boat in Northern Europe apart from the Humberside finds. It is a round-bottomed boat made of five overlapping planks, stitched together, edge to edge. But the particular interest of the boat rests in its stem and stern. These comprise solid blocks carved out to form bows and stern, with the bottom plank projecting outside the boat proper at either end almost like a runner, so that the general appearance is not unlike that of Professor Marstrander's and Paul Johnstone's skin boat, though the boat herself is a wooden clinker-built craft, entirely plank-built apart from the end blocks and in what appears to be an earlier form of the Scandinavian tradition. It may well be that she represents a mingling of boat-building traditions.

The evidence for the existence of the skin boat in Britain is very limited. A gold boat model found in 1891 near Limavady in the north of Ireland was part of a horde

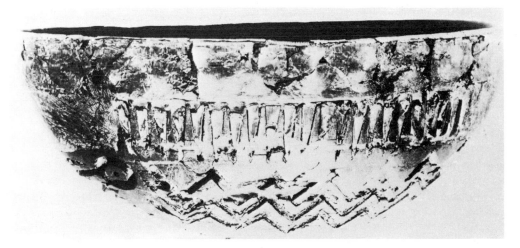

Figure 74   The Caergwrle bowl.   *National Museum of Wales*

or votive deposit, Figure 73. It is believed to represent a skin boat with oars and a mast and it has been dated at the 1st century AD. The model is only 7½ ins (19 cms) long, 3 ins (8 cms) in the beam and lacks any details of construction. The Caergwrle bowl, an oak bowl found in a bog near Caergwrle Castle, Flintshire, in 1823 and now in the National Museum of Wales at Cardiff, Figure 74, is even less evidence though it is generally considered to represent a Bronze Age skin boat formalised in the limitations of its bowl function. It measures 8 ins (20 cms) across its largest axis, the gold band around the rim includes twenty sun disks, a Bronze Age decorative feature, as are also the *occuli* in the 'bows'. The vertical triangular cuts are believed to represent oars and the three horizontal zigzags the sea, but all this is rather hypothetical, as is the evidence provided by a carving on an 8th century pillar near Bantry in County Cork, Figure 75, usually considered to represent a skin boat of generally curragh form.

Figure 75   The Bantry boat.   *National Maritime Museum*

Coracles have been the subject of detailed study by Geraint Jenkins of the National Museum of Wales. They are very simple skin boats made in latter days by stretching fabric over a rough framework. There is a fine example in the National Maritime Museum built by Mr J. C. Thomas of Brotiog Cenarth and used on the river Teifi for salmon fishing. The model shown here in Figure 68, is of a river Teifi coracle.

The Eskimo culture, dependent very largely on what could be won from the sea, developed the skin boat to perhaps its finest forms in modern times. They were an aquatic hunting people in a very hostile environment, lacking in timber but rich in skins, with driftwood and whale bone also available. They developed one of the most specialised of boat types—the kayak, built by making a light wooden framework and sewing seal skins over it. The kayak is a one-man boat, but a bigger skin boat, called in some Eskimo dialects the *umiak*, was used for conveying goods and people. Both types were very safe and seaworthy in skilled hands but not, I suspect trials will prove, for long voyages, heavily laden in rough water.

National Maritime Museum

Figure 76   Kayaks in use by eskimos at Churchill on Hudson Bay.

Bibliography

ADNEY, E. T. and CHAPELLE, H. I.   *Bark Canoes and Skin Boats of North America*, 1964

BARNWELL, E. L.   'Caergwrle Cup', 1875

BRØNDSTED, J.   'Oldtidsbaden fra Als', 1925

ELLMERS, D.   'Keltischer Schiffbau', 1969

EVANS, A. J.   'Votive Deposit of Gold Objects', 1897

JENKINS, J. G.   *Nets and Coracles*, 1974

JOHNSTONE, P.   'A Medieval Skin Boat', 1962

JOHNSTONE, P.   'The Bantry Boat', 1964

JOHNSTONE, P.   'Bronze Age Sea Trial', 1972

MARSTRANDER, S.   *Østfolds jordbruksristninger: Skjeberg*, 1963

ROSENBERG, G.   'Hjortspringfundet', 1937

Chapter 7

The Third Root,
The Bark Boat

WITH THE BARK boat we are back in the boatbuilding tradition of shell construction, for despite a superficial resemblance to the skin boat the bark boat is in fact of completely different origin. In the skin boat the skin is a watertight cover. It is skeleton-built, and derives its shape from the frame around which it is wrapped. The simple bark canoe is shell built, the bark being the main strength member determining the shape of the boat and only supported by an internal framework made to fit it. Perhaps the terms skeleton-built and shell-built can be applied most accurately to skin boats and bark boats. Even more than the skin boat, the bark boat is not able to take the stresses imposed by long voyages at sea or in very rough water when heavily laden.

The bark canoe is particularly associated with the North American Indian. Certainly these people developed it to its most perfect form, particularly in the

Figure 77   Model of Beothuck canoe.   *National Maritime Museum*

124

Ottawa valley region, but it also existed elsewhere in the world—Australia, South America, Africa, Siberia and Indonesia.

Even North American Indian canoes varied greatly in shape and structure. The model illustrated here, Figure 77, used by the now extinct Beothuck Indian tribe of Newfoundland, who, from their habit of daubing themselves with red clay, were responsible for the dubbing by Europeans of the whole North American race as red, is of particularly interesting construction, with its raised sides. The Ottawa valley canoe, Figure 78 was made by lumbermen at the beginning of this century and is an excellent and rare example of the North American Indian bark canoe in her most developed form. Her framing bears little resemblance to the complex structure of twigs used by the Indians before they adopted the methods of their European contacts, but its shape is still determined by the bark shell and the frames have been carefully made to fit. This canoe was probably made by Sarazin of the Algonquin Reserve in Ontario. Sarazin's son was still building bark canoes in the 1960s. The raw materials of the canoes he built were spruce roots, cedar wood, ash wood, spruce gum, bear grease, moose hide and the bark of the white or canoe birch tree, though spruce bark and other barks could be used.

National Maritime Museum

Figure 78   Ottawa valley bark canoe.

The white birch was preferred because the bark is more waterproof than that of most substitutes. It was gathered in the largest available pieces in the early summer when the sap was flowing. Roots of the black spruce which lie close to the surface were collected at the same time. From the black spruce also came the spruce gum used to cement the seams in the bark and this also was gathered in the first warm May weather after the April thaw.

Sections of bark were stripped from the white birch trees for the hull; white cedar wood was used for the ribs, gunwales and sheathing; ash (or possibly maple) for the thwarts. A flat wooden pattern weighed down by stones was used to shape the steamed bark and temporary stakes kept the sides of the bark vertical.

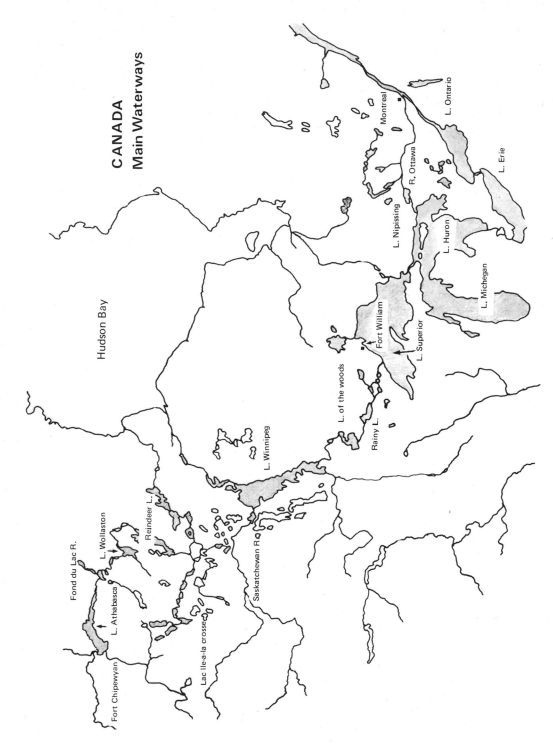

CANADA
Main Waterways

Hudson Bay

Fond du Lac R.

L. Wollaston

Reindeer L.

Fort Chipewyan

L. Athabasca

Lac Ile-a-la crosse

Saskatchewan R.

L. Winnipeg

L. of the woods

Rainy L.

Fort William

L. Superior

L. Michegan

L. Huron

L. Nipissing

R, Ottawa

Montreal

L. Ontario

L. Erie

National *Maritime Museum*

Figure 79   The fur trader's canoe route across Canada.

Steamed gunwales were then fitted and the bark allowed to dry in shape. At bow and stern the pieces of birch bark were sewn together with spruce roots, subsequently sheathing was fitted under tension inside the bark and 'U'-shaped ribs forced into position to tauten the bark shell. The gunwales were temporarily secured by nailed planks, thwarts were fitted and finally the seams in the outer bark caulked with spruce gum. Properly handled the bark canoe could stand up to hard wear and it was a vehicle of serious transport, on inland waterways, not only of human beings but in its larger forms of heavy goods, and big bark canoes played a major role in the development of Canada.

Half the fresh water in the world is to be found in Canada. There are as many miles of inland waterway as there are in all the other countries of the world combined. You can put a canoe in the water in any Canadian city and paddle to the Atlantic, Pacific, Arctic Ocean or through the United States to the gulf of Mexico. This fantastic pattern of natural water routes was the highway of the bark canoes of the 'voyageurs', mainly French speaking, who opened up the trade of the northern part of the continent. There was a regular east-west trade across Canada thirty years before settlers in the United States had crossed the Mississippi. The greatest of the bark canoe trade routes was the 'Voyageurs' Highway' of the fur trade, three thousand miles of canoeing from Lachine near Montreal to Fort Chipewyan on Lake Athabasca, Figure 79. Only with the coming of the railways in the 1880s did this route cease to be the fastest way of crossing Canada. The fur trader's canoe was larger than the usual Indian canoe, it could be up to 36 ft (10·97 m) in length, Figure 80. Its reign was from the 17th century to the early part of the 19th century,

Figure 80   The cargo canoe of the voyageurs.   *Public Archives of Canada*

and it played a fundamental part in the development of the North American continent.

But these North American Indian bark canoes were very sophisticated craft. Bark canoes used in Australia, South America and Africa were a great deal simpler. In some cases a long piece of bark was peeled off a tree and the ends in turn placed over a fire. They became soft and pliable and the edges were doubled over and secured with skewers of wood, light pieces of timber were then placed between the edges of the bark to prevent the sides from collapsing. In many of the Australian bark canoes a few stretchers were present but no frames. Most of these primitive bark canoes were made from a single piece, but more sophisticated builders from northern Australia developed techniques of joining together wide strips of bark, extending the sides with bark weatherboarding and using gunwales and frames made of mangrove stick.

Bibliography

ADNEY, E. T. and CHAPELLE, H. I.   *Bark Canoes and Skin Boats of North America*, 1964

MORSE, E. W.   *Canoe Routes of the Voyageurs*, 1962

MORSE, E. W.   *Fur Trade Canoe Routes of Canada, Then and Now*, 1968

Chapter 8

The Fourth Root, The Dugout

THE FOURTH ROOT was of much greater significance in the origins of boats than any of the first three. Far more types of boats and vessels in the world owe their origins remotely to a hollowed-out log than to a raft, skin boat or bark boat, for the hollowed log is susceptible to almost limitless development while the very nature of the structure and materials used in rafts, skin boats and bark boats restricts their development in varying degrees. The lines of descent from the dugout are extremely complex, starting and stopping again at different times in different parts of the world, inter-relating in some areas, developing in other places without any apparent influence from other areas. The greater part of the remainder of this book will be taken up with an examination of some of the complex lines of descent traceable back to dugouts of one form or another.

In England and Wales alone the remains of over 170 ancient dugouts have been recorded, which means that very many have been discovered and either not recorded or not recognised at all for what they are. Of those recorded about half survive in various museums in different states of disintegration. There are records of more than another 150 discoveries of ancient dugouts in Ireland and Scotland. Probably every country in Europe could add its quota. Most of these dugouts have not been excavated scientifically, nor have they been published adequately—indeed many have not been published at all. At the time of writing Sean McGrail of the National Maritime Museum is preparing a new survey of dugouts found in Britain.

The oldest examples of dugouts we have today are several thousand years old. Radio-carbon dating shows that dugouts were used in England and Wales from at least 1500 BC to about AD 1000. In fact they were probably used both earlier and later. Dugouts are still being made in the last quarter of the 20th century in Asia, Africa and South America for everyday use as working boats. They vary in shape and structure from hollowed logs, so crudely made that they derive most of their buoyancy from the lightness of the wood used rather than from the air they envelop,

Figure 81
Making of a
dugout in Brazil.

National Maritime Museum

to light graceful structures with shells so thin that they are indistinguishable from plank-built boats, indeed it is often difficult to tell whether a particular boat has been carved out from a single hollowed log or built up of planks, especially when she has been much repaired with planks and her sides extended.

The undertaking of making a dugout is a considerable one. Suitable trees must be available near to the water, and the community concerned must have a great deal of time available for this kind of specialised work, for making a dugout frequently takes more time than building houses, or cattle pens or fencing fields. It is a kind of large scale capital investment requiring a sufficient surplus of food production to enable the dugout makers to give the considerable amount of time demanded by the work. They must have reasonably efficient tools. It follows that to make such a big investment the community must be a prosperous one in a certain stage of technical development.

In 1973 a big dugout was specially made in Brazil for the Development of the Boat display in the National Maritime Museum. The accompanying photograph, Figure 81 illustrates dugout making at its most sophisticated. But the men who made her did so as a normal job, for these vessels are still being cut out for use in beach and

National Maritime Museum

Figure 82 A one-man
dugout from Ceylon.

river fishing, and can in fact be seen lying on the beach beneath the expensive hotels on the fabulous foreshore at Copacabana in the southern suburbs of Rio.

By way of contrast the little Ceylonese dugout shown in Figure 82 was used for harbour net-fishing. It is a one-man boat and like the huge Brazilian vessel it is a simple hollowed-out log, neither expanded nor extended, although the shaping of the top of the sides appears to be an imitation of an extensive plank or wash strake. Low relief transverse bands inside this and similar canoes have been taken by some authorities including Hornell as evidence of the influence of skin boat-building techniques on the dugout. A much more probable explanation for their presence is to provide a toe-hold and prevent the crew slipping on the wet wood.

A well-made dugout from a small log can be an efficient, light and seaworthy small boat. In her bigger versions inevitably, because of the dimensions of the tree from which she was made, she is too long and narrow to be either very seaworthy or very handy. The efficiency of a larger dugout was greatly improved by softening the sides with fire and water and then forcing them apart with wooden struts. This treatment:

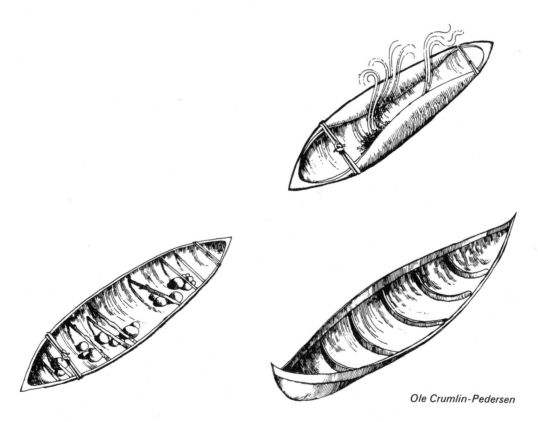

Ole Crumlin-Pedersen

Figure 83   Three stages in making an expanded and extended dugout.

Figure 84   Dugouts at the Mariners' Museum at Newport News.   *Basil Greenhill*

(a)   made the sides curve into a boat shape; and
(b)   made the ends of the dugout lift so that they were higher than the middle thus
      giving the dugout 'sheer', the characteristic curve of a traditional wooden boat
      in profile.

Ole Crumlin-Pedersen's diagram, Figure 83, shows one way in which a dugout can
be made.

The result was a shape still to be met with in many parts of the world. If the solid
ends were shaped away at the bottom and sides a graceful dugout canoe could result.
The third and fourth dugouts down from the top in the wall display in the Mariners'
Museum at Newport News, Figure 84, correspond almost exactly with stages two
and three in Figure 83.

Where the tools and skills existed to make planks from logs, and once a dugout had
been expanded, it could be made more efficient still by extending the sides with
planks. These were fastened to the sides of the dugout, and when metal fastenings
were not available the planks were sewn on with natural fibres, or pegged with wood
pins. A second and a third plank could be added to make a seaworthy boat. This
process was applicable even to the largest dugouts and some expanded and extended
dugout built boats still in use in Bangladesh today are seagoing ships 70 ft (22·86 m)
long, carrying many tons of cargo.

Such vessels are far more able than might be imagined to resist the working
stresses met with by a laden boat or vessel at sea, because of the great strength and
rigidity of the dugout shell which comprises the lower part of the hull. They do not
tear themselves apart as quickly as might be supposed. Nevertheless, the wear and
deterioration of fastenings and caulking is such that these boats are stripped down
into their component parts and rebuilt many times during a long working life,
sometimes even as frequently as every year. This, I suspect, happened to most sewn
boats in history.

It must not be assumed from the foregoing that this process of development was
inevitable. The great majority of dugouts were quite adequate for the limited
requirements for which they were made, without expansion, extension, or, indeed,
much shaping. Once again the dugout must be judged by the purpose for which she
was made. For use on a lake, small river or sheltered arm of the sea a simple log will
do. Sometimes dugouts were extended without expansion. The great majority of
dugouts surviving in Britain do not appear to have been expanded, although some
were probably extended.

But it is from this root, that of the expanded and extended dugout, that many
different types of boat developed in different parts of the world; in particular most
European edge-joined boats and vessels, including it is now widely but not
universally agreed, those in the North European and British clinker tradition.

A series of photographs, Figures 85 to 88, which I took in Bangladesh in the early
1950s shows how fishermen from Chittagong extended an expanded dugout base to
make a substantial and seaworthy little boat. Here the extending strakes were sewn
to the dugout base with split bamboo.

Basil Greenhill

Figure 85   An expanded dugout lies at the water's edge. On the mud above her lie three similar dugouts, each extended with a single plank each side to make a seaworthy fishing vessel.

Figure 86   The first plank being fitted into position on the dugout base. The planks are secured with split bamboo sewing, the holes for which have already been drilled in the dugout, but not in the plank which has not yet been finally shaped.

Basil Greenhill

Basil Greenhill

Figure 87   Both planks are now shaped and sewn into position,
the seams sealed with twisted reeds on the inside.

Figure 88   A few props to act as side frames, stringers and a
shallow top strakes are added to complete the boat.

Basil Greenhill

Basil Greenhill

Figure 89   A *balam*, a large expanded and extended dugout used as a coastal cargo vessel, under sail.

Figure 89 shows the ultimate development of this local boat form, a Chittagong *balam*. The traditional *balam* from this part of the Bay of Bengal is a sewn boat, built entirely without metal. It is essentially an expanded and extended dugout with up to five strakes sewn on each side, nothing more than an enlarged version of the little boat the fishermen were building by the side of the road near Chittagong when I happened along many years ago. Seagoing *balams* are impressive vessels, some of them being 60 ft (18·29 m) long, 7 ft (2·13 m) deep and 12 ft–14 ft (3·66 m–4·27 m) in the beam. The floors are secured to the dugout base with trenails while the frames and deck beams are lashed into position with split bamboo. Figure 90 shows in detail the criss-cross of frames and stringers lashed together and secured to the sewn outer planking at the seams of a *murina* a very similar Bangladesh expanded and extended dugout type.

The planks could be joined to an expanded dugout and to each other in several ways. As with the Chittagong boats, the fishing boat, the *balam* and the *murina*, they could be joined flush, edge to edge, so that the outside of the boat presented a smooth surface. They could be joined to overlap one another at the edges, clinker-style, so that the outside of the boat had the ridges of the plank edges running along its length, or they could be joined to overlap one another with a bevelled edge on each

Basil Greenhill

Figure 90   Framing of a *murina*.

plank or a half rabbet on each plank. Such boats, although the planks may in fact overlap quite as much as in the second form, may have smooth skins. The four different methods are shown very clearly in Figure 91.

Though until recently both simple and expanded and extended dugouts were still widely used in many parts of the world, at the same time, plank-built boats were developed. The process depended on the availability of timber and tools to make planks. Depending on the tools used—splitting wedges, axes, adzes or saws —the planks which resulted lent themselves to being used in different ways, and this influenced the types of boat which developed.

In some societies early plank-built boats were deliberate copies of the lighter and better shaped types of dugouts. Indeed, in some parts of the world this process of copying still goes on; the planks are always joined to one another to make a wooden shell as in the original dugout, and perhaps afterwards strengthened with frame timbers, cut to fit. Thus the dugout determines the shape of the final boat. Figure 92, drawn by Kurt Kühn for Dr. Wolfgang Rudolph, shows a boat made on a dugout base which can easily be converted into a keel plank and thus a round-hulled, plank-built boat evolves. It is one of the processes of such evolution, and appears to be that of at least some local boats in the South-Eastern Baltic, and also in Bangladesh.

Japanese seafarers and boat and shipbuilders were by deliberate administrative decision isolated from outside contacts for more than two centuries. It is not

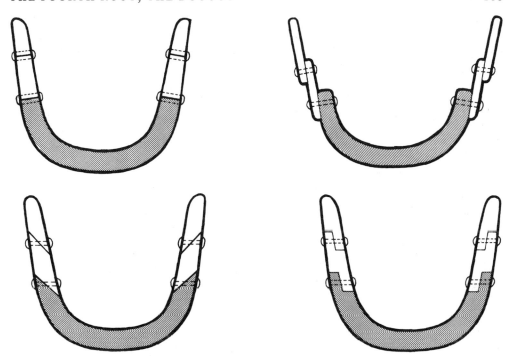

Figure 91   Methods of edge-joining the planks of an extended dugout.   *Kurt Kühn*

surprising, therefore, that the history of Japanese boatbuilding traditions demonstrates the development of the dugout and evolution from it in a very pure form, without significant outside influences. Apart from a few dugouts found in fresh water environments no discoveries of ancient boat remains have been made in Japan. But there is an outstandingly rich field of detailed contemporary illustrations of boats and ships from the 14th century onwards. From these, from the detailed legislation enacted in the late 19th century designed to discourage the building of large traditional vessels, and from the evidence provided by small vessels built to the old traditions in recent years, it is possible to reconstruct the evolution of Japanese traditions with a reasonable degree of confidence—perhaps more confidence than with any other medieval vessels except the Viking ships.[1]

Despite the great influence of Chinese culture in many ways in old Japan, traditional Japanese boatbuilding seems to have owed nothing to China—a phenomenon which has been the subject of much speculation. While, as we have already seen, the raft is generally accepted to have played a large part in the evolution of Chinese boats and ships, it appears to have played no part in the

---

[1] This account of the development of Japanese boats and vessels is derived from discussion with Professor Satoru Matsuki of the Kobe University of Mercantile Marine, and from examination of the structures of traditionally-built boats and vessels during two and a half years' residence in Japan.

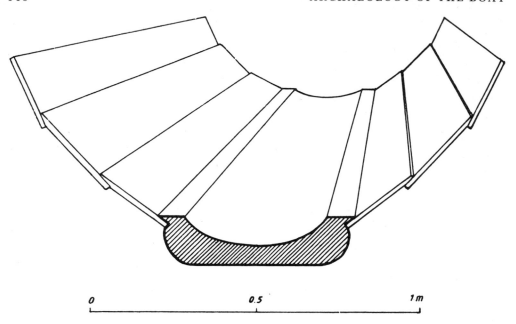

0   0.5   1 m

Figure 92   Plank-built boat on a dugout base.   *Kurt Kühn*

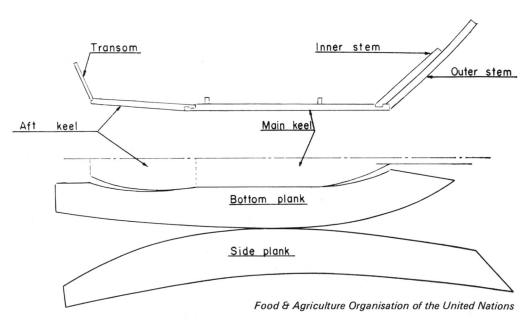

Food & Agriculture Organisation of the United Nations

Figure 93   Strake diagram of a *Yamato-gata* vessel.

development of those of Japan. Illustrations of the 14th century show highly developed dugouts built in three parts, a central hollowed-out log with two more hollowed logs, joined to it, one at each end, set at an angle to the basic dugout to give a sheer to the whole structure, usually higher in the stern than in the bows. These dugout structures are perhaps reminiscent in some ways of the Utrecht ship described and illustrated in Chapter 11.

The basic dugout appears never to have been expanded but only extended. An entirely plank-built, completely frameless, edge-joined tradition, copying the three dugout form, was apparently developed in the 16th century, after which time no more illustrations of big dugouts appear. This frameless plank-built tradition, the *Yamato-gata*, Japanese-style, was to persist for three hundred years with relatively little development. This persistence was the product of Japanese political history. In the 1630s the Tokugawa Shogunate prohibited foreign voyaging and, apart from very restricted entry to designated ports, prohibited visits by foreign ships. At first a restriction was imposed forbidding the building of vessels over approximately fifty tons gross, and though this was soon lifted for merchant ships, the embargo on foreign trade was very rigorously enforced. It was at roughly this period that the big *Yamato-gata* vessels were perfected for the trades round and among the Japanese islands and, in the absence of any foreign contact, the tradition persisted in detail for big ships until Japan was opened up in the last quarter of the 19th century, and it survived into the early 20th century.

Yamato-gata is best represented by a strake diagram, Figure 93, and a photograph of a model, Figure 94, in the National Maritime Museum. The diagram shows an edge-joined vessel without frames built of broad strakes. She has no keel but a massive hog. Cross beams just below deck level were a long-term characteristic of the tradition in all sizes of boats and vessels. One of the relatively few contemporary models surviving, that shown in Figure 94, has been dated by Professor Satoru Matsuki as of the very early 19th century. Later in the century as cargoes became bigger the lines were changed a little with greater beam and higher sides.

After the Meiji Restoration in 1868 the building of big *Yamato-gata* vessels was progressively discouraged by government policy and the introduction of a degree of framing was encouraged in small vessels. In 1887 the building of *Yamato-gata* vessels of over fifty tons was forbidden and the last big traditional cargo vessels vanished before 1930. The government's object was, of course, the encouragement of work in traditions which would permit the building of much bigger wooden vessels. Since there was no restriction on small vessels the old tradition lingered on among the beach fishing boatbuilders. The extra strength needed to withstand the stresses imposed by the semi-diesel engines adopted after the First World War forced fishing boatbuilders to adopt variations of skeleton-construction even for small vessels, though edge-joining was retained.

For some types of fishing, however, motors had still not been adopted even in the late 1950s or were specifically forbidden in the interests of conservation (as they were in the Maryland oyster fishery of Chesapeake Bay and in the Truro river oyster fishery in Britain). In these circumstances almost completely traditional vessels

Figure 94   Model of a *Yamato-gata* cargo vessel.

National Maritime Museum

Basil Greenhill

Figure 95   A mid-20th century *Yamato-gata* fishing vessel.

survived—indeed I was able to examine and record an almost pure *Yamato-gata* vessel built as late as 1957. She was a seine-net boat working off the beach of Kenada-wan at the mouth of Tokyo Bay, Figure 95. Thus it was that in Japan, more clearly perhaps than elsewhere in the world, the boats and small vessels of the 20th century were the true descendants of the big vessels of previous centuries.

The photographs which follow show dugouts and a few of the boat types which have developed from the dugout in different parts of the world. The Maori war canoe, Figure 96, (not the double canoe used on the trans-Pacific migrations of this great seafaring people) was the most ornate of all the traditional Pacific craft. It could be up to 70 ft (21·34 m) in length with a beam of 5 ft (1·52 m) and was dug out from a single kauri pine tree. These canoes were normally paddled but occasionally a sail of an inverted triangular shape was used.

The single outrigger canoe is a model from Manus in the Admiralty Islands and the outrigger, which is braced by four booms lashed to the gunwale of the canoe, makes the basic dugout more stable and hence more seaworthy, Figure 97. The first

National Maritime Museum

Figure 96   Model of a Maori war canoe.

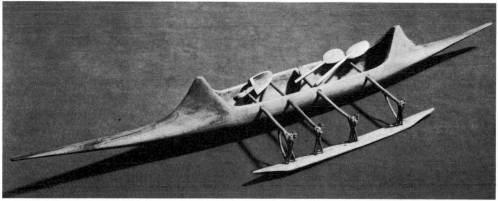

National Maritime Museum

Figure 97   Model of an out-rigger canoe from the Admiralty Islands.

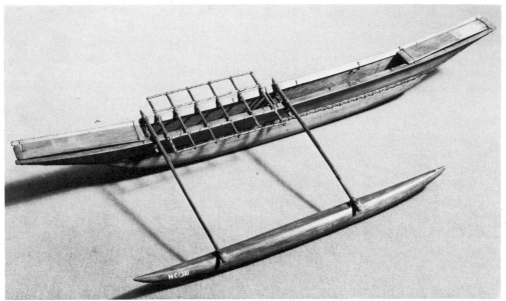

National Maritime Museum

Figure 98   Model of an extended dugout from Ceylon.

stage in the evolution of the plank-built boat from the dugout is shown in the illustration from Ceylon where the outrigger dugout has a single strake sewn onto the dugout to give more freeboard, Figure 98.

The Shalish dugout, Figure 99, is a North American Indian vessel from British Columbia. They are the largest dugouts in the modern world, made from trees of enormous size.

The Tepuke dugout, Figure 100, is a sailing dugout with an outrigger from the Solomon Islands group. Here the outrigger and its booms are of complex design; a

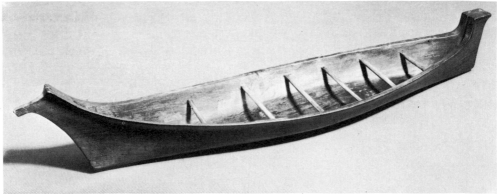

National Maritime Museum

Figure 99   Model of a dugout from British Columbia.

Figure 100   Model of a sailing dugout from the Solomon Islands.

characteristic feature is the half moon matting sail. Like other advanced forms of outrigger canoe this type was capable of ocean voyages; the crew living on the platform structure.

I have already referred many times to one of the richest boat cultures surviving in the world, that in Bangladesh in the valley of the Brahmaputra and its tributaries, where today there are still thousands of rowing and sailing cargo boats. The majority of them are variations on the same basic types, they are of different shapes and proportions but of the same construction. They are round-hulled boats built of edge-joined planks, in different ways, sometimes with the lower plank laid outside the

Basil Greenhill

Figure 101   The solid block ends of Bangladesh cargo boats reach out over the water like the stems of Viking ships, see Figure 135.

upper, in the reverse of the main European tradition, more frequently built in this way but with the planks half rabbeted so that the outside of the vessel presents a smooth skin, sometimes built in ordinary North European clinker style. The frames are then shaped to the shell and inserted. Some boats are never framed at all except for a few floor timbers. The evidence strongly suggests that the boats of this great floating world developed from expanded and extended dugouts. Indeed, it is still possible to see boats at every stage of development from the dugout—so light and so similar to small plank-built boats as to be distinguishable from them only on close examination—to the sophisticated plank-built boat. All have the solid block ends which are characteristic of some types of boats of dugout origin. The planking of most of these boats coming up to the gunwale at bows and stern instead of into the bent-up keel plank, shows a solution to the problem of the plank ends adopted in few places in the modern world. As I have already said in Chapter 3 of this book, this solution resembles a form of planking shown on pictures of European vessels which were called hulks in the 14th century and with which I shall be dealing later.

Besides the round-hulled boats there are flat-bottomed vessels, some of the largest of which, with sides clinker-built in European style, resembled the cogs of medieval Europe which will also be discussed in a subsequent chapter.

When Europeans first penetrated the Arab trade routes in the late 1400s using their relatively newly perfected non edge-joined skeleton-built big ships to give them the necessary range and fire power, they found the great Arab trade of the Indian Ocean was conducted in highly developed plank-built boats and ships, the planks of which were sewn together edge to edge. Such vessels were not gimcrack affairs but strong and seaworthy, provided they were well maintained—which usually meant rebuilding them each year.

Under European influence Arab vessels rapidly developed to copy features of contemporary European hull forms, like the ornate stern of the 16th century European traders. Eventually in some places the shell-constructed vessels gave way locally to partly skeleton-built or entirely skeleton-built non edge-joined vessels. But until recent years a thriving trade was still conducted in Arab vessels little different in general shape and sailing rig from some of those the first European travellers met with five hundred years ago.

The two photographs show a pointed-stern *bhum*, Figure 102, and a transom-sterned *baggala* from the Persian Gulf, Figure 103. Both these merchant vessels are

Basil Greenhill

Figure 102   A double-ended Pakistan cargo vessel of similar shape to an Arab *bhum*.

Figure 103   A *baggala*, a square-sterned Arab cargo vessel.

types which until recent years ranged far and wide in the Arabian Sea. The principal long-range vessels were based at Kuwait. The *baggalas'* quarter galleries show the influence of 17th and 18th century European merchant ships, even though I took these photographs in the early 1950s.

The *bhum* is a derivation from the double-ended, edge-joined, plank-built sewn vessels and examples of similar types survived in use until comparatively recent years. The National Maritime Museum holds two of the dozen or so models known to exist of one of these types, the *mtepe*. The *mtepe* was built in the Lamu Archipelago of East Africa and is a recently surviving example of a large wooden sewn ship with many parallels with early Arab vessels. As the photograph, Figure 104, of the Museum's model clearly shows the strakes are sewn together with coir twine, pegs are then driven into the stitch holes from the inside to secure the stitches and to prevent leaks. The exposed twine is then cut off flush with the outside of the boat. Frames are subsequently inserted and stitched direct to the strakes and beams provide athwartship strength.

As I have already said clear evidence of a probable origin in an expanded and extended dugout is provided when a boat type has solid or block ends to a planked hull, in place of a stem and stern post or transoms or any other of the terminations described and illustrated in Chapter 3. These block ends represent of course the solid ends of almost all dugout structures. There are groups of boats of this type in the Southern Baltic, a distinctive environment where the raw material available, the technology used and the function of the boat have all remained much the same for many centuries. Thus early boat types have survived to the present day and provide authentic first-hand evidence for boat historians and archaeologists. These boats have been studied by Dr Wolfgang Rudolph who has pointed out that in this region the principle of shell-construction being given by the dugout model, the progressive evolution of the technique led to craft of higher quality being developed along two different lines;

(a) by way of the extension of expanded dugouts, which became in the end no more than bottom shells

National Maritime Museum

Figure 104   A model of a *mtepe*.

(b)   by way of three or five part bottom plank boats which were shaped so as to
       resemble closely the form of the dugout, and in the building of which the use of
       hollowed-out massive baulks of timber for the boat ends was a favourite
       solution to the problem of the plank ends.

Bottom shelled boats developed at Rostock around the mouth of the Oder and
around that of the Vistula, while the longitudinally-laid bottom plank boat with
block stems developed around the Lower Oder, the east Pomeranian lagoons and at
Rügen among other places.

Big dugouts were in commercial use in the United States, for instance in the Long
Island Sound oyster fishery, as late as the beginning of the present century. Perhaps
the most remarkable dugout originated vessel in use in the modern world was
developed in the United States. She was the Chesapeake Bay log bugeye, used in the
oyster fishery on the Maryland shore of the great Bay. She was the more remarkable

Figure 105 Chesa-
peake Bay log canoe un-
der construction.

the late Marion Brewington

Figure 106   Chesapeake Bay log bugeye *Sanxton Hubbard*, built at Solomons, Maryland, in 1891.

in that she was a late 19th century development of the dugout and at the same time one of the larger types of dugout based vessels to be developed anywhere in the world.

After the War between the States the Maryland oyster fishery, rich from several years of no fishing and with prices sky-high, faced a period of great potential prosperity. The fishery had been carried out by scraping with tongs from canoes and small sailing vessels. Now a change in Maryland legislation allowed the dragging of dredges to scrape the oysters off the beds. To drag these heavy dredges bigger and more powerful sailing craft were needed, but there was little capital available. To build a non edge-joined skeleton vessel was a shipwrighting job, the building traditions of the oystermen were traditions of edge-joining. Canoes had developed from Indian dugouts and were made up by bolting together shaped logs to create a massive frameless boat the main part of the shaping of which was done with the axe or adze from the solid mass of timber bolted together, Figure 105. The tradition, in fact, was for carving jobs rather than boat or shipbuilding. There is one point of some interest here. Figure 105 clearly shows the change in the run in the logs of a log canoe between bottom and sides. The bottom logs run hulk-fashion, the sides fore and aft. The parallel with the planking pattern of a Bangladesh boat, see Figure 41, is obvious, as is the parallel with the European hulk—see Chapters 3 and 18. It is just possible that the origins of this particular solution to the problem of the plank ends may rest in the vessel carved out from a series of edge-joined logs. But it is rather unlikely that further evidence either way will be forthcoming.

The situation was met by the development of the log bugeye in the late 1860s. In the words of their historian, Marion Brewington, '—some person added a couple of extra wing logs, put a deck on his dugout, and with that the bugeye was born'. In fact they had massive solid edge-bolted bottoms (the bolts were $\frac{3}{4}$ in (1·9 cm) thick iron) of shaped logs with no floor timbers, frames fastened to the made up bottoms which were planked up in the ordinary way, and ordinary decks and low bulwarks. They were very distinctive vessels in appearance with clipper stems and long trail-boards and a very simple two-masted rig which anticipated much of modern yachting practice, Figure 106. They have not been built for very many years. The big logs needed to make them soon became difficult to obtain and many vessels were built of the same form and appearance but of conventional non edge-joined skeleton construction. But the log bugeye, while she lasted, was a most remarkable American ultimate development of a simple dugout canoe.

Bibliography

BREWINGTON, M. V.   *Chesapeake Bay Log Canoes and Bugeyes*, 1963

CRUMLIN-PEDERSEN, O.   'Skin or Wood', 1972

HADDON, A. C. and HORNELL, J.   *Canoes of Oceania*, 1936–8

HOURANI, G. R.   *Arab Seafaring in the Indian Ocean in Ancient and Early Medieval Times*, 1951

MCGRAIL, S.   Unpublished study of the dugout canoes of England and Wales, undated

MCGRAIL, S. and SWITSUR, R.   'Early British Boats and their Chronology', 1975

PRINS, A. H. J.   *Sailing from Lamu*, 1965

RUDOLPH, W.   *Inshore Fishing Craft of the Southern Baltic from Holstein to Curonia*, 1974

VILLIERS, A. J.   *Sons of Sinbad*, 1940

PART THREE

Aspects of the Evolution of Boats and Vessels in Europe and North America

Chapter 9

The Classical Traditions

by J. S. MORRISON, Wolfson College, Cambridge

THIS CHAPTER WILL be concerned with the structure of vessels belonging to the Greek and Roman civilisations of the Mediterranean. The account has to rely on information which is derived mainly, but owing to the achievements of recent underwater exploration not entirely, from indirect sources. In general, though not perhaps as we shall see at the beginning of the period, there are two distinct types: the 'long' ship, a war galley rowed by many oarsmen on occasion[1] and using sail in transit on the high seas, and the 'round' ship, a cargo carrier with a small crew[2] using sail on the high seas and towed in and out of port.[3] The galley is hauled ashore in harbour, the merchantman rides at anchor or ties up to a quay.[4] Between these two contrasted types there is, throughout the whole period, a useful hybrid, a cargo carrier which employed a small number of oarsmen on occasion. The difference in shape between the 'round' and 'long' ship, apart from that indicated by their names, is that in silhouette the former was up-curving at bow and stern ('symmetrical' in P. M. Duval's[5] convenient phrase) while the latter had a projecting forefoot, which came to be developed tactically as a ram. The shape of the oared merchantmen

---

[1] In Homer oars are normally used in moving in and out of port or beach, Morrison and Williams, *Greek Oared Ships*, 1968, p. 62. Later they were used in battle.

[2] Swiney and Katzev, 'The Kyrenia Shipwreck', 1973. 'The recurrence of the number four' in the list of eating utensils found in the Kyrenia shipwreck (4th century BC) 'may indicate the size of the crew'.

[3] Cf. the common name *holkas, holkadikon* (towed vessel) for a merchantman.

[4] *Greek Oared Ships*, pp. 62, 135, 186, 311: for merchantmen at anchor, e.g. Thuc. II 91 3. Theophrastus says that cargo ships had keels of pine as opposed to *triereis* which had keels of oak to stand up to hauling ashore. We find also that merchantmen were lead-sheathed (Blackman, 'Further Early Evidence of Hull Sheathing', 1972) whereas galleys were not.

[5] 'La forme des navires romains d'après la mosaïque d'Althiburus', 1948, p. 121.

probably approximates to that of the 'long' ship. The mosaic of Althiburus[6] from the end of the 2nd century AD, which presents a sort of illustrated catalogue of ship types, contains a number of merchantmen with a projecting forefoot, and the type is represented in another mosaic of the same period[7] as proceeding under oar.

Marine archaeology in the last few decades has excavated a number of ancient wrecks. The earliest, that of a Bronze Age merchantman of the end of the second millennium BC, is certainly relevant to the ships described by Homer.[8] Others are Greek, Roman and Byzantine merchantmen from the 5th century BC to the 7th century AD. A small Punic ship has very recently been excavated at Marsala, the ancient Lilybaeum.[9] The hulls of these wrecks are sufficiently preserved to show a common tradition of construction, which this chapter will examine in the light of the other information which the texts and representations provide. The chapter will be divided into two sections covering: (**1**) the early pre-classical period, and (**2**) the classical period of Greek and Roman civilisation.

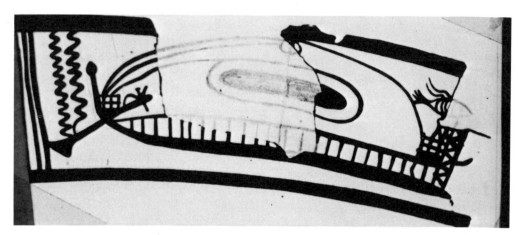

Figure 107   Mycenaean ship of about 1400 BC.   *W. Dodds after Kourouniotes*

(1) The earliest Greek ships

The earliest representations of Greek ships show the up-curving stern and projecting forefoot,[10] in particular the Pylos ship, Figure 107, and the Minoan seal stones.[11] In the case of some, Casson has argued that the up-curving end is the bow, but this

    [6] Casson, *Ships and Seamanship in the Ancient World*, 1971, gives as Plate 137 the 'rationalisation' of the mosaic with Gauckler's indications of direction which had best be forgotten. The accurate, clean, delineation of the mosaic is given by Duval as Pl. I.

    [7] Casson, *Ships . . . in the Ancient World*, Pl. 140.

    [8] Bass, 'Cape Gelydonia, a Bronze Age Shipwreck', 1967.

    [9] Frost, 1973, 1974A, 1974B, and a sister ship has been reported, Frost, 1975.

    [10] Casson, *Ships . . . in the Ancient World*, Pl. 22–30.

    [11] Betts, 'Ships on Minoan Seals', 1971.

Figure 108   Greek and Tyrrhenian ships in combat: 700–650 BC.

interpretation is most unlikely to be right.[12] Others show the symmetrical shape. It is doubtful whether the symmetrical shape at this period is to be regarded as confined to cargo ships. The sea-battle between the Egyptians and the Peoples of the Sea shown in the Medinet Habu reliefs of 1160 BC[13] show two types of symmetrical warship, but neither is likely to be Greek. And again in the Assyrian reliefs of 700 BC symmetrical and asymmetrical types seem to be equally warships.[14] By 700 BC Greek naval influence would certainly have been felt on the coast of Asia Minor, and it seems reasonable to assume that the asymmetrical ships are Greek and that a mixed naval force of Greek and non-Greek ships is depicted.

The function of the up-curving stern is plain. The steersman must have a clear view ahead. And the up-curving stern facilitates the manoeuvre of beaching, which in Homer is always carried out stern first.[15] The function of the projecting forefoot has given rise to argument. It seems unlikely, though not of course impossible, that the earliest oared ships which have the forward projection were built to ram. But there is no direct evidence of the tactic of ramming before the 6th century BC.

[12] Casson, *Ships . . . in the Ancient World*, Ch. 3 Appendix, and Morrison, 'Review of Casson 1971', 1972. Casson, 'Bronze Age Ships: The evidence of the Thera Wall Paintings', 1975 claims that the stern projection above the waterline in the larger (but not in the smaller) ships on the Thera fresco of about 1500 BC (Gray, *Archaeologia Homerica*, 1974) proves conclusively that what I have called the forefoot in Bronze Age ships is in fact a projection in the stern. But the projection in the Bronze Age ships illustrated in Casson, *Ships . . . in the Ancient World*, Pl. 22, 23, 27, 34, is an extension of the keel; and there is in these ships no upward curving of the end of the ship at which this projection occurs. In the large ships on the Thera fresco, on the other hand, the projection is plainly a structural feature built on to a sharply upward curving stern. This difference seems to me to rule out the use of the stern projection in the Thera ships to explain the projection of the keel in the Bronze Age ships in question. The larger Thera fresco ships in fact curve upwards higher in the stern, and more sharply, than they do in the bow. I am inclined to explain the unique stern projection in these ships as an embarkation step (cf. the Homeric *threnus*, see p. 164 below), which we may now perhaps recognise in the ship on the 12th century vase from Asine (*Greek Oared Ships*, Pl. 1c) and on a Cretan bell crater (*Greek Oared Ships*, Pl. 1d). If it is an embarkation step, its absence on the smaller ships is understandable. They did not stand high enough to need one.

[13] Casson, *Ships . . . in the Ancient World*, Pl. 61.

[14] Casson, *Ships . . . in the Ancient World*, Pl. 78.

[15] *Greek Oared Ships*, p. 63.

Hipponax mentions the ram then in connection with a *trieres*, and Herodotus speaks of pentekontors having the bronze sheaths of their rams wrenched off at the battle of Alalia in 535 BC.[16] Representations of ships with the forward projection, however, go back well into the second millennium. The tactic of ramming is a tactic of battle-fleets, not of individual ships, and requires a high degree of oar-power and training. We must, I think, infer that the projecting forefoot was not designed for ramming, but that it was later used for that purpose armoured with a bronze sheath. The use of the ram can probably be put back to the first half of the 7th century, since from that period we have a picture of two warships in combat,[17] one of the usual Greek shape, the other, probably Tyrrhenian, has the symmetrical shape except that a ram has been added, Figure 108. The adaptation seems to indicate that ramming had been introduced by that date. A bronze fitting which similarly adapts an up-curving bow to mount a ram was recently recovered from the sea off the North African coast and is now in the Fitzwilliam Museum at Cambridge. Its date is 3rd–1st century BC,[18] Figure 109.

On two representations the bow projection is shown as having trivial uses. In one[19] a member of the crew is apparently using it as a convenient place at which to relieve himself, and in another[20] a man is about to step from it into the sea. Neither offer a reason for its existence. If the projection is not functional, it must be structural. If, as it is reasonable to suppose, the long ship derives from the monoxylous dugout boat, brought by the Greeks from the better-wooded Black Sea area, where pine and oak would have been plentiful, then the projecting bow is the continuance of the keel with the upper bow formed above by stepping a stem post perpendicularly into it. At the stern, on the other hand there are functional requirements, lacking in the bow, for an upward curve. We must suppose that when this bow projection came to be used as a ram, the fore and aft up-curving, probably indigenously Mediterranean, ship type was modified by the addition of a ram to the upward curving prow, as in the case of the Tyrrhenian ship and the North African bronze ram-fitting. In a small Punic ship recently reported by Miss Honor Frost (the 'Sister ship'), probably as L. Basch has suggested a liburnian, there appears to have been an upward curving ram, which was a continuation of the keel attached by side timbers. These side timbers were nailed to it on each side and project like tusks from the keel in its present state, since the ram itself and most of its bronze sheathing is missing.[21] This upward curving attached ram is a feature of the later warships, as L. Basch has shown, and does not conflict with the apparent fact that in the earliest ships the

---

[16] Hipponax Fr. 45. He uses the word *embolos* which can only mean an offensive ram. Herodotus I 166 1–2.

[17] *Greek Oared Ships*, pp. 74–5.

[18] Nicholls, *Archaeological Reports*, 1970–71.

[19] *Greek Oared Ships*, Pl. 10d.

[20] *Greek Oared Ships*, Pl. 20d.

[21] Basch, 'Another Punic wreck in Sicily: its ram. 1. A typological sketch', 1975 and Frost, 'Another Punic wreck in Sicily: its ram. 2. The ram from Marsala', 1975.

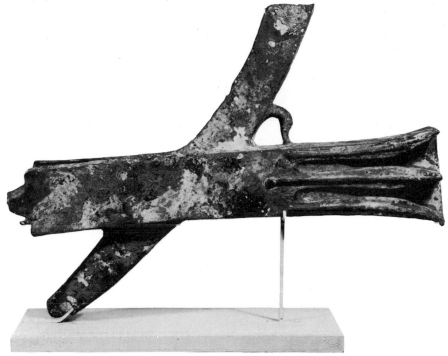

Fitzwilliam Museum, (photo: D. Schofield)

Figure 109   Ram fitting for upcurving prow.

forefoot was the keel itself, and that in classical times this forefoot, now developed as an actual ram, was reinforced on each side by wales.

(a)   Round ships

For the structure of the early 'round' ships we have the evidence of e.g. a model boat in the Heraklion Museum belonging to the 8th or 7th century BC, Figure 110,[22] and a description in Homer[23] of the boat which Odysseus builds on Calypso's island. Calypso first tells Odysseus 'where tall trees grow, alder and poplar and pine, dry long ago, well seasoned'. 'He then set to, cutting the planks and quickly got on with the job. He dragged out twenty felled trees, and adzed them with the bronze. He cleverly planed them and made them straight to the line.[24] Then Calypso brought drills and he bored holes in all the planks and fitted them to each other. He hammered the boat together with *gomphoi* and *harmoniai*. As

[22] *Greek Oared Ships*, p. 17.
[23] *Odyssey* 5 243–61.
[24] Cf. *Iliad* xv 410–2.

Figure 110   Clay model of a round boat of 8th–7th century BC.

Heraklion Museum, (photo: Androulake)

broad an *edaphos* of a wide merchantman as a man skilled in carpentry will round out (*tornōsetai*), so broad an *edaphos* did Odysseus fashion for his wide boat'. The word *gomphoi* pl. may be taken to mean the pegs, dowels or trenails by which the mortice and tenon joints were secured; it may also mean the tenons themselves. The word *edaphos* means the whole rounded hull of the vessel, which is plainly no raft as used to be supposed, but a complete, if makeshift, boat. The word *tōrnosetai* emphasises the rounding of the hull. The Kyrenia ship[25] was about 39 ft (12 m) long and 16½ ft (5 m) broad and had about twelve planking strakes and wales on each side of the keel. The Cape Gelydonia Bronze Age ship[26] was about 29½ ft (9 m) and on the basis of the Kyrenia ship measurements would have been over 11 ft (3·35 m) broad. Made of twenty 29½ ft (9 m) planks, Odysseus' boat would have closely resembled the Cape Gelydonia ship in size. The latter ship, unlike the Kyrenia ship, probably had no keel. In

[25] Swiney and Katzev.
[26] Bass.

both wrecks, like Odysseus' boat, the hull planking was joined edge-to-edge by dowel, mortice and tenon.

It is obviously unwise to infer too much from two isolated wrecks. Nevertheless, the fact that the earlier wreck has no keel while the later wreck has one may be significant, since there is no mention of a keel in Odysseus' boat nor is there a keel in the earliest preserved ship, the Cheops ship of 2600 BC.[27] Herodotus[28] in the 5th century BC writes about the construction of cargo-carrying ships in contemporary Egypt:

'their ships for carrying cargo are made of acantha . . . From this acantha then they cut timbers of two cubits length,[29] and assemble them like bricks using the following method of shipbuilding: they make courses of planking around long, close set pegs (*gomphoi*, here certainly tenons); and when they build ships in this way they stretch frames over the surface of (*epipolēs*) the planks. They use no *nomeis*; and reinforce the joints from within the *byblos*. They make one rudder oar and this is passed through the keel. The mast is of acantha wood and the sails of *byblos*.'

The recent publication of the Cheops ship by Landström throws light on this passage in two places. The hull timbers of the nearly flat bottom of the boat are joined edge to edge by mortice and tenon; and the cords are passed through pairs of holes in each plank making a 'V'-shaped passage,

[27] Landström, *Ships of the Pharaohs*, 1970
[28] Herodotus II 96.
[29] Cf. the illustration of Egyptian boatbuilding in Casson, *Ships . . . in the Ancient World*, Pl. 11. The men of course, as ever, are portrayed, in proportion to the boat, larger than their proper size. The carpenters are using mallets, adzes and drills.

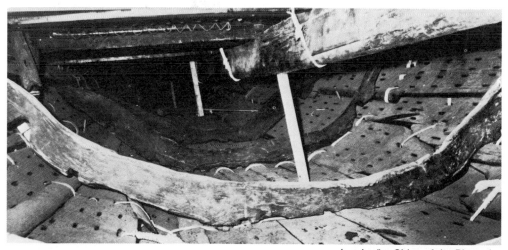

Landström, Ships of the Pharoahs

Figure 111   Floor timbers in Cheops' ship of 2600 BC.

Figure 111, thus reinforcing the mortice and tenon joint. It looks therefore as if the sentence in Herodotus hitherto translated: 'they caulked the seams from within with *byblos*' refers rather to the use of cords, for which *byblos* was the normal material, [30] to reinforce the joints. Caulking is at any rate better done from outside than from within. In the second place when Herodotus says: 'they stretch *zuga* over the surface of the planks' the *zuga* have been taken to mean thwarts, the usual meaning of the word in a nautical context. However, the Egyptian ships described are cargo carriers not galleys, and thwarts would have been as few as possible. Furthermore *epipolēs* means over the surface of (and touching) the planks. It is plain that these *zuga* are not thwarts but frames, and are exactly illustrated in the Cheops ship. The fact that the latter is two thousand years earlier than the ships Herodotus describes should not make the comparison less useful. Not only in Egypt but throughout the world methods of shipbuilding are notoriously unchanging. In describing the construction of the planking of the merchantman Herodotus mentions no keel: but he does so when he speaks of the rudder mounting. Now single rudders mounted in a groove or fork in the stern, in contrast to the side-slung rudders normal in the Mediterranean, are noticeable in the smaller Egyptian ships of the Middle and New Kingdom,[31] which are almost certainly keel-less. Herodotus may be speaking loosely and mean no more than that the rudder was mounted on the middle line. In any case the keel proper could hardly be said to continue to a height in the stern such that the rudder could pass through it. If that is so, we may regard the type of keel-less shell-constructed cargo ships built in Egypt from the third millennium to the time of Herodotus as the prototype of the Cape Gelydonia ship and of the boat which Homer describes as built by Odysseus.

After completing the hull, Odysseus turns to the superstructure, the *ikria*, ie, the raised poop where the helmsman and important passengers sat.[32] Such a poop is a noticeable feature of oared warships. The side view shows uprights and a longitudinal rail, together forming a short fence on each side of the platform or seat on which the steersman sits.[33] So Odysseus 'sets up and fashions the *ikria*, fitting it with many uprights, and completes it with long *epēnkenides*'. The meaning of *epēnkenides* depends on what is thought to be the object of 'completes'. I have no doubt at all that the poet is still telling us about the *ikria* (which would certainly need more than uprights). In the pictures mentioned there are longitudinal timbers

---

[30] *Greek Oared Ships*, p. 57. The word in the passage under reference in the *Odyssey* (21 390–1) is *bublinon*. Ropes in the small Punic ship were made of esparto grass (Frost, 1974B).

[31] Landström, pp. 75ff, 122ff.

[32] *Greek Oared Ships*, pp. 47–8. See also Gray for the larger Thera ships.

[33] *Greek Oared Ships*, BA2; Geom. 8(3); 9; 25; 28: Arch. 2; 31. See also particularly the model cargo ship dating from the 6th century BC illustrated in Casson, *Ships . . . in the Ancient World*, Pl. 94.

also, and what is more they touch the steersman's elbows. Now 'elbow timbers' is just what the word appears to mean. Other interpreters have supposed that the object of 'completes' is 'the boat' against the run of the passage, and have regarded them as e.g. 'long planks bolted to the top of the ribs'. But if that is the case, since the word derives from *ankōn* an elbow, the word is more likely to mean something bent, e.g. 'knees' to carry the upper planking. Oared galleys also have *ikria* in the bow[34] but cargo ships have them only in the stern. Odysseus needs one there 'high to carry him over the misty sea'.

Odysseus also equips his boat with wattle screens to keep out the spray,[35] and 'spreads much brushwood'. The latter presents a momentary puzzle. Brushwood was found specially cut in the Gelydonia wreck, and has been found in others.[36] Since it has been found under the cargo, and in one case cut to fit between the frames, it seems reasonable to suppose that its function was to serve as dunnage, a springy layer to protect the cargo and also to protect the planking. Odysseus however had no cargo in prospect. We must, I think, take this detail to confirm what is now becoming accepted,[37] that Homer is describing the construction of a real cargo vessel.

(b)   Long ships

There is no reason to suppose that the method of construction of the long ship differed from that of the 'broad merchantman'. Homer's galleys are usually pentekontors, ships of twenty-five oarsmen a side with two officers. They were probably about 98 ft (30 m) long and had a mast of at least 35 ft (10·7 m). They had a substantial keel. When Odysseus' pentekontor broke up in a storm he lashed mast and keel together and rode on them. The use of the word *steira* which means the forepart of the keel[38] indicated that it is the keel which projects forward of the stempost to form the distinctive forefoot. There is some evidence that the edge-to-edge joints of the early long ships were reinforced with cord lashings in the manner of the Egyptian ships. In the *Iliad* (11 135) it is said that after nine years at Troy the planks of the Greek ships were rotten and the cords had worked loose. As Casson has pointed out[39] Roman writers assumed that Homer was talking about the cord by which the planks were joined together. It seems likely that as in the case of the Egyptian ships the mortice and tenon joints were reinforced by cord lashings.

[34] Cf. *Odyssey* 12 229–30.
[35] *Greek Oared Ships*, pp. 55, 302.
[36] Bass, and Casson, *Ships . . . in the Ancient World*, pp. 177 n. 45, 199.
[37] Casson, *Ships . . . in the Ancient World*, pp. 217–19.
[38] *Greek Oared Ships*, pp. 50–1.
[39] Casson, 'New Light on Ancient Rigging and Boatbuilding', 1974. See also *Greek Oared Ships*, p. 50 for the ancient references to this method.

Figure 112   Attic triakontor of
the early 6th Century BC.

(photo: the Sopraintendenza alle Antichita, Florence)

Other structural features of the early galleys are the substantial cross-timbers projecting on each side of the ship fore and aft, in addition to the twenty-five internal thwarts on which the oarsmen sat. The after cross-timber, the 7-ft *thrēnus*, may be so called, since *thrēnus* means a footstool, because the steersman's foot rested on it. But in the 5th century model of a galley[40] the projection is too far aft for that. I am inclined to think now that it is so called because when the ship was beached the projection was at a convenient height for a man to step on it when climbing aboard the stern platform. In the later, larger, galleys a stern ladder was used. It was also a convenient fulcrum against which to lift the rudder.[41] A similar projecting timber on each side of the bow, the *epholkaion*, was used, as its name implies, as a towing bar; and was also useful for going over the side.[42]

In conclusion it must be emphasised that these early galleys were light craft in spite of their many oarsmen. The best impression of this lightness,

[40] *Greek Oared Ships*, Pl. 27b.

[41] Alternatively the word *thrēnus* may have the first meaning 'cross-timber' with 'foot-rest' as subsidiary. The cross-beam in the stern is seen in some representations, e.g. *Greek Oared Ships* Arch. 34, 52; Casson, *Ships . . . the Ancient World*, Pls. 144, 170, to serve as a fulcrum on which the steering oar could be raised or lowered.

[42] Cf. *Odyssey*, 14 350–2.

perhaps slightly exaggerated because of the disproportionate size of the human figures, is given by the Dipylon vase triakontor shown in Figure 112.

(2)   Ships of the Classical Period of Greece and Rome

(a)   Round ships

The round cargo-carrying ship seems to have remained as a predominant type throughout the period. It is illustrated in pictures from the 6th century BC, Figure 113, and is particularly well attested by representations from the Roman period.[43] In the 5th and 4th centuries BC the merchant ship is called a *ploion strongulon* (round ship), *holkadikon ploion* or *holkas* (towed ship). The latter terms give a useful indication of practice. There were still, as there had been earlier and continued to be in Roman times,[44] cargo ships which employed a few oarsmen. Demosthenes[45] mentions a twenty-oared ship which carried three thousand amphorae. Such ships, like the oared galleys, were more independent than the ordinary cargo ship, which would need a tow into and out of harbour. Aristophanes[46] mentions specially thick ropes for *holkades*, i.e., presumably towing ropes. The ordinary round ship was not oared, as Aristotle makes plain.[47]

The 5th and 4th century wrecks of merchantmen[48] have keels and hulls constructed of planks edge-joined by mortice and tenon and dowels. The result is a hull of planks and wales on the inside of which are applied half-frames alternating with futtocks and floor timbers, the whole sheathed in lead at any rate below the waterline over some kind of cloth. These features are found in wrecks of merchantmen continuously until the 7th century AD,[49] and may be regarded as a fixed type. There is a hint however that the shell method of construction was not the only one in the 5th century BC. Herodotus describes the building of coracles on the Euphrates[50] by erecting a frame of *nomeis* and covering the frame with hides; and in the description of the Egyptian method of building cargo ships, which we have noticed, he says 'they use no *nomeis*'. Lucien Basch has rightly interpreted *nomeis* as 'active' frames, regulators, a framework to which the skin subsequently applied is made to conform, as opposed to

[43] Casson, *Ships . . . in the Ancient World*, Pls. 142, 144, 147, 149, 151, 156.

[44] Casson, *Ships . . . in the Ancient World*, pp. 139, 140.

[45] Demosthenes 35 18.

[46] Aristophanes *Peace* 36–7.

[47] *IA* 710 a 15.

[48] E.g., Kyrenia—Swiney and Katzev: Messina—Owen, 'Excavation Report', 1972.

[49] Lead sheathing, see Blackman. See also the convenient table in Casson, *Ships . . . in the Ancient World*, pp. 214–6.

[50] I 194.

British Museum

Figure 113   Greek merchant ship and two-level pentekontor of the late 6th Century BC.

the passive frames used in the shell method.[51] Now the fact that there was a word with the meaning Herodotus requires, and that he denies that the Egyptians used *nomeis* for their cargo ships suggests that active frames were sometimes used. The isolated case of the Euphrates quffas would not be enough. But this is the only hint we have. Alternatively of course active frames could have been used for the upper strakes, passive for the lower.

The fact that round ships were normally kept afloat, and were not hauled ashore, would account for the lead sheathing. They would have been specially vulnerable to worm. Also the additional weight[52] would have been useful as ballast. There is no evidence for lead sheathing in galleys. Had it been used in the 4th century the fact would have emerged

[51] Basch, 'Ancient Wrecks and the Archaeology of Ships', 1972.

[52] Blackman. The lead sheathing of the preserved parts of the Kyrenia ship's hull was 0·125 in (3·18 mm) thick.

in the dockyard lists,[53] but its use in light ships built for speed and normally hauled ashore is quite inconceivable.

Ballast was found in the Bronze Age merchantman[54] and has been suspected in the Mahdia wreck (probably 1st century AD). There are references to ballast (*herma*) in the literature of the 5th and 4th centuries BC and of the 1st century AD[55] which indicate that its use was recognised as a stabilising factor in rough weather.

(b)   *The oared galley*

Whereas the round ship and the oared merchantman seem to have shown no major structural change in the Mediterranean from the Bronze to the Byzantine Age, the oared galley developed in a spectacular fashion. It was essentially a ship of war; and the stimulus of naval rivalry led to technological development no less urgently than in modern times.

The first development of the simple long ship consists in the employment of fleet tactics by which the forefoot, suitably armoured, is used to ram. The tactic of ramming then seems to have led to considerations of oar power, since ramming required great manoeuvrability and a high ratio of oar power to length. It also ruled out the employment of symmetrical ships as warships. If we accept the apparent two-level ships on the late Geometric vases[56] as actually using two-level oar-systems (and not as attempts to show the oarsmen on both sides of the ship by a primitive kind of perspective), we may attribute this development to the 8th century. It undoubtedly appears in the 6th,[57] Figure 113. The effect is to increase the oar-power in relation to the length, and to produce a more manoeuvrable ship. I have suggested elsewhere[58] that the further evolution in the same direction, which produced the *trieres*, may have taken place in the 7th century when Corinth, the foremost naval power of the time, was engaged in acute naval rivalry with her colony Corcyra. That dating would fit the attribution by Herodotus of a force of *triereis* to the philhellenic Saïte Pharaoh Necho at the beginning of the 6th century,[59] and the first appearance of the word *trieres* in the poet Hipponax in that century. The two-level ship became a *trieres* by the construction of an outrigger extending outwards about 2 ft on each side of the ship and the imposition of a third row of oarsmen directly above but nearer the gunwale than the

[53] *Greek Oared Ships*, see General Index 'naval lists'.

[54] Bass.

[55] Aristophanes *Birds* 1428–9, cf. Aristotle *HA* 597 b 1, 626 b 25; Plutarch 2 782 b, and see below p. 169.

[56] *Greek Oared Ships* 19, p. 28, Pl. 4e.

[57] There is however no word for a two-level triakontor or pentekontor at this date.

[58] *Greek Oared Ships*, pp. 158f.

[59] Lloyd, 'Triremes in the Saite Navy', 1972. See now against L. Basch's attribution of the invention of the *trieres* to the Phoenicians.

lower row of the two-level ship (the upper row sitting between them both horizontally and vertically). The numbers of oarsmen in the three rows of the *trieres* were (each side), thirty-one, twenty-seven, twenty-seven, the reduction in beam towards the stern apparently accounting for the smaller numbers that could be accommodated at the lower levels, though there may have been other reasons.

(i)   The hull

The evidence for the structure of the hull in these advanced galleys is mostly indirect, but there is no reason to suppose then that it was any different from that of contemporary merchantmen. The small Punic ship recently excavated at Marsala, since it is asymmetrical in shape and carried no cargo, may probably be regarded as a warship. It has a hull constructed by the shell method in the normal way with subsequently inserted frames and floor-timbers.[60] There is also a relief dated to the late 2nd or early 3rd century AD showing a shipwright adzing a frame for insertion into the hull of an already constructed asymmetrical ship. When Aristophanes in the 5th century BC has occasion to describe dockyards in which ships are being prepared for sea, he speaks of *gomphoi* (dowels, tenons: see page 160) being hammered;[61] and he speaks elsewhere of the noise of adzes in a shipwright's yard.[62] On commissioning it appears that *triereis* were given a coat of pitch; we hear also of white and black *hupaloiphe* among naval stores,[63] a word which probably means paint, but could mean wax or tallow which we know was applied to ships' keels to make them run easily on the slipways. Ships did however become 'heavy' fairly quickly; eighteen months was regarded as a long time to pass before the hull was dried out properly. And ships out of water too long also became leaky. Keels appear to have been made of oak to stand up to the constant wear of the slipways (see above p. 155, n. 4). The internal timbers[64] of ships in general were of mulberry, elm, poplar and plane since they needed to be flexible and strong. Theophrastus says that some shipwrights make frames of pine-wood in *triereis* to save weight. This statement confirms, what one would otherwise expect, that these galleys were designed as rowing machines in which everything was sacrificed for lightness, and must dispose of the suggestion that Casson has made[65] that *triereis* normally carried ballast in the form

[60] See Frost, 1973, 1974A, 1974B.
[61] *Acharnians* 552.
[62] *Birds* 1156.
[63] *Greek Oared Ships,* pp. 280, 296.
[64] Aristophanes *Knights* 1185; Theophrastus *H.P.* V 73.
[65] Casson, *Ships . . . in the Ancient World,* p. 90.

of sand in the bilges. Theophrastus can hardly have believed that the frames of a *trieres* were made of pine for lightness if he knew that a layer of sand had been deliberately inserted in the bilges. Casson's only evidence is a passage in Procopius, who died in the second half of the 6th century AD, speaking of Belisarius' ships in the invasion of Sicily.

Of course when an oared galley was being towed empty of its oarsmen on the high sea it might well have taken temporary ballast, since otherwise it would have been very unstable. I suggest that this may account for the ballast reported in the wreck of the small Punic ship, which had a forefoot and no cargo, recently excavated at Marsala.[66]

The tactic of ramming had implications for the structure of the galley, as it did for the modern battleship during the brief period of its adoption before advances in naval gunnery brought it to an end.[67] But the Greek shipwrights seem to have met the problems not, or not only, by structural means but by the employment of a rope girdle, the *hypozoma*,[68] a swifter which seems to have performed for the superstructure of the warship in battle what the seat belt does for the passenger in a modern motor car in a collision. Athenian *triereis* were fitted with these girdles on commission in the dockyards.

(ii) Superstructure

The developed *trieres* retained the sideways projecting forward cross-timber, the ends of which were now given the name *epōtides*, earpieces, a very apt name since the forepart of a galley was usually painted to represent the head of an animal. These *epōtides*, made, Theophrastus says,[69] of specially strong wood, served to protect the outrigger in collision; and appear to have projected each side of the bow to a distance of 2 ft (0·61 m). A 4th century Apulian rhyton in the shape of a galley's prow, when the vase-elements are left out of account, gives a very good idea of what a *trieres*' prow must have looked like in three dimensions, Figure 114. When the Athenians'

---

[66] Frost, 'First season of excavation on the Punic Wreck in Sicily', 1973. The fact that it had an asymmetrical shape does not rule out the possibility that it was a small merchantman. I know of no evidence that oared warships carried ballast. Arrian, *Anabasis,* ii 19 (Frost, 'Another Punic Wreck in Sicily; its ram. 2. The ram from Marsala', 1975, p. 220) is only evidence that when a ship was damaged in the bows ballast was taken on in the stern to bring the bows out of water, not that it was normally carried.

[67] Robertson, *Evolution of Naval Armament*, 1921, p. 261 and Clowes, *History of the Royal Navy VII*, 1923, p. 24. By 1865 the ram had become a regular feature of the battleship; and in the battle of Lissa (1866), which was the first engagement of ironclads in any number, ramming played a part even more important than the broadside in the tactics of the opposing Austrian and Italian fleets.

[68] *Greek Oared Ships*, pp. 294–8. See now D. H. Kennedy, Mariners Mirror 62, 2 (1976), pp. 159–68.

[69] Aristophanes *Knights* 1185; Theophrastus *H.P.* V 73.

Figure 114   Vase in the
shape of a *trieres'* bow.

Musée du Petit Palais

fleet at Syracuse in 414 BC was unable to employ their usual tactics
in the open sea,[70] but being confined to the harbour was forced to
meet the enemy ships head-on, they found that the Syracusans on
Corinthian advice had strengthened their *epōtides* with side
supports.

[70] *Greek Oared Ships*, pp. 317–20.

The 'seven-foot *thrēnus*', the equivalent cross-timber in the stern, now appears to have been responsible for the name of the third row of oarsmen rowing through the outrigger, presumably because they sat at that height, slightly higher and further outboard than the zugian oarsmen who sat on the thwarts and rowed over the gunwale. They were called *thranitai*.

The bow and stern platforms, the Homeric *ikria*, now called *selmata*,[71] became, as the galley developed, linked by a medial-line gangway, seen best in the representation of a two-level ship on the Ficoronian chest.[72] Casson has put forward the highly acceptable suggestion that when Thucydides (I 14 3) said that the Greek ships at Salamis did not have a deck overall (*diapasēs*) he did not mean a deck throughout their whole length (as has been supposed) but a deck over their whole breadth. On the old explanation it was puzzling to read at Herodotus VII 194 1 that the Persians could mistake Greek ships for their own, if their were decked throughout their length and the Greek ships were not. But if the difference lies in the breadth of the deck the problem disappears, since in silhouette there would be no difference. Casson links his suggestion neatly with the policy of Cimon after Salamis as reported by Plutarch: he 'took the 200 triereis that Themistocles had originally built particularly for speed and manoeuvrability and made them broader and gave the decks *diabasin* (overall breadth) so that carrying many soldiers they might attack the enemy with greater offensive power'.[73] Cimon now had on his side the Ionian Greeks who had fought with the Persians at Salamis, where they had many fighting men on their decks, as opposed to the ten on each ship in the Greek fleet. Cimon was reverting to the more old-fashioned tactic, as Thucydides called it, whereby a sea-battle is fought like a land battle with ships locked together. The deck, in an ancient warship, is never a place from which oars are rowed; it is always, to a greater or a lesser extent, a fighting platform.[74]

(iii) Later oar-systems

The next major development in the war-galley was the introduction of the multiple-handed oar-system. The method and pace of its introduction in the second quarter of the 4th century BC indicates that the system was not regarded as an improvement, but was the result of the lack of skilled oarsmen.[75] With more than one man to an

[71] *Greek Oared Ships*, Index.
[72] Casson, *Ships . . . in the Ancient World*, Pl. 106.
[73] Casson, *Ships . . . in the Ancient World*, Ch. 5.
[74] The deck *(katastroma)*: *Greek Oared Ships*, pp. 163, 184.
[75] *Greek Oared Ships*, pp. 249, 290, 291.

oar the number of men representing the single oarsman in the simple long ship (and hence the numerical denomination of the type) could rise to four and five and then in the navies of Alexander's successors quickly jump to ten and upwards, until the ridiculously cumbersome double hulled *tessarakonteres* of Ptolemy Philopator was reached.[76] Some of these high denominations were still called *trierika ploia* because presumably the large multiple-handed oars were rowed, as in the *trieres*, at three levels. Most of the later Greek and Roman representations of war galleys show oars at two levels, and we must suppose that this was normal. In Roman republican times the capital ship of the Roman and Carthaginian navies was the quinquereme. Compared to the *trieres* these ships were large, and naval battles were decided less with the ram than from the deck. There is no reason to suppose that any changes were made in the basic principles of construction.

[76] Casson, *Ships . . . in the Ancient World,* p. 108ff, and my criticism in *IJNA* i pp. 230–33.

Bibliography

BASCH, L.   'Ancient Wrecks and the Archaeology of Ships', 1972

BASCH, L.   'Another Punic wreck in Sicily: its ram. 1. A typological sketch', 1975

BASS, G. F.   'Cape Gelydonia, a Bronze Age Shipwreck', 1967

BETTS, J. H.   'Ships on Minoan Seals', 1973

BLACKMAN, D. J.   'Further Early Evidence of Hull Sheathing', 1972

CASSON, L.   'New Light on Ancient Rigging and Boatbuilding', 1964

CASSON, L.   *Ships and Seamanship in the Ancient World,* 1971

CASSON, L.   'Bronze Age Ships. The evidence of the Thera Wall Paintings', 1975

CLOWES, L.   *History of the Royal Navy VII,* 1923

DUVAL, P-M.   'La forme des navires romains d'après la mosaïque d'Althiburus', 1949

FROST, H.   'First season of excavation on the Punic Wreck in Sicily', 1973

FROST, H.   'The Punic Wreck in Sicily, second season of excavation', 1974A

FROST, H.   'The Third Campaign of Excavation of the Punic Ship, Marsala, Sicily', 1974B

FROST, H.   'Another Punic wreck in Sicily: its ram. 2. The ram from Marsala', 1975

GRAY, D.   *Archaeologia Homerica,* 1974

JOHNSTONE, P.   'Stern first in the Stone Age?', 1973

LANDSTRÖM, B.   *Ships of the Pharaohs,* 1970

LINDER, E.   'Naval warfare in the El Amarna Age', 1973

LLOYD, A. B.   'Triremes in the Saite Navy', 1972

MORRISON, J. S.   'Review of Casson (1971)', 1972

MORRISON, J. S. and WILLIAMS, R. T.   *Greek Oared Ships*, 1968

NICHOLLS, R. V.   *Archaeological Reports*, 1970–71

OWEN, D. I.   'Excavation Report', 1972

ROBERTSON, F. L.   *Evolution of Naval Armament*, 1921

SWINEY, H. W. and KATZEV, M. L.   'The Kyrenia Shipwreck', 1973

TAYLOR, J. du PLAT   *Marine Archaeology*, 1965

Chapter 10

The European Clinker-built Boat before the Viking era

T HE REST OF this book deals with the development of boats in Northern Europe and North America, particularly between the beginning of the Saxon migrations in the 4th century AD and the development of the skeleton-building techniques which gradually became standard practice for the building of big ships from the early or middle 1400s onwards. After this date no new strands come into North European wooden boat and ship building traditions until the development of plywood and wood reinforced plastic in the mid 20th century. Big ships were skeleton-built, while boats continued to be built in the traditions which had evolved in the preceding nine hundred years and which are described in the following chapters. Some small ships continued to be built in these traditions also. Thus it was in boats and a few small vessels that the ancient traditions were still very apparent in Northern Europe in the first half of the twentieth century, just as they were in Japan. They can, indeed, still be found in rapidly decreasing numbers of boats today.

As has already been said, one of the types of boatbuilding which developed from the dugout was clinker or lapstrake, with planks overlapping, lower edge of upper planks outside upper edge of lower, or much more rarely, the other way round. Though this technique of boatbuilding occurs elsewhere in the world, it was in Northern Europe that it achieved its greatest development in the various kinds of Saxon and Viking ships. Clinker-building with planks fully overlapping became the main tradition in Britain, Scandinavia and Northern Europe generally as long as wooden boats were built and although lapstrake was never the central tradition it was more widespread in North America than is generally realised. Among the North European boatbuilding traditions described in the third part of this book, therefore, the history of clinker-building is dealt with in special detail.

As a reminder of what is meant by clinker-building in this context, Figure 115 shows fully overlapping clinker planking. The persistence of the tradition is shown in Figure 116 of a big clinker-built fishing *jagt* which is still sailing in the Sound

174

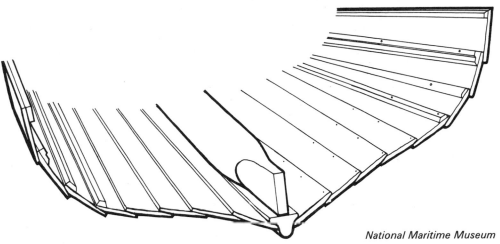

National Maritime Museum

Figure 115   Clinker or lapstrake construction.

between Denmark and Sweden, not any longer as a commercial fishing vessel but as a carefully preserved example of an ancient tradition.

This is perhaps the stage at which to ask, why clinker? Why did overlapping edge-joined techniques develop in some places and smooth-skinned edge-joined traditions elsewhere? We have seen that the question is misleading because of the various different ways in which the planks of smooth-skinned boats were joined edge to edge with varying degrees of overlap to produce a strong and (when the wood was saturated) reasonably watertight join, see Figure 26. It has been perhaps a minority of the world's edge-joined boats in which the planking has lain with only the squared-off edges in contact. The mechanical difficulty of joining planks strongly in this way; the difficulty of cutting timber to absolutely matching edges; the difficulty of making watertight such a narrow seam; and the inherent weakness of joints with so little bearing edge—all these factors indicate the desirability of some kind of overlap.

As to why the fully overlapped tradition in two forms developed in widely separated areas of Bangladesh and in Uttar Pradesh hundreds of miles away in India (see page 268) might be worth some further study. As far as Bangladesh is concerned it is most unlikely to have been a European innovation, not only because this was unusual and indeed very difficult at the level in rural society at which the boatbuilding *mistris* operate, but because the forms of the traditions in Bangladesh are essentially alien to 19th century Britain. Moreover, the tradition is to be found in the most basic forms, in the extension of the simplest expanded dugouts with fully overlapping clinker planking in, for instance, the valleys of the wild border mountains between Assam and Bangladesh, and it runs right through the boatbuilding of the most eastern parts of Bangladesh to large sophisticated cargo boats.

Figure 116   Danish fishing *jagt, Otto Mathiasen.*   *Basil Greenhill*

There may be some special reason why fully overlapping planking developed in Northern Europe. The use of cleft planking (see Chapter 15) was widespread, and cleft planks in their untrimmed state are triangular in section. The originators of boatbuilding traditions were using planks of which one edge was materially thicker than the other. Flush-joining edge to edge with such material was very difficult indeed and it could be that the natural solution, a full overlapping of the edges, followed from this historical situation. The whole matter requires more investigation, but I think this possibility worth examining.

Because the remains of many ancient boats have been discovered in Scandinavia and elsewhere in Northern Europe, in bogs and marshes, old harbours from which the sea has long receded and been excluded, and in burial mounds, there is quite a lot of evidence from which to follow the development of the Northern European clinker-built boat through more than two thousand years of history. In particular, the development of boatbuilding within two hundred and fifty miles of the Skaw over the period AD 800 to 1200 is relatively well covered by archaeological finds.

But it is extremely important to remember in considering the evidence provided by these archaeological finds that each gives information only about itself. Though similar features in the boats can be compared, these similarities do not mean that a later boat is necessarily, or even possibly, a direct descendant of an earlier one. The finds are far too scattered both in time and place to enable us at this stage to come to even tentative conclusions about the general evolution of more than one or two particular boatbuilding traditions of the many in Northern Europe in the past two millennia, and only the most tentative conclusions covering very short periods of these. The study of the archaeology of the boat is still in its infancy, even in this one part of the world, and just as in parts of Asia today very primitive boats still co-exist with very sophisticated local vessels, so much the same thing very probably happened in Europe at the time of the Saxon and Viking migrations, indeed it has continued to occur with boats right down into the present century.

As more archaeological finds come to light, so the history of the clinker-built boat in Northern Europe will become more accurately and completely understood. At the present moment a great deal of what follows is still conjecture. This fact and the study of the clinker tradition is of particular interest in Britain, because the clinker-building technique is our own strongest boatbuilding tradition and persisted until a few years ago as the normal method of boatbuilding in this country.

The accompanying map, Figure 117, shows the location of an important few of the most complete of the hundreds of remains of ancient clinker-built boats found in Northern Europe. There are more than four hundred and twenty graves in which a boat was buried alone known in Northern Europe and Iceland. Many of these and other finds have not been fully published, and in very few have the boat remains been fully studied.

I shall be describing some of the principal finds and the evidence they provide in detail, and it will therefore be convenient to list them. In rough chronology, the finds date from—

pre AD 700:

(1) Als or Hjortspring boat
(2) Björke boat
(3) Nydam boat
(4) Sutton Hoo ship
(5) Gredstedbro boat
(6) Kvalsund boat
(7) Barset boat

AD 700–1100:

(8) Bruges boat
(9) Utrecht ship
(10) Oseberg ship
(11) Gokstad ship
(12) Tune ship
(13) Ladby ship
(14) Graveney boat
(15) Årby boat
(16) Skuldelev finds

It may be useful to recapitulate the basic facts about the clinker-building tradition. The shell of edge-joined planks is built first. The ribs or frames, such as they are, are added afterwards and shaped to the shell of planks. It is the planks, not the frames, which first determine the shape of the boat. In clinker work in its purest form the builder builds by eye alone, that is he forms the shape with the planks without the use of any patterns or moulds.

This was the primitive skill of this kind of boat and shipbuilding. It was very difficult, given in particular the ways in which knowledge of boatbuilding traditions was conveyed from generation to generation, for the boatbuilders to innovate and experiment with new forms. Traditions of boat form and shape, therefore, tend to persist for many hundreds of years where these non-innovative techniques and traditions existed. This fact is demonstrated perhaps most clearly in the boats of Norway. But nevertheless major developments could take place rapidly at times, as it is possible they did in Southern Norway in the 9th century.

Björke boat

The earliest clearly dugout-based clinker-built boat found so far in Northern Europe is the Björke boat, 23½ ft (7·16 m) long and attributed to about AD 100. It was discovered on an island west of Stockholm.

It is a simple boat comprising a log hollowed out to leave a very thin and gracefully-shaped shell to which two planks have been added, one on each side, see Chapter 8. They are fastened to the basic dugout with iron rivets and laid fully overlapping, clinker style. The planks, like the dugout itself, have been cut with lugs or cleats left outstanding on the inner surface. Holes have been drilled in these cleats

THE GREAT DISCOVERIES

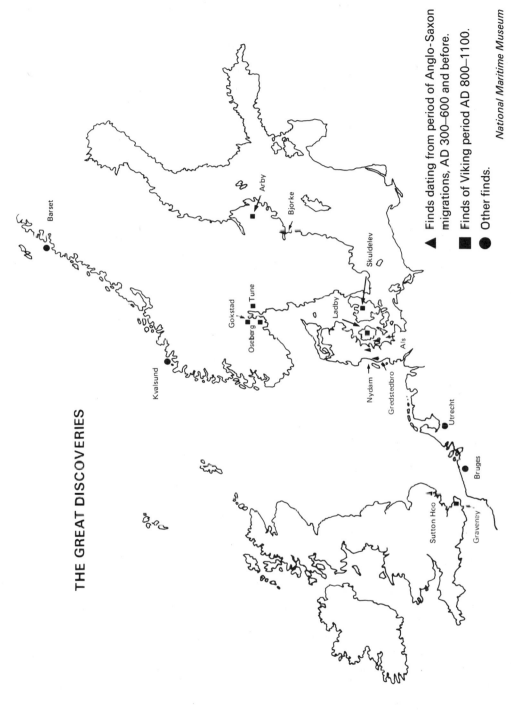

Barset

Kvalsund

Arby

Bjorke

Gokstad

Oseberg

Tune

Ladby

Skuldelev

Als

Nydam

Gredstedbro

Utrecht

Bruges

Sutton Hoo

Graveney

▲ Finds dating from period of Anglo-Saxon migrations, AD 300–600 and before.

■ Finds of Viking period AD 800–1100.

● Other finds.

National Maritime Museum

Figure 117 Some of the principal discoveries of remains of ancient boats in Northern Europe.

and strong natural grown frames, six in number, have been lashed to them with withes. At the top of the planks the timbers have been fastened to the plank direct with iron rivets. The long broad planks are each in one piece and with the cleats, which make them twice as thick, very few planks can have been obtained out of the tree from which they were made.

The boat, inevitably from its construction, is long and narrow, her proportions dictated by her dugout base and the planks used to extend it. The dugout was never expanded. The evidence which leads to the widespread agreement that the North European clinker-built boat evolved from the expanded and extended dugout rests elsewhere, in the method and order of construction of early clinker-built boats and in the archaeological evidence provided by boat graves and expanded dugouts fished up from the sea off the Swedish coast. The argument is brilliantly summarised by Ole Crumlin-Pedersen in 'Skin or Wood', his contribution to *Ships and Shipyards, Sailors and Fishermen*.

Nydam oak boat

Four extremely important boats have all been found in areas associated with the migrations of Saxon peoples to Britain and date from the general period of these migrations—about AD 300–600. They are not, however, all necessarily Saxon boats. The Björke boat was a relatively small vessel, but some of the same general characteristics occur in the first big clinker-built boat find, the Nydam oak boat, dated in the late 4th century AD. She was found in southern Jutland near the present Danish/German border in an area inhabited by Angles at the time of her construction.

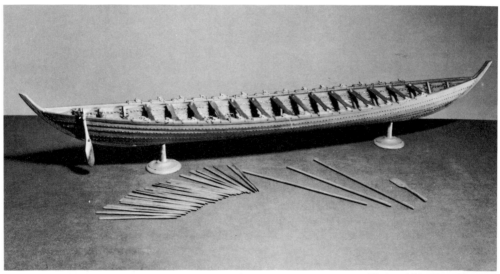

National Maritime Museum

Figure 118   Model of the Nydam oak boat.

She is entirely plank-built of oak but has the proportions of a dugout-based vessel, long and narrow, and the relevant shape athwartships, Figure 118. She is built of broad planks, only five on each side, each at least 50 ft (15·24 m) long, with double cleats each twice the thickness of the planks themselves. Such a system of building was prodigiously wasteful of wood and labour, since here again only a relatively few planks can have been made from each tree. The boat was the product of a well organised society rich in both timber and time. The materials used strictly limited its shape to something like that of a dugout.

The bottom of this first Nydam boat is more of a hog than a keel, as it is really nothing more than an extra heavy plank shaped to take the garboard strakes and thickened in the middle to take the strains of beaching on sand. This plank is joined to the stem and stern posts by a shallow horizontal scarf at each end. The overlapping planks are joined to one another with iron rivets, and grown timber frames are lashed to the cleats with withes

The vessel is constructed entirely of oak. She was a rowing boat with curved wooden single thole pins to which the oars have been secured with twisted withes. Thus with the Nydam oak boat a rowing boat, pulled not paddled, appears for the first time in the archaeological evidence of the remains of an actual boat in Northern Europe.

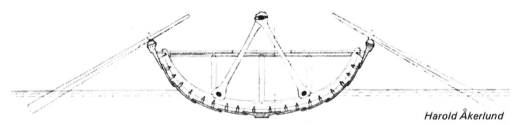

Harold Åkerlund

Figure 119   Harold Åkerlund's reconstruction of the midships section of the Nydam oak boat.

There is much controversy about the details and indeed about the real shape of the Nydam boat. The Swedish authority Harold Åkerlund has suggested that she may have been wider and rounder than was at first thought. She has been reconstructed in the form shown in the model in the National Maritime Museum, Figure 118. This model shows the hull form which would require much ballasting. Harold Åkerlund has suggested that she may have had a fuller midships section, Figure 119, and may have been strengthened by a rope truss running fore and aft and that the stem and stern posts rose more steeply than is shown in the model. It may also be that what has previously been taken as the stem was in fact the stern, and *vice versa*—the study of the remains of ancient boats is likely increasingly to give rise to controversy of this kind in which the assumptions of earlier eras, often based on suppositions and deductions inadequately recorded, are coming under a new challenge.[1]

Nydam soft wood boat

With the Nydam oak boat was found substantial fragments of another built of soft wood. Both boats were found in a bog in which they had been sunk evidently as ritual sacrifices. This second boat was built of some kind of fir, and has been dated from about AD 400. She was smaller than the first boat and differed from her in several important respects.

(1) She was built of more and narrower planks.
(2) She had a 'T'-shaped keel, which is the earliest keel of this type, as opposed to the keel plank, so far known to have been discovered in actual boat remains in Northern Europe.
(3) The stem and stern posts were joined to this keel with a different form of scarf from that used in the first Nydam boat, the one built of oak. This scarf form may have developed from the Björke boat form. It has been suggested also that the Nydam soft wood boat may have had a much more developed form of stem than the boats of earlier periods so far discovered.

This second Nydam boat appears to show structural characteristics—keel, stem and stern posts, narrow and numerous planks—which were to survive into the Viking Age and show a possibly later and certainly different tradition from the keel plank boats described in this chapter. Built as she is of different material she may well have originated in Norway. The drawing by Harold Åkerlund, Figure 120, shows a conjectural shape for the Nydam soft wood boat. Indeed neither the Nydam oak boat, nor the soft wood boat, despite the location in which they were found, were necessarily built by Angles. Like the Als boat found nearby, and already described (page 121), they may well have been vessels from some other area lost in a raid on Angle country or captured by Angles; just as the soft wood boat may have come from Norway, the oak boat may have come from North Germany and represent a different local tradition. It would be most unwise to assume an evolutionary connection between these two; all three, with the Björke boat, may represent units in the complex of a North European tradition in which boats co-existing in simple and sophisticated forms showed in their construction the influence both of the expanded and extended dugout and, to a lesser extent, possibly the influence of skin boats.

Gredstedbro boat

Although only a few fragments were recovered, the next boat find, the Gredstedbro boat, discovered also in south west Jutland near the Danish/German border, gives vital evidence. The three fragments preserved are the most important parts for

---

[1] The reconstructed Nydam oak boat is now on display in the Schloss Gottorp in Schleswig, Northern Germany.

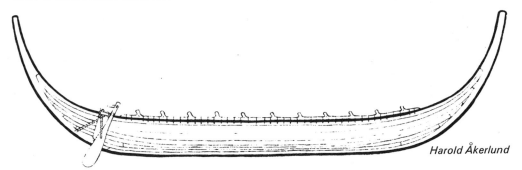

Harold Åkerlund

Figure 120   Harold Åkerlund's reconstruction of the Nydam fir boat.

learning about the structure of the boat. They are a frame and pieces of the keel and a stem or stern post, joined to the keel by a shallow horizontal scarf. These fragments of timber have been dated by radio-carbon analysis at AD 600–650. The boat has a broad keel plank, much worn on the underside, thus showing she was frequently pulled ashore, and a horizontal scarf of post to keel very much like the scarf of the oak-built Nydam boat.

But she also shows several very important developments on (but by no means necessarily from) the Nydam boat.

(1)   She has eight narrow planks on each side, in place of the five broad planks of the Nydam oak-built boat.

(2)   The planks are smooth without cleats and the framework which survives was secured direct to them with wooden pins—trenails—as the frames of a modern clinker-built boat were fastened direct to the planks.

This is a completely different form of construction from the lashed frame cleat construction of the Nydam boats. Less flexible, in some ways less durable, but far simpler, quicker and more economical both in timber, time and labour. It is a great step forward in boatbuilding. It is possible that the cleat and lashed frame form of construction of Nydam and some later boats may represent boatbuilding craftsmen's allegiance to the dugout origins of the boats they built. Although in some societies dugout hulls were and are pierced while the dugout is being made in order to measure thickness, in some primitive communities possibly the custom was that the precious dugout made with such labour must not be pierced. It is easy to leave cleats in the basic dugout to lash the frames to when they are inserted. The tradition died hard in the plank-built boat but the obvious advantages of the hull-piercing trenail won completely in the long term.

Sutton Hoo ship

In 1939 an Anglo-Saxon burial mound was excavated at Sutton Hoo near Woodbridge in Suffolk. Buried in it with a hoard of magnificent treasure had been a

Figure 121   A general view of the impression of the Sutton Hoo ship taken during the first excavation in 1939.

British Museum

Figure 122   This model of the Sutton Hoo ship is based on early assessments of her probable form, but it gives a good general impression.

great boat, about $88\frac{1}{2}$ ft (27 m) long. The timber had all rotted away, but the imprint of the hull and of the long rows of iron rivets remained in the sand. Through careful excavation in 1939 and again between 1965 and 1967 it became possible to see that the boat had the same kind of shallow horizontal keel scarf as the Gredstedbro boat, a keel plank of similar cross section and nine strakes a side. There appear to have been no cleats. The frames were secured to the planks with trenails, the strakes were narrow and ran beautifully up the gently rising stem and stern posts. They are each made up of several lengths of timber scarfed together—they are not in one piece, as with the Nydam oak boat. The Sutton Hoo ship is broader than the reconstructed Nydam oak boat and would generally appear likely to have been a better sea boat, even if the Nydam boat is reconstructed in a manner which makes her broader, more full-bodied and more seaworthy than she is thought to have been in the past, Figures 121 and 122.

Although the Sutton Hoo ship burial is dated by the accompanying finds at about AD 625 it seems probable that the ship was actually built around the year AD 600, or perhaps a little earlier, as several patches of repair work suggest a fairly long working life. She represents a great development on (certainly not necessarily from, since she may emerge from a quite different local tradition) the Nydam oak boat.

This fact suggests once again that, as has occurred throughout history, boats of widely differing sophistication existed together in Dark Age Northern Europe. The Sutton Hoo ship may represent a main stream of the migrants' boatbuilding techniques at the time of the invasion of Britain by the Angles, Saxons and Jutes, even though she may represent it in one of its most refined and luxurious forms, and these traditions may have persisted for many centuries.[2]

Graveney boat

This theory perhaps receives some further support from chronologically the next important boat find made in England, the Graveney boat, discovered near Faversham in Kent in the autumn of 1970 and excavated jointly by the National Maritime Museum and the British Museum. This very important find, dating from about AD 950, is described in exact sequence in Chapter 14 of this book.

The last two boats described, Sutton Hoo and Gredstedbro, possibly the last four, the two Nydam finds as well, may represent variations on the boatbuilding traditions of the peoples who invaded Britain from North Germany and Denmark in a migration which lasted for approximately two hundred years, from AD 400–600, the so-called Anglo-Saxons, families of Angle, Saxon, Jute and Frisian origin.

None of the four boats described may be typical. The Nydam oak boat may already have been obsolete when she was built. The Sutton Hoo ship may have been an exceptional Royal vessel, but these boats show that the people who made the migration could construct very well-built clinker-built open rowing boats which were seaworthy and could be very big. At least two types of boat may have developed, a long narrow vessel of war, or royalty, and a slower, wider, more stable type which would be better able to carry many passengers and goods in general seafaring.

Such boats brought family and village groups—young and old, women, children and animals. It has been argued that they cannot have crossed the North Sea direct from Schleswig and must have made long circuitous journeys. Such journeys must have taken months and many boats which started out no doubt never arrived. The hardships in such journeys can be imagined. Only the fittest even of these people, who had already lived through the rigours of infancy and childhood in the Dark Ages, can have survived to reach Britain and form a strand in the ancestry of many British, American, Canadian, Australian, New Zealand and South African citizens today.

---

[2] A fibreglass positive has been made from the image in the sand of the Sutton Hoo ship, and part of this is on display in the boat archaeology gallery at the National Maritime Museum.

Figure 123   Model of the larger Kvalsund boat.

Norsk Sjøfartsmuseum

Kvalsund and Barset boats

The next major North European boat finds, in chronological order of probable date of construction, comprise the finds at Kvalsund in Western Norway. Their date has been much disputed, but the two boats are usually thought to have been built around AD 700. The planks of the larger boats are narrow and the frames are secured to the upper strakes with trenails and iron spikes, to the lower planks with lashings to the cleats. In the smaller boat the frames are fastened with trenails throughout. As the model in the Norsk Sjøfartsmuseum, Oslo (Figure 123) shows, these boats are long and narrow and the larger of the two has seven narrow strakes on each side of a keel rather like that of the Nydam soft wood boat, that is, of a very shallow 'T'-section. The boat is built of oak and is about 50 ft (15·24 m) long, with its softwood frames in one piece. The hull is quite full-bodied and could have been sailed, but there is still no evidence at all of a mast or sail and the boat was rowed with single tholes with withy lashings to secure the oars.

Another boat dating from the same period and found in northern Norway is the Barset boat. Her uppermost strake is sewn to the next, the rest are fastened together, clinker fashion, with iron rivets.

By AD 700, therefore, there is still no positive evidence of the appearance of the sail in the North European wooden boatbuilding traditions, as represented by the finds described in this chapter. The boats—long, narrow and varying in depth, keel structure and cross section in a manner which suggests adaptation to use in shallow or deep waters, involving beaching or lying to moorings afloat—are rowing boats, apparently increasingly efficient for this purpose, both in the open sea and in more restricted waters.

It can be argued that the adoption of the sail in the development of the boat tends to happen as necessary. When large numbers of people have to be carried for reasons of transport, as in migrations, or warfare as in raiding parties, or fishing, they can provide predictable and reasonably reliable motive power, and under these conditions a rowing boat is more efficient and usually safer than a long, narrow, squaresailed sailing boat and there is no cause for the adoption of sail. Sail comes when it is necessary to propel large boats with few men, or for great distances, under conditions when sails can be used favourably. The fishermen of Shetland, operating ninety miles offshore, did not adopt the sail until early in the 19th century. It may well be that the sail was not widely used in the great northern Norwegian fisheries until much the same period. When the use of the boat is considered and the economic and social background to that use, the fact that the utilization of the sail in Northern Europe may not have developed on a large scale until widespread seafaring began at the onset of the Viking Age is not so surprising as it might otherwise seem.

Bibliography

ÅKERLUND, H. *Nydamskeppen*, 1963

BRØGGER, A. W. and SHETELIG, H. *Viking Ships, their Ancestry and Evolution*, 1951

BRØNDSTED, J. 'Oldtidsbaden fra Als', 1925

BRUCE-MITFORD, R. L. S. *Sutton Hoo Ship Burial*, 1968

CHRISTENSEN, A. E. *Boats of the North*, 1968

CRUMLIN-PEDERSEN, O. 'Cog-Kogge-Kaage', 1965

CRUMLIN-PEDERSEN, O. 'Gredstedbro Ship', 1968

CRUMLIN-PEDERSEN, O. 'Skin or Wood', 1972

EVANS, A. C. 'The Sutton Hoo Ship', 1972

GJESSING, G. 'Båtfunnene fra Bårset og Øksnes', 1935

HUMBLA, P. 'Om Björkebaten från Hille socken', 1949

ROSENBERG, G. 'Hjortspringfundet', 1937

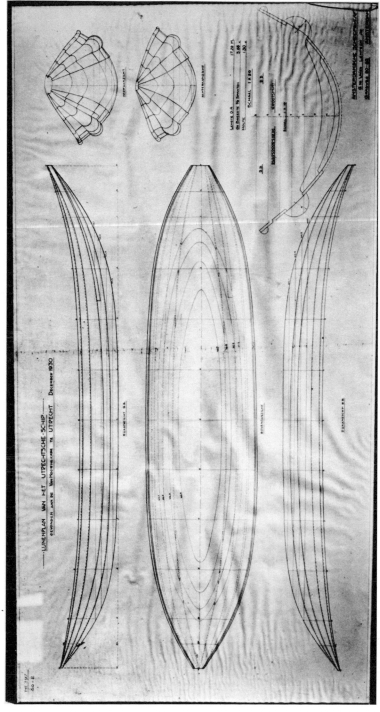

Figure 124   Conventional lines drawing of the Utrecht ship.

Chapter 11

The Round-hulled Boat before the Viking Era —a Different Tradition

THE UTRECHT SHIP was discovered in 1930 in a dried-up former bed of the Rhine. She is dated from about AD 800. As Figure 124 shows, she comprises a great expanded dugout made from a long narrow tree so that its proportions are near to those of a massive keel plank. This dugout in fact comprises a hog, that is a

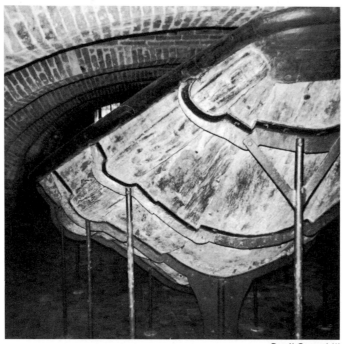

Basil Greenhill

Figure 125 The Utrecht ship in her cellar in Utrecht.

Figure 126   A clinker-
built extended dugout in
Sylhet district, Bang-
ladesh.

Basil Greenhill

member to accept the garboard fastenings, rather than a keel, which by definition is
the principal longitudinal strength member of a vessel. The natural upward curve at
either end of the expanded dugout is carried on by huge extension pieces scarfed
onto the rising end; Figure 125 shows the construction. Two planks and a wale made
from half a log extend on each side of the boat, the planks laid overlapping, clinker-
style. She has massive floor timbers, the main purpose of which would appear to be
to prevent the expanded dugout from closing again, since they extend only a short
way above its sides.

   The structure is a larger and more sophisticated version of one currently in use in
Bangladesh in areas where the narrow straight trees available reduce the dugout
base of the local boats to little more than a keel plank, or hog, as shown in Figure 126.

   The Utrecht ship was perhaps an inland waterway vessel herself, like the
Bangladesh boats illustrated, and she may well be an example of an early and
primitive form, co-existing in the Europe of AD 800 with much more sophisticated

Figure 127 Flat-bottomed boat at Ketelhaven Maritime Archaeological Museum.

Basil Greenhill

vessels in the same tradition. Certainly conditions in the Low Countries in the second half of the first millennium were such that this type of vessel would have been suitable for trading in the great areas of marsh, fen and tidal innundation and on the great rivers of this part of Europe. From a common ancestor with the Utrecht boat could have developed in one direction some forms of keel plank clinker-built boats, in another perhaps the European hulk of the 14th and 15th centuries (though I do not think this very likely) and in the third direction possibly some forms of flat-bottomed boats.

A recent example would appear to be a type of barge used in Norfolk in the 19th century, and her general form may owe something to the building traditions which influenced the construction of the Utrecht ship. Another 19th century boat in the same tradition but developed in the direction of the flat-bottomed boat may be seen in Figure 127, a flat-bottomed boat of the 19th century preserved at the Ketelhaven Maritime Archaeological Museum of the North East Polder in Holland, showing structural parallels with the Utrecht boat. She may well demonstrate a persistence of similar building traditions in the same general area for more than a thousand years. Once again the small boats of a later age may show the traditions in which long vanished, much greater ships were once built.

Bibliography

CRUMLIN-PEDERSEN, O. 'Cog-Kogge-Kagge', 1965
PHILIPSEN, J. P. W. 'Utrecht Ship', 1965

Chapter 12

The Flat-bottomed Boat
before the Viking Era

I HAVE ALREADY suggested that where the nature of the materials available dictated, the expanded and extended dugout could develop into a flat-bottomed boat—half a long narrow log hollowed out and expanded could make almost a flat bottom for an extended dugout. In this way a different kind of hull form could develop from those which we have examined so far in this part of the book, flat underneath in shape with straight sides and a sharp angle at the turn of the bilge where the sides joined the bottom.

Once planks were available at a price the flat-bottomed boat need no longer have a dugout base, but could be built simply with broad planks making a bottom and sides. Thus one form of the flat-bottomed boat appeared at a very early period, perhaps in the last centuries BC in the area between southern Denmark and northern France. Such a simple flat-bottomed boat is the Somerset turf boat, described and illustrated in Chapter 2. Here a dugout origin is perhaps indicated by the massive block ends which may reproduce the solid ends of the original basic dugout structure.

The turf boat represents a very old boatbuilding tradition on the Somerset levels and illustrates the simplest form of plank-built flat-bottomed boat extremely well. To recapitulate, the block ends, locally 'nosers' (there is no differentiation between bow and stern) are kept as low as possible so as to minimise the effects of local winds on the boat and make it easier to pole. It was poled with a special pole, locally known as an 'oar'. The floor timbers were called in local dialect 'hrungs' (which appears to be a variation of the old Scandinavian *hrong* floor timber) and the side frames 'drashels', which word was used also in the local dialect for a flail.

From the simple dugout beginnings both the flat-bottomed boat and the keel plank round-bottomed boat could develop. The drawings by Kurt Kühn for Dr Wolfgang Rudolph reproduced here of 19th century boats of the East German Baltic coast show examples of how these two different lines of development could grow, Figures 128 and 129.

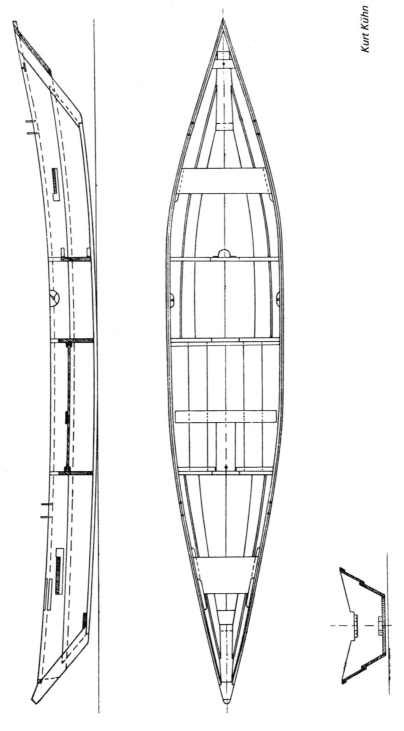

Kurt Kühn

Figure 128   A flat-bottomed clinker-built boat, generally similar to the Somerset turf boat, of the East German Baltic coast.

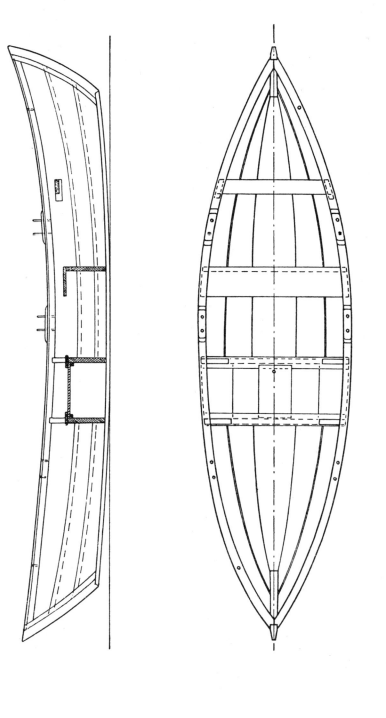

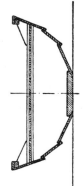

Kurt Kühn

Figure 129   A round-hulled flat keel plank boat from the same coast.

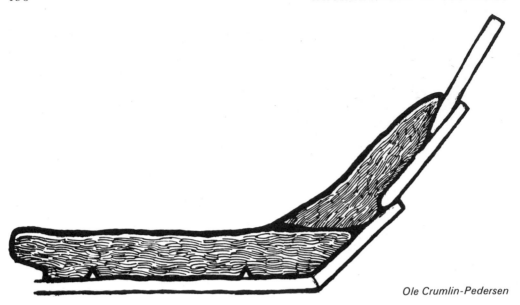

Ole Crumlin-Pedersen

Figure 130   A reconstruction by Ole Crumlin-Pedersen of part of the structure of the Bruges boat.

There is evidence that already by the 5th and 6th centuries AD the flat-bottomed boat had reached a high state of development in what are now the Low Countries. Fragments of what appears to be a flat-bottomed boat of sophisticated construction were found in 1899 in a river at Bruges, during excavations for an extension of the harbour, and they have recently been reassessed by Ole Crumlin-Pedersen. The vessel was flat-bottomed, with a sharp angle to curved sides planked in reverse clinker style. Her stem was almost straight; she had a mast; she is believed to have been between 40–50 ft (12·19–15·24 m) long and about 18 ft (5·49 m) wide; and she would appear to represent a type of trading vessel well suited to the shallow seas between the mouths of the Rhine and the South Baltic. Ole Crumlin-Pedersen's diagram, Figure 130, shows very well the basic section as he envisages it from the surviving fragments. Remains of apparently somewhat similar boats from the 13th century were found at Antwerp in the 1880s.

The history of the flat-bottomed boat has been generally neglected and it is only very recently that the type has begun to be recognised as an important and very old strand in the development of the boat in Northern Europe and North America. Recognisable remains of simple flat-bottomed boats are less likely to be found than those of round-hulled vessels, which are more likely to remain intact and on discovery to be recognised as obviously parts of ships or boats. Round-hulled ship fragments are also less likely, because they have been extensively and characteristically worked in a way which makes the timber hard to adapt to other purposes, to be torn apart and used again for purposes not associated with boatbuilding. This is only too likely to happen to the flat and relatively unworked boards used in simple flat-bottomed boat construction. For in some forms of flat-bottomed boat, including the Somerset turf boat and the whole vast international tradition of boats of similar form and varying degrees of sophistication, there need be only four curved edges in all the planks of the boat—the curves of each side of the flat bottom and the curves of the lower edge of the bottom strakes which fit them.

This simple fact is fundamental to the appreciation of the history of the flat-bottomed boat. In its simplest forms it was the boat which presented the fewest problems of construction, because it has the fewest and simplest curves to the plank edges. In Chapter 3 I said that historically a boat has been thought of as a reasonably watertight shell of strakes made up from planks joined at the edges, and held in shape by such minimal internal reinforcement as may be necessary. I pointed out that since wooden planks are flat, boatbuilders have been successful to the degree in which they have been able to convert flat material into shapes which, when joined together at the edges, will make a hollow object of the shape of the sort of boat they are trying to build. The formation of the boat will depend on the shape of the edges of the planks more than anything else. The success of the boatbuilder depends on his ability to foresee the flat shapes which will make up into the three dimensional form of the boat he wants.

I went on to point out that this skill of judging the shapes of the plank edges is an extremely difficult one to acquire, and that this difficulty had played its part in the history of the development of boats—again and again. Just how complex the shapes of planks can be is shown by the strake diagram of the Gokstad *faering* in Figure 29.

In Chapter 2 I showed that in flat-bottomed boats, like George Adams' skiff, the great problem of the boatbuilder was reduced to its very simplest terms. George Adams had to know the bottom curve of his sides, and almost nothing else presented him with any difficulty. Boats in the tradition of the Somerset turf boats give their builders an even easier time. Here the only curve to worry about is even simpler—Figures 29 and 31 show the contrast between the complexity of the strake shapes of the Gokstad faering and those of a boat of the turf boat tradition.

Given this relative simplicity it is little wonder that the flat-bottomed boat has had its own building traditions, probably for at least two thousand years in Northern Europe; for much longer in Egypt. Even in its most complicated forms, where the sides are curved, as in the Bruges boat, the medieval cog and the 19th century Bridgwater boat (Chapter 17), its construction requires much less of the boatbuilder's peculiar skill than does that of a round-hulled vessel. I do not think this fact can be illustrated more clearly again than by the photograph in Figure 131 of an exploded banks dory. Here are all the component parts of a classic flat-bottomed boat, another fisherman's dory from the Lawrence Allen dory shop in Lunenberg, Nova Scotia (bigger and more complex than that in Figure 31), set up so that you can see how they are shaped and where they fit together. And the only complex shape is in the bottom edge of the lowest strake. Yet within certain limitations and for certain purposes this boat form is efficient enough. I shall have a lot more to say about the origins, characteristics and development of the banks dory in Chapter

Figure 131   An exploded dory from Lunenberg, Nova Scotia, at Mystic Seaport, Connecticut.

17 of this book. No wonder the basic form has persisted for centuries and is still in use all the way down the east coast of North America and in Portugal and was in use very recently in north-western France. Very similar craft are still to be found on the sea coasts of Somerset in Britain, in Holland, in Western Germany, and in Denmark, and on the coast of the Southern Baltic and in southern Sweden—and once again in Bangladesh, see Figure 19, among many other places. However the parts of a boat of this kind are only too likely to be utilised for other purposes once the boat they have comprised is finished with, so flat-bottomed boats are unlikely to make archaeological finds.

The absence in the Low Countries and Western Germany, where the flat-bottomed boat type appears to have developed most in Europe, of the boat burials and sacrifices which have proved such a valuable source of information on some other North European vessels, also means that little is positively known of these 'Frisian' boats of the centuries before the Viking era. But on the evidence of place names, and the visual evidence of ships represented on coins found in Scandinavian trading centres and on stone carvings on the Baltic island of Gotland from the pre-Viking era, and in view of information coming to light on the probable trade routes of the people of West Germany and the Low Countries at the same period, it is now

National Maritime Museum

Figure 132 Two stone carvings from Gotland.

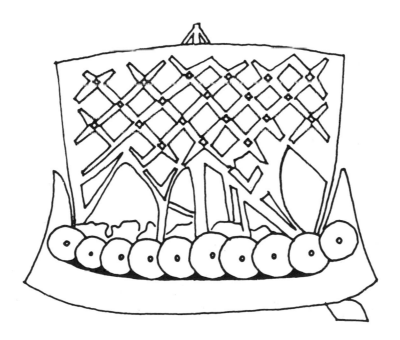

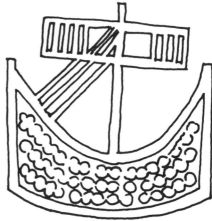

Figure 133   Ships on coins from
Birka and Hedeby.   *National Maritime Museum*

beginning to be thought possible that big Frisian vessels of the flat-bottomed type
traded as far north and east as the vicinity of Stockholm, until the Viking expansion
at the beginning of the 9th century made such long range trading far too dangerous
because of piracy.

Two stone carvings from the island of Gotland reproduced here, Figure 132, and
dated about AD 700 are among the earliest illustrations of sailing ships in
Scandinavia. They show the sharp transition between keel and stem, characteristic
of the flat-bottomed boat and later to be characteristic of the cog, see Chapter 17.
The two early 9th century coins from Birka and Hedeby, Figure 133, show ships with
straight stem and stern posts.

These vessels appear clearly to have used sails, and it was possibly from these ships
that Scandinavians learned to use the sail. It seems likely that the flat-bottomed
Frisian vessels were more suited to sailing than the early boats in the Scandinavian
clinker tradition can have been. All the illustrations reproduced here show angular
projections at the junction of the stem and stern posts with the bottom structure of
the vessels. These projections would certainly increase the directional stability of the
ship and thus enhance her sailing characteristics. Ole Crumlin-Pedersen believes
that this stem feature, known in Danish as the *barde*, may have been incorporated in
ships and boats of the Scandinavian clinker tradition when sail was first introduced.
Certainly something very like it appears in the Graveney boat—see Chapter

14—which provided the first archaeological evidence of the existence of this feature, which appears in a number of drawings of ships from widely different parts of Northern Europe over a long period. Subsequent improvements in shipbuilding methods made the *barde* unnecessary in the later Norse ships, though, as we shall see later, it is probable that their sailing virtues always lay in certain specific directions.

Quite apart from the rowing characteristics of vessels in the North European clinker-building tradition and the use to which they were put, and the economic and social background against which they operated, it may well be that the early use of the sail by the Frisians and the later use by the Scandinavians may have been conditioned partly by the availability of suitable fabrics for sail-making in the two areas. There is a great deal of work still to be done on this whole question of the history of the development of the squaresail in Northern Europe and I shall have more to say about it later.

Bibliography

CRUMLIN-PEDERSEN, O. 'Cog-Kogge-Kaagc', 1965
RUDOLPH, W. *Inshore Fishing Craft of the Southern Baltic from Holstein to Curonia*, 1974

Chapter 13

The Viking Age

Tʜᴇ Vɪᴋɪɴɢ Aɢᴇ is of irresistible interest to many people in Britain and in North America. It was a period of great, almost incredible, expansion by the Scandinavian peoples which resulted in the settlement of large areas of the British Isles by peoples of Scandinavian origin, so that there is a very good chance that any reader of this book whose mother tongue is English has an element of Scandinavian in his or her ancestry. It resulted in the settlement of Iceland and of Greenland, and in the discovery, followed by frequent visits, of North America.

This Age is thought of as one of plunder, piracy and violence. In fact, these were commonplaces of the age. The Scandinavian expansion, though it contained these elements, was also an era of colonisation, settlement and of trade as peaceful as the circumstances of the times allowed. The Scandinavians sailed to Newfoundland in the west, and into the Mediterranean and through the great rivers of Russia down to the Black Sea in the east, for purposes of trade as well as piracy and war.

We know today more about the evolution of the ship within two hundred and fifty miles of the Skaw between AD 800–1200 than about the development of almost any other kind of ships and boats until modern times. The large number of archaeological boat finds which have been made in Scandinavia, the finds of Scandinavian ships elsewhere, and other evidence, notably in literary sources, have been studied more intensively and more ably perhaps than the evidence of the development of any other boats until the finds of very recent years in Britain. The fact of the physical survival of the remains of boats has served the memory of the Vikings well. But the story is still fragmentary and very incomplete, and the conclusions which have been reached must be regarded for the most part as tentative until more evidence is found. In particular we know very little about Viking sails and rigging and about the way the Vikings handled their ships, particularly under sail.

202

Because of the widespread Scandinavian influence in Britain, the Scandinavian tradition of boatbuilding during the Viking Age is part of the British heritage, and is particularly and obviously so in some areas of the country more than in others. But it is only a part of our heritage, and many boatbuilding traditions in Britain probably spring from other sources, some of which may be partly influenced by Scandinavian traditions. Eric McKee's current detailed study of the structures of selected British boat types may cast some more light on this matter.

Our own clinker-built boatbuilding traditions were, recent evidence suggests, highly developed at the time of the Viking invasions. We still know very little of them, but the discovery of the Graveney boat has revealed a boatbuilding tradition as developed as the Scandinavian but quite different in many ways. Moreover, the Scandinavian traditions about which we know so relatively much, probably paralleled and sprang eventually from the same roots as the traditions indigenous in Britain and elsewhere in Europe at the time of the Viking expansion. We are just beginning to learn a little about the origin of these traditions, with the Sutton Hoo and Graveney finds and other evidence, but much more is needed before any but the most tentative conclusions can be formulated.

For all these reasons it is justifiable to examine what we know of the development of the Scandinavian boatbuilding traditions at the time of the Viking expansion in some considerable detail. They are part of our heritage and parallel the development in this country of earlier traditions which in turn form perhaps a large part of our heritage of boatbuilding traditions also, but about which we still know very little.

Viking ships, that is vessels constructed generally in the traditions revealed by the Scandinavian evidence for the period, may well have been built in Britain. Viking boats almost certainly were. But many more boats were built in different traditions of clinker, and perhaps, for all we know, of smooth-shelled edge-joined building, about which we still know nothing. There is a tendency today among writers superficially involved with the development of the boat to treat clinker construction and boatbuilding of the period of Scandinavian expansion as synonymous. Arguments are put forward for the preservation of this or that clinker-built boat or vessel on the grounds that it is a descendant of the Viking ships, regardless of the fact that not one single feature of her construction may correspond with the characteristic features revealed by archaeological evidence as part of the Scandinavian building practices at the relevant period. Some British boats are probably in origin of the opposite limit of a wide North European clinker-building pattern of traditions of which the Scandinavian—the Viking—is only one part, about which we happen to know quite a lot at present.

It may well be, even, that the Scandinavian tradition was a specialised one on the edge of a wider tradition, rather than being its principal branch. It may be that remote influences from skin boatbuilding traditions played a larger part in the Scandinavian than in the main European developments of the period and led to the development of this special family of sensitive, aristocratic boats, boats associated with the activities of a very energetic and virile people well recorded in the vivid poetry of the sagas, and sufficiently alien from the modern world to grip the imagination today.

In the years immediately before the onset of the Viking Age in the late 8th century AD it appears, from the available evidence already described in this book, that the Scandinavian and some other North European round-hulled boats had the following general characteristics:

(1)   They were clinker-built with the strakes laid with the lower edge of the upper outside the upper edge of the lower.
(2)   Their timbers were each in one 'U' or 'V'-shaped piece cut to shape.
(3)   The strakes of entirely plank-built boats were by now narrow and made up of several planks joined end to end.
(4)   The timbers could either be fastened direct to the strakes or secured with ties to cleats left upstanding on the strake when they were cut out. There are a number of examples of both nailed and lashed timbers from pre-Viking remains besides those which have already been described in this book. On the whole the indications are that cleats had become obsolescent, if not obsolete, south of Norway by the beginning of the Viking period.
(5)   They had no permanent beams, though even early Viking ships were to have permanent beams at *every* frame.
(6)   Two traditions seem clearly to have emerged—the keel plank boat, associated with the shallow waters of the rivers, creeks, waterways and coastal seas between northern Denmark and the north of France; and boats with 'T'-shaped keels, some of them very small, associated especially with Scandinavia.
(7)   Within the family of keel plank boats different traditions had developed which were to give rise to different types of boats and ships.
(8)   Round-hulled boats were rowed with oars worked on single thole pins with lashings of thongs or withes and there is no firm evidence that sails were used.
(9)   These boats were steered with a side rudder, perhaps sometimes with a steering oar.

Besides round-hulled boats a different tradition of flat-bottomed boats was already probably highly developed. Perhaps it was ultimately derived from a common root with some forms of keel plank boat. These boats had smooth plank bottoms and clinker-built sides, though some of the smaller ones may have had their sides made from one or two broad planks joined end to end. There is evidence that at least some of the big flat-bottomed boats had masts and sails. These flat-bottomed boats are also associated with the area between northern France and south Denmark where the seas are shallow, tidal and steep.

These in very broad terms seem to have been the vessels, as far as is at present known (and very little is known) of the peoples of Scandinavia before the Vikings, and the vessels with which the trade, commerce, travel and raiding of the peoples of what is now north Germany, Holland, Belgium, northern France and Britain were carried on about the year AD 800. There almost certainly have been many other types, or developments from the types described above. Future archaeological discoveries will add to our knowledge.

Bibliography

BRØGGER, A. W. and SHETELIG, H.   *Viking Ships, their Ancestry and Evolution*, 1951
FOOTE, P. G. and WILSON, D. M.   *Viking Achievement*, 1970
JONES, G.   *A History of the Vikings*, 1968
SAWYER, P. H.   *Age of the Vikings*, 1971

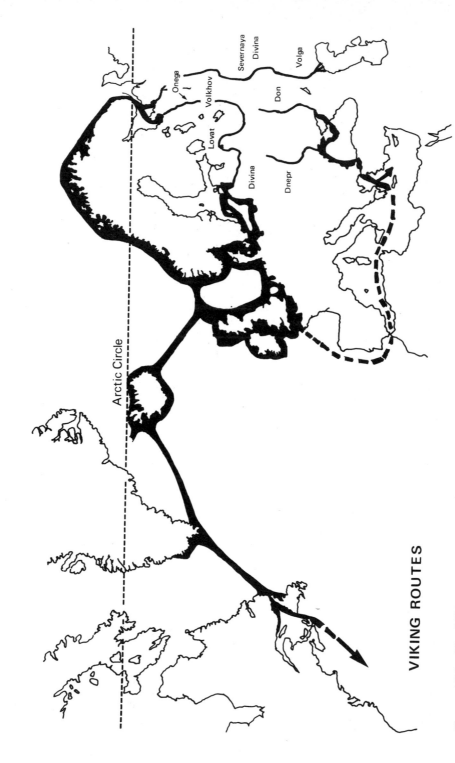

National Maritime Museum

VIKING ROUTES

Figure 134   The Viking expansion.

Chapter 14

The Viking Ships and the Graveney Boat

IN THE LATE AD 700s Europe was entering the two hundred and fifty years of Scandinavian expansion—the years of the Vikings. This was the period when kings and earls, local chieftains and merchants and bands of villagers from what are now Denmark, Norway and Sweden, using the clinker-built boat as the chief tool and agent of their expansion, colonised, traded and raided from southern Russia to North America. They settled in Iceland, Greenland, northern France, Britain and Ireland, and worked their great open boats into the Mediterranean and down the great rivers into the Black Sea.

The story is complex; trading on long established routes, colonisation and raiding went on all at the same time. But in very simple terms the Danes' sphere of interest was northern Europe, including eastern and southern Britain, where they appear to have settled extensively, leaving a legacy of place names, words in local dialect and a strain in the ancestry of some people who come from those parts of Britain. The Swedes penetrated the great rivers of Russia to the Black Sea. The Norwegians occupied the Scottish Isles, parts of western Britain, the Isle of Man, Ireland, Iceland and Greenland from where they made voyages to the North American mainland. The map, Figure 134, shows the approximate routes taken by the Vikings. The dotted lines show routes which are conjectural. In central Europe when moving from river to river the Vikings are assumed to have transported their boats overland across watersheds.

The regular maintenance of this kind of deliberate open boat sailing often in rigorous climatic conditions is one of the most remarkable, if not the most remarkable, of seafaring achievements in the history of European man. Until the voyages and colonisation of the 16th and 17th centuries no people from European homelands ever spread so far by sea as the Scandinavian peoples during the Viking Age. As to the size of their fleets, a carving on a rune stave dating from the 13th century, Figure 135, found during the excavation of the old quays at Bergen in

207

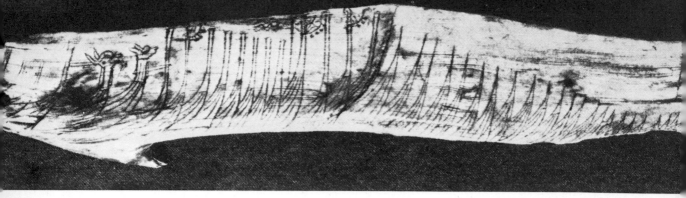

Figure 135   A Viking fleet.

Bergen Sjøfartsmuseum

Norway shows the stems of a great Viking fleet of 48 ships. In the light of knowledge as it now stands of Scandinavian shipbuilding of the period, it is possible from this rune stave to identify several of what are thought to have been the basic types of Viking ship.

Five of the ships associated with the period of the Scandinavian expansion which still survive today in greater or lesser degree of completeness will be described. These, and numerous other finds, most of them more fragmentary, give clear evidence of the scale and sophistication of Viking shipbuilding. These ships were the principal technical achievements of the people who built them. In the words of the Danish historian Johannes Brøndsted:

> 'The ships of the Vikings were the supreme achievement of their technical skill, the pinnacle of their material culture; they were the foundation of their power, their delight, and their most treasured possession. What the temple was to the Greeks, the ship was to the Vikings; the complete and harmonious expression of a rare ability.'

There is no generally accepted explanation of the origin of the word 'Viking', though the Danes themselves were using it in the 11th century. It has become synonymous with an expansion which was to effect most of Europe and the North Atlantic islands. The reasons for the sudden outflowing of the Scandinavians beginning in the late 8th century are still a matter of speculation, amongst them may have been the development for the first time in the north of the use of the sail, allied with significant improvements in shipbuilding. Probably partly in search of new land to settle; for political reasons; in pursuit of trade; as pure raiders and pirates or as mercenaries in the service of other powers, the Scandinavian peoples moved outwards for over two centuries.

Oseberg ship

In 1905 the richest and most magnificent of all Viking archaeological finds was made on Oseberg farm near Tønsberg in Norway. This was the grave of a rich woman and the find comprised a cart, sledges, beds, household utensils, all inside a magnificently decorated clinker-built boat. The finds date from about AD 800 and, coming from the beginning of the age of the Scandinavian expansion represent the greatest single find of the art of the Vikings—vigorous, highly skilled surface decoration with its roots deep in the Scandinavian art of the preceding centuries, and influences from Europe to the south.

The ship was taken from the burial mound and when reassembled was found to be of a form which, it has been suggested, probably represents an early Viking *karve*, a ship on the whole intended for service in relatively sheltered waters. The model illustrated here, Figure 136, was made in the workshops of the National Maritime Museum and it illustrates the general form of the ship very well. The sail and rigging, which did not survive in the burial mound, are highly conjectural, based on contemporary rock scribings found on the island of Gotland in Sweden. But all the reconstructions of rigging and sails of this and later periods for sometime are still only theoretical. I shall have more to say on this subject later.

Though the ship probably was of a type meant for service in fjords and the network of sheltered waters in southern Norway and Sweden, this one was evidently

National Maritime Museum

Figure 136   Model of the Oseberg ship.

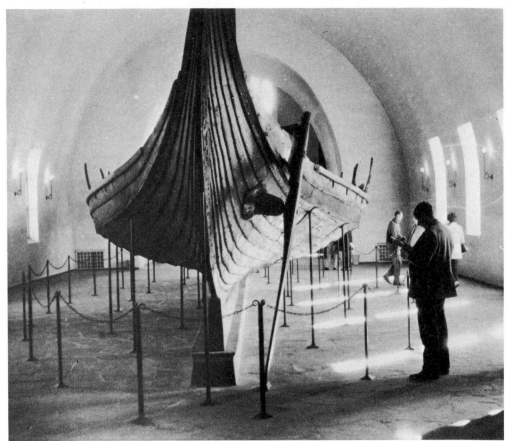

Figure 137   The Oseberg ship.   *Basil Greenhill*

very special, used as a family boat for a chieftain or chieftainess. She is exceptionally elaborately decorated and as she was recovered almost in her entirety, it is possible to see the full shape of the vessel and her bow and stern without so much speculative reconstruction as in some other cases. Today she stands reassembled in the Viking Ship Museum of the University Museum of National Antiquities at Bygdøy, outside Oslo, and although there is no detailed record of the work done and the assumptions made in reassembling her, she gives a very good impression of what she must have looked like when in use, Figure 137.

This remarkable structure is now nearly twelve hundred years old. Her construction is of great interest. The strakes are narrow and numerous, the frames are secured to them with lashings to cleats. There is a fully developed 'T'-shaped keel. The ship had a mast and evidently had a squaresail. For the first time there are permanent beams joining the heads of the frames. These beams are a great characteristic of the Viking ship; their development is one of the possible keys to her evolution.

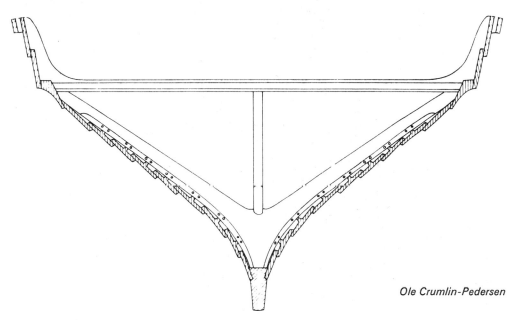

Ole Crumlin-Pedersen

Figure 138   Section of the Oseberg ship.

But the most important feature of the Oseberg ship is that the boat is really in two distinct parts. The timbers are in one piece and at their heads amidships, where the gunwale of a pre-Viking ship would have been, is a strong 'L'-shaped plank. This was called the *meginhufr* in old Norse, that is, the strong middle plank of the three plank strake. Thus, it can be argued that there is a complete boat of pre-Viking shape, something like the Nydam fir boat but with a more highly developed 'T'-shaped keel, below the *meginhufr*. Above the *meginhufr* and at a sharp angle to the lower strakes, are two more strakes, supported by knees secured to the *meginhufr* and the beams above the frame heads. The shape is very clearly shown in the drawing, Figure 138, by Ole Crumlin-Pedersen. Thus a basic boat shape has become the bottom of the boat and the extra strakes the sides. To put it very roughly, there are two boats, one above the other. And thus, in terms of archaeological finds, the Oseberg ship represents a distinct and clearly demonstrable development, a landmark in the evidence for the history of the Scandinavian shipbuilding traditions. A very recent find, the Klåstad ship in Norway, Arne Emil Christensen tells me, apparently shows an even more complex structure of the same kind from about the same period. She appears to have been a merchant ship and she was laden with a cargo of whetstones.

Basil Greenhill

Figure 139   The Gokstad Ship.

Gokstad ship

A vessel like the Oseberg ship, for all her beauty, must have been uncomfortable and dangerous if she ventured on North Sea crossings, particularly with heavy cargo. The Gokstad ship, shown in Figure 139, was also found south of Oslo, but twenty-five years earlier than the Oseberg ship, in 1880. She dates from about AD 850 so she was built fifty years or so after the Oseberg ship. This was a time of intense maritime activity for the Vikings when in the first flush of their expansion some of them were raiding the coasts of England, Ireland, Scotland and France almost annually. The Gokstad ship, for all that she is still probably a vessel intended for trading within a relatively restricted area of sheltered water, and also certainly the boat of a very prosperous family and not a vessel of the type used on the raiding or colonising voyages, shows a really considerable development on, but by no means necessarily from, the Oseberg ship. She is a fine seaworthy vessel, superbly constructed as far as can be told from the vessel as she is to be seen today.

She still shows her ancestry. The *meginhufr* dividing the lower boat from the upper planks is still there, though in a much less obvious form than in the Oseberg ship and the imposition of one ship on top of another is not at all so obvious, the change in shape of the structure at the critical point being far less acute. The timbers are still in one piece, secured by lashings to cleats on the planks of the lower boat. The beams are secured to the timber heads but the sides are higher and the strakes above the beams are secured to the knees with metal fastenings. The whole structure is clearly seen in the diagram, Figure 140, by Ole Crumlin-Pedersen. There is thus a difference of structure between the lower boat and the upper, but the basic boat is a less significant part of the structure as a whole and the beams are nearer the floor. The basic boat is built like the Nydam boat, the top part in a newer and more economical style. The Gokstad ship perhaps represents the ultimate development of an old Norwegian and north Swedish tradition, already obsolescent when she was built, in which radially split oak planks with cleats were used. Perhaps (one can speculate) the men who built her did so in what may already have been to them an old-fashioned way, with cleats and lashings instead of trenails securing the frames directly to the strakes, because she was a royal ship.

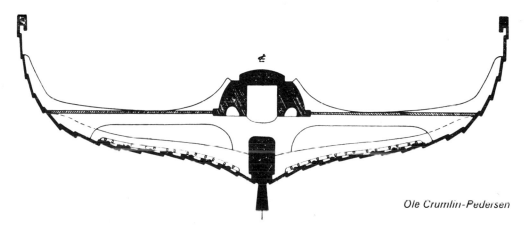

Ole Crumlin-Pedersen

Figure 140   Section of the Gokstad ship.

The hull has more body to it and the vessel is altogether more seaworthy than the Oseberg ship. For the first time there was found a *beitiass*, a wooden bowline or reaching spar, which is believed to have been used to thrust the luff of the squaresail out to the wind, and this has been taken as clear evidence that attempts were being made to improve the windward qualities of the sail. But all statements and theories about Viking sails and sailing should, at this stage of knowledge, be taken with some reserve.

It could be that the expansion of the Viking seafaring activity which did actually take place in the fifty years between the Oseberg and Gokstad ships is sufficient to account for the tremendous improvement in design represented by the latter. On the other hand the improvement may have been responsible, at least in part, for the expansion in voyaging. More likely, they were just two separate special purpose vessels, the one archaic, the other incorporating some of the current features of vessels built in the middle of the 9th century for long-range voyaging.

Ladby ship

Neither the Oseberg ship nor the Gokstad ship, magnificent structures though they are, fully represent the ordinary run of vessels in which the Vikings made their long voyages overseas either to raid, trade or colonise. These were probably very different. The raiding vessels were long narrow ships, and at least two representatives of these have been found. One, the Ladby ship, was excavated on the island of Funen in Denmark in one of the four boat graves that have been found to date in that country. She is long and narrow, $67\frac{1}{2}$ ft (20·6 m) long and only $9\frac{1}{2}$ ft (2·9 m) broad. Though smaller than the bigger longships she probably represents the nearest type of vessel yet found to the sort of warship in which the Danish Viking raids on eastern Britain were carried out. A similar vessel dating from about AD 1000 has been identified in the Skuldelev finds in Roskilde fjord, only a few miles from Copenhagen. Others are illustrated in the Bayeux Tapestry, which shows the transports of the Normans—five generations removed Danish Vikings—who invaded England in 1066.

A replica of the Ladby ship, Figure 141, was built in Denmark some years ago and subjected to some informal sea trials. She proved to be seaworthy and easy to row and sail in good conditions downwind. She was an ideal transport for short journeys in relatively sheltered waters because she could be run ashore very easily in the right

Figure 141   The replica of the Ladby ship lands horses.   *Ole Crumlin-Pedersen*

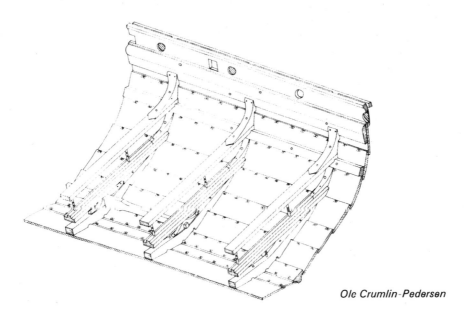

Ole Crumlin-Pedersen

Figure 142   Skuldelev Wreck 5—midships section.

conditions. The Ladby ship, like the Sutton Hoo ship, was found as a ghost in the sand and little detail could be learned of her construction. But Skuldelev Wreck 5, the smaller of two longships found in Roskilde fjord and raised in the early 1960s has the same length/beam ratio of the Ladby ship of about 7:1 and sufficient of her was recovered to show her midships cross-section, Figure 142.

The Bayeux Tapestry scene illustrated here, Figure 143, shows horses being transported in vessels very similar in general appearance to the Ladby ship. The experiment was tried of embarking horses on board the Ladby ship replica and putting them ashore again. This was completely successful on the shallow, sheltered, non tidal coasts of the Danish islands.

It is convenient now to compare the midships sections, in so far as they can be reconstructed with varying degrees of conjecture, of some of the principal vessels so far discussed. The drawings here, Figure 144, show the conjectural midships sections of the Als or Hjortspring and Nydam boats, and the Oseberg, Gokstad and Ladby ships. In considering the proportions of the Ladby ship it should be borne in mind that she is nearly as long as the Gokstad ship, but half the breadth and depth; a long, narrow, fast rowing boat reminiscent perhaps in her proportions of the 20th century Swedish church boat from Lake Siljan of which a photograph appears in Figure 145, and, when bereft of the fanciful head and stern ornaments given to the replica, somewhat similar to the church boat in general appearance. It will be noted that the

from *Bayeux Tapestry* by F. Stenton, Phaidon Press

Figure 143   Scene from the Bayeux Tapestry.

Ladby ship had the same extra heavy strake, this time number four, like the *meginhufr*, so clearly demonstrated in the Oseberg ship and to a much lesser extent in the Gokstad ship. The shadow of the strakes in the sand clearly showed this *meginhufr* and from its existence it has been assumed that the Ladby ship, like her two Norwegian contemporaries, was something of a mixture of building traditions though in this case, as in the Gokstad ship, in a very refined form.

It will be noted that the beams in the Ladby ship are a feature of the upper boat, holding its bottom together and secured to the heads of the timbers of the lower boat. As the two become merged into one another, the lower boat gradually assumes the status of simply the bottom of the boat, and the beams tend to sink lower and lower in the structure. This tendency is demonstrated even more clearly in the most recent find of vessels of the period of the Scandinavian expansion described in detail here, also made in Denmark—the Skuldelev find.

Skuldelev find

The Skuldelev find, one of the most important of all archaeological finds of boats, was made in Roskilde fjord, twenty miles west of Copenhagen, in the late 1950s.

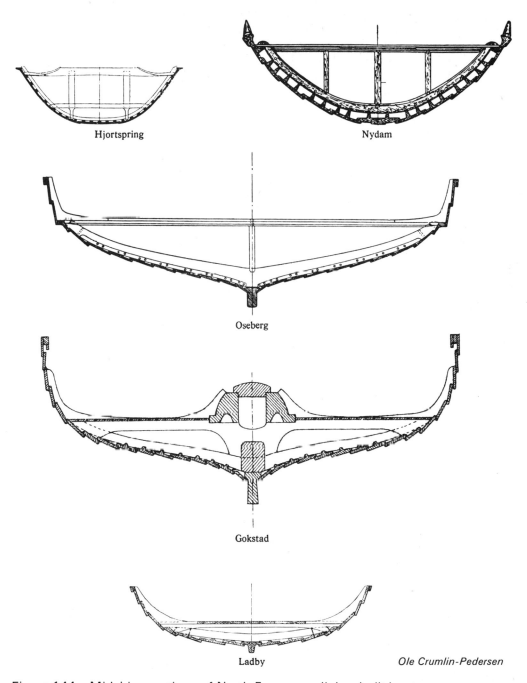

Hjortspring

Nydam

Oseberg

Gokstad

Ladby   *Ole Crumlin-Pedersen*

Figure 144   Midships sections of North European clinker-built boats.

Figure 145 Church boat from Lake Siljan in Sweden.

Parts of five vessels, a fishing or ferry boat, two longships, two cargo ships, all dating from about AD 1000 were found blocking a shallow part of the fjord. They had been deliberately sunk to make an obstruction against maritime raids, probably by the Wens, the then inhabitants of north Germany, who were attacking southern Denmark at this time. As I said in the first chapter of this book, the modern study of the archaeology of the boat really dates from the excavation and study of these boats by the Danish National Museum in the early 1960s.

One of the longships, of which only fragments survive, is almost certainly a dragon ship, the principal Danish Viking raiding vessel type about 92 ft (28 m) long with twenty to twenty-six pairs of oars. This was the kind of ship in which a further Danish invasion of England took place in about the year 1000, a successful invasion which led to the rule in England of King Canute of Denmark. The other longship is of the type found at Ladby and already described.

The first cargo ship was the most complete of all the finds. She represents a small vessel, and the model, Figure 146, was made in the workshops of the National Maritime Museum and is based on reconstruction from the wrecked timber by Ole Crumlin-Pedersen. Not too much significance should be attached to the sail, in the present state of knowledge of Viking sailing this gives no more than a suggestion of what it may have been like. Indications from recent experimental work show that in fact its proportions may have been rather different.

This small Skuldelev cargo ship is a vessel of great interest. She is about 40 ft (13 m) long and 10 ft 3 ins (3·2 m) in beam, primarily a sailing vessel with provision for seven oars as auxiliary power. She was light enough to be hauled overland for short distances when empty of her cargo, shallow enough to be used in rivers, yet with enough keel to be an effective sailing vessel by the standards of Viking ships. It is thought that she was probably a Danish coaster for service among the islands and in the southern Baltic, perhaps down the German and Dutch coasts and across to Britain, though such a round voyage would have taken her months.

Her construction shows a further development and is in the tradition which employed trenails to secure the frames direct to the strakes. There are no cleats with lashings and the two boats one above the other have at last become faired into one.

The frames are no longer in one piece with knees above them; there are separate floor timbers. The beams are even lower than in the Gokstad ship. The stem and stern post comprise carefully carved sets of plank ends—on the lines of the solution to the plank end problem illustrated in Figure 37. The strakes of the Skuldelev vessel are not brought to the stem and stern post as in almost all the other boats so far described, and as in most full-size clinker-built boats of modern times, but the upper sections of both the stem and the stern post are cunningly carved to provide the ending for several strakes together.

The Scandinavian peoples of the Viking period colonised much of Britain and established settlements in Iceland and western Greenland, and for over two centuries sent a series of expeditions to Canada—starting with unsuccessful attempts at colonisation and continuing as expeditions to collect timber. They transported small armies which harried France and Britain; they traded in the Mediterranean. In the course of this great maritime activity they moved many thousands of men, women and children, horses and cattle, tools and agricultural equipment, trade goods, weapons and timber cargoes.

National Maritime Museum

Figure 146   Model of the small Viking cargo ship, Skuldelev Wreck 3.

Though there is dispute about the early Greenland voyages in particular, and on economic grounds some authorities suggest they may have been made in local vessels of a type developed in Iceland, these great movements of peoples and goods were not made in longships like the Ladby ship, or in *karves* like the Gokstad and Oseberg ships, or coasters like the small Skuldelev cargo ship. The great ocean voyages to Iceland, Greenland and Canada are unlikely to have been made in these vessels either, despite the proven seaworthiness of the Gokstad ship. A lot of them must have been made in vessels with greater cargo-carrying capacity, relatively short, broad, sailing cargo ships of the type referred to in the sagas as *knarr*. The big cargo ship found at Skuldelev, built with pine planking, probably in Norway, represents perhaps the first example of a vessel of this general type to have been found.

She is 54 ft (16·5 m) long and nearly a quarter as broad as she is long, very strongly built and a burdensome vessel with full round stern and bows. The bows of the *knarr* were so characteristic that in one or two places in the sagas, the prose poems of the Viking peoples written down in Iceland long after the events they purport to record, some Icelandic women are called *knarr bringa*, 'knarr breasted'.

Constructed with a shell of narrow strakes, strengthened by timbers, separate futtocks and knees and beams at the timber heads, the massive *knarr* still shows a sudden change in the run of planking above the fifth strake up from the keel. Thus, perhaps, the influences at work in her ancestry can still be seen. Like the Oseberg ship she may be a development of the basic plank-built boat shape of an earlier age. She is also herself one of the ancestors of some of the wooden sailing ships of the Middle Ages. The *knarr* has few oars, her sailing efficiency under her squaresail appears to have been dependent partly on her beating spar. Like all the Viking ships so far described she was steered with a side rudder.

Ole Crumlin-Pedersen has made a preliminary reconstruction, Figure 147, showing a longitudinal section. Today this vessel is as fully re-erected as she can be in the Viking Ship Museum by the shores of Roskilde fjord in Denmark, and Figure 148 shows her as she is now, with a framework of black metal to indicate the likely shape of the complete vessel.

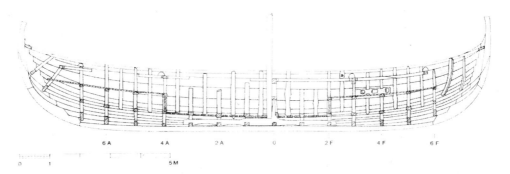

Ole Crumlin-Pedersen

Figure 147   Big Viking cargo ship—reconstruction of Skuldelev Wreck 1.

Basil Greenhill

Figure 148   Skuldelev Wreck 1 as she is today in the Viking Ship Museum at Roskilde.

It may be helpful at this point to summarise in very general terms the changes which appear to have taken place in the development of Scandinavian shipbuilding traditions over two hundred years between AD 800 and about AD 1000. In a very oversimplified way this can perhaps best be done by the three diagrams reproduced here which have been drawn by Ole Crumlin-Pedersen, Figure 149. They show the midships sections of the Oseberg ship, with its sharp transition of the *meginhufr* above the lower hull, the basic boat and the upper structure with the high beams at the top of the lower hull. Transition is far less marked, though still present, in the Gokstad ship, the lower hull less significant, the beams lower in the vessel. In the Skuldelev small cargo ship, the lower hull has become the bottom of the vessel. The upper structure has grown to be at least half the side of the ship. The beams have sunk to just above the floor timbers and additional beams have come in above them. It is the inside structure which reveals the apparent development of the tradition.

Graveney boat

There is plenty of evidence that during the two centuries the Vikings came to Britain as raiders, traders and colonisers they met with a great deal of opposition, some of it at sea. There must have been in Britain highly developed boatbuilding traditions,

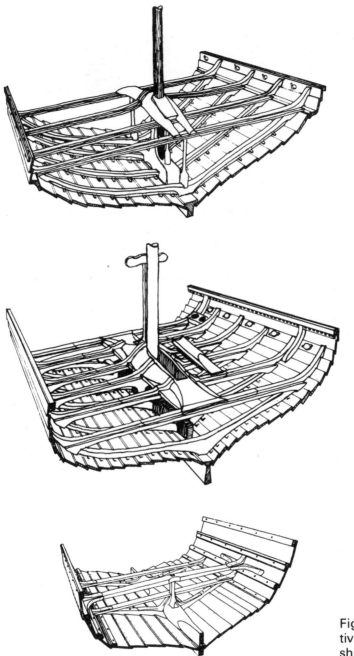

Figure 149 Comparative structures of Viking ships, AD 800–1000.

Ole Crumlin-Pedersen

perhaps almost as highly developed as those of the Scandinavians, sharing some common ancestry.

But until very recently there has only been shadowy evidence as to the nature of these traditions. Rather more information is now available through the discovery in 1970 in marshes near Faversham, Kent of the Graveney boat, which has been provisionally dated as from the middle of the 10th century AD—half a century after the Danish attacks during the reign of King Alfred. She is no grand great chief's ship, like the Oseberg or Gokstad ships. The parallel is more with the two workaday Skuldelev cargo boats and she is between the two in size, clinker-built with a plank keel, or hog, instead of the 'T'-shaped keel of the Scandinavian finds. The stern post, which survived, and the way the ends of the planks were fastened to it, which have a near parallel in a 15th century Thames find which is even more recent, is quite outside the Scandinavian tradition as are the massive floor timbers and the apparent absence of cross-beams. Her great beam and sturdy framing distinguish her as a carrier of bulky cargoes. The massive frames are joined straight to the strakes with trenails. Her stern post has a sharp knee at the foot which appears to provide the first archaeological evidence for the *barde*—see Chapter 12—a feature which has been seen in various forms in contemporary illustrations of Scandinavian vessels. She is probably a boat which had an everyday job of work to do. A coaster, perhaps operating between creeks and rivers of south-eastern England, occasionally across to the Low Countries, it may well be that the highly developed clinker tradition which she represents had roots in what is now Holland and Belgium and southern Germany. The Graveney boat's structure has been the subject of more thorough examination and report than any comparable boat find made previously in Britain, and few boat finds anywhere in the world have been more thoroughly researched. But the full significance of the find will only be assessable in the light of further discoveries of this period. Meanwhile the Report on her produced under the editorship of Valerie Fenwick is a model of its kind.

The hypothetical lines of the Graveney boat prepared by Eric McKee have been the source of hydrostatics prepared by Burness Corlett and Partners, the naval architects. Analysis suggests that the vessel was intended to be a moderately fast carrier of heavy concentrated cargoes, such as stone or salt. For this purpose the design is good and there is little to fault. She is seaworthy, reasonably fast and capable of making seagoing voyages under sail carrying six or seven tons of cargo, though in these conditions she will have had a tendency to ship water amidships. Her seagoing qualities are much in excess of those required for a vessel for service only on the river. It is hoped to put these conclusions into practice in due course by trials with a full-sized replica which the National Maritime Museum plans to build, not only for the trials, but also because to solve the problems which faced the original builders will be an excellent way to press even further the detailed study of the structure of this very important vessel.

The three photographs are an admirable illustration of boat archaeology in action, since the Graveney dig was one of the most difficult, because of the conditions in which the boat was found. The first, Figure 150, shows the boat after its

Figure 150   The Graveney boat after initial excavation.

National Maritime Museum

Figure 151   The Graveney boat being dismantled by National Maritime and British Museum staff.

National Maritime Museum

Figure 152   The keel of the Graveney boat.

initial excavation, indicating her position relative to the Graveney Marsh dyke. The second, Figure 151, shows dismantling in process, a joint operation carried out by National Maritime Museum and British Museum staff, and the third, Figure 152, the underside of the keel being cleaned and recorded.

Eric McKee spent over a year examining and recording the timbers and with the aid of a $\frac{1}{10}$th scale model made by himself has arrived at a preliminary hypothetical reconstruction of the whole boat which has gained widespread acceptance. The scale model, which gives a general indication of the possible full shape of the parts which were found, but which is no more than a working tool, is shown in Figure 153. Working drawings, Figures 154 and 155, both in conventional naval architects' and strake diagram form, indicate the generally agreed hypothesis of the form of the minimum boat and they will be the basis (but no more than the basis) of the full-scale reconstruction in due course. It is hoped that in this way in the course of ten years or so of work to learn as much as possible from the substantial timbers found 8 ft (2·44 m) under the blue clay of the Graveney marshes in the cold October of 1970. The original builders would indeed be very surprised to know of the money and effort which is being spent to learn from their work as much as possible of the traditions which conditioned them.

National Maritime Museum

Figure 153   A working tool model of part of the hypothetical Graveney boat.

Årby boat

In an era of nationally popular small boat sailing the question is often asked, what were the small boats of the Vikings like? Surely, it is said, they must have developed fast rowing and sailing boats which, within the limitations of their traditions, were of quality comparable with that indicated by the big ship finds which have been described here. They did indeed. Fragments of many small Viking boats have been found in Scandinavia. Among the principal finds are the parts of boats found inside the Gokstad ship and the boat found at Årby near Upsala in middle Sweden. Dating from about the period of the Skuldelev ships, AD 1000, she is a nicely shaped, simple little structure, about 13 ft (4 m) long made of a keel plank with two strakes on each side. She has three timbers, each in a single piece, fastened direct to the shell with trenails. She was rowed by one man who sat amidships and pulled his oars against two single thole pins, cut out of planks secured to the upper strakes on each side. The oars were secured with grommets. She had no gunwale and was a light canoe-like craft, unstable and needing skilled hands to get the best from her, but light and no doubt a pleasure to row once mastered.

Gokstad boats

The boats of the Gokstad find were larger. The smallest, the *faering* or four-oared boat has three strakes on each side. She also has three timbers secured direct to the plank shell, together with inclined frames at the bows and at the stern, where a miniature side rudder may have provided the means of steering her. She has solid carved stem and stern posts like the Skuldelev finds and parts of the Gokstad stem, that is the plank ends are carved out of the solid and are in one piece with the stem itself.

The smallest of the three boats—see Figures 28, 29 and 30, Chapter 3—has thole pins similar to those of the Årby boat. She is 20 ft (6 m) long, and is also light, very easy to row and will take three people in comfort. She is rowed by two men but one can handle her well enough. She is most beautifully shaped and built of very thin planking, so finely constructed as to be almost a work of art in her own right.

We do not know for certain what considerations were made by those who reconstructed her from the planks found in the Gokstad ship, for no detailed record was left. Nor can we be absolutely certain what new work was put into her. The boat as she is today in the Viking Ship Museum at Bygdøy therefore, is herself an approximation, but so right for her purpose as a fast rowing boat, that she is probably fairly close to the original form. More than one replica has been made of her including the one built at the National Maritime Museum, Greenwich (in order to gain experience for the work on the Graveney boat replica), which has been subjected to extensive sea trials. The building and trials of this boat have been published in the Museum's Maritime Monograph Series, see Chapter 3.

Oselver boat

It is probable that these two small boats from Sweden and Norway represent types which had already been developed for several centuries when they were built in approximately AD 850 and AD 1000. The type has continued to be built down to the present day and can be seen in its modern form in the Oselver from the Hardanger area of Norway near Bergen. The Oselver has correctly been described

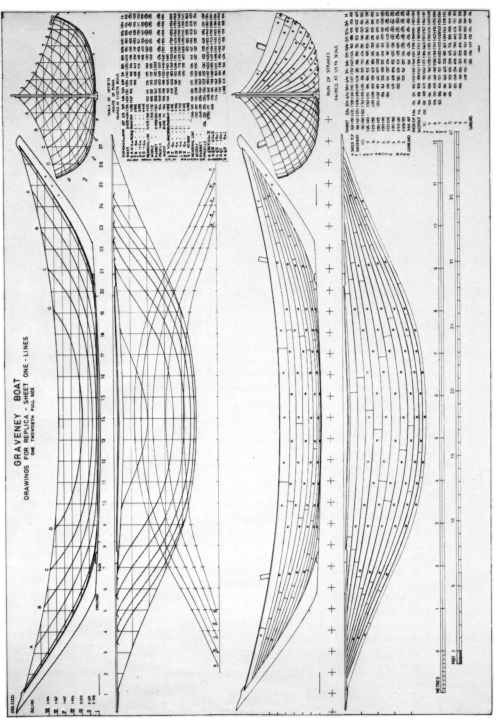

Eric McKee

Figure 154   Lines of the Graveney boat, the conventional drawing.

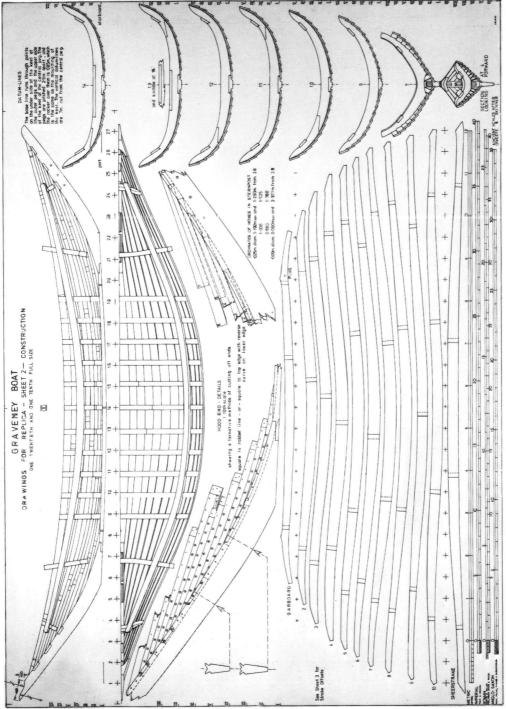

Figure 155   Structural drawing and strake diagram of the Graveney boat.

Eric McKee

as the boat of a thousand years. She is a perfect example of a simple boat built with overlapping strakes which has changed scarcely at all in that time. The Oselver illustrated here, Figure 156, was built especially for the National Maritime Museum to represent a type of boat used in Norway from Viking times until today, and exported in large numbers to the Shetlands, from where it influenced boat construction and shape in the north of Britain and gave rise to the very similar *fourern* used by Shetland fishermen until very recently. While few strakes make for relatively easy building and flexible strength for low weight, her shape is restricted to an almost straight 'V' section. Built without moulds with frames fitted after planking, the boat demonstrates two points very clearly. The first is the tendency of small wooden boats built by people in remote communities to continue to show the basic constructional characteristics of their very remote ancestors. The second is the importance of size in the longevity of boat design. In the larger examples of this constructional method the desirable quality of flexibility in a small boat becomes a weakness in a ship, and the method was replaced by designs using heavier structures, fuller sections and more and narrower strakes. The building of small boats in wood represents a deep folk culture. Bigger vessels came and went, but the world of small boats remained insolubly bound up with the life of humble watermen. Though big ships changed out of all recognition in the 15th and 16th centuries, all over the world small boats continued, as long as they were built of wood, to show the basic constructional characteristics of their remote ancestors—the big ships of eight or more centuries ago.

National Maritime Museum

Figure 156   The Oselver, a modern boat very similar in form to small boats of the Viking period.

It is possible today to build a Viking boat, a copy of the National Maritime Museum's Oselver, in the Museum's boatbuilding shop, and thereby to learn much of one of the oldest of the more complex human skills.

It is through smaller boats that some progress is being made towards learning more about the sails and rigging the Vikings and their contemporaries may have used and the ways in which they sailed their vessels. More accurately, perhaps, experimental work in England and in Denmark being conducted at the time of writing is directed towards discovering more of how boats and vessels rigged with only one squaresail, more or less amidships, sailed and were handled. For although Viking ships and some of their fittings have survived in greater or lesser degree, their sails and their rigging have not and we know remarkably little about them. We do not really even know what the sails were made of, what shapes they were, or how they were cut and sewn.

The Danish National Museum began practical experimental work in 1974 with a Nordlands *ottring*, Figure 157, (see Chapter 16). The Nordlands boat was probably the last European seagoing boat type to work in any numbers under a single squaresail. Eric Anderson, working in association with the National Museum, has made a very detailed study of these boats (which were in use until about seventy

Basil Greenhill

Figure 157   The Danish National Museum's Nordlands boat under sail in the Sound in 1974.

years ago), their sails and rigging and the way they were handled. With a number of volunteers in 1974 he restored and re-rigged the National Museum's Nordlands boat and slowly began to learn to sail her. In the summer of 1975, working closely with Eric Anderson, the National Maritime Museum's replica of the Gokstad *faering* was rigged and experience gained in sailing her. It was hoped to hold measured trials with each of these boats with a view to definite knowledge of the performance of Viking-type hulls under a type of sail which is known to have been used with such hulls at sea. These trials may be extended by the use of simulations of contemporary materials for the sails, both with the Gokstad boat and with the full-sized Graveney boat when she is built.

It must be remembered that for a boat to go well to windward both hull and sail must be capable and be matched. A good sail on a poor hull and *vice versa* is of no avail. We do not know what kind of sails the Vikings used, a poor homespun sailcloth, if that was the material used, must have held the Viking ships to a broad reach at the best. With a hull like the Oseberg ship a tightly woven canvas sail, or more likely a heavily shrunken woollen one almost certainly gave her a good sailing performance at least in smooth water—but a good deal of experiment is needed before we can be sure.

The Nordlands boat requires five men to handle her and she needs skilful sailing, but she is a beautiful boat to handle within these limitations, far more close winded than might be expected, and very fast. Indeed the sailing of this boat has demonstrated that the flexibility of the squaresail is much greater than has been supposed in recent years, now that the tradition of single squaresail sailing has completely died away. The squaresail is highly flexible and adaptable, and should perhaps be thought of in the same way as the dipping lug of British fishing boats of the late 19th century. By definition the differences from the lug are, of course, that the luff of the squaresail changes from one side of the sail to the other as she goes about and the sail is always set outside the shrouds. But its aerodynamic characteristics are perhaps not so different from those of the dipping lug.

Bibliography

ARBMAN, H. 'Der Årby-fund', 1940
BRØGGER, A. W. et al *Osebergfunnet*, 1917–28
BRØGGER, A. W. and SHETELIG, H. *Viking Ships, their Ancestry and Evolution*, 1951
BRØNDSTED, J. 'Oldtidsbaden fra Als', 1925
CHRISTENSEN, A. E. *Boats of the North*, 1968
CRUMLIN-PEDERSEN, O. 'Viking Ships of Roskilde', 1970
ELLMERS, D. *Frümittelalterliche Handelsschiffahrt in Mittel-und Nordeuropa*, 1972
ESKERÖD, A. *Kyrkbåtar och Kyrkbåtsfärder*, 1973
FENWICK, V. H. (ed) *The Graveney Boat*, (in press)
FOOTE, P. G. and WILSON, D. M. *Viking Achievement*, 1970

GJELLESTAD, A. J. 'Litt om Oselverbäter', 1969

HAASUM, S. *Vikingatidens segling och navigation*, 1974

JONES, G. *A History of the Vikings*, 1968

KRISTJÁNSSON, L. 'Graenlenzki Landnemaflotinn og Breidfirzki Báturinn', 1965

MCGRAIL, S. and MCKEE, J. E. G. *Building and Trials of the Replica of an Ancient Boat: The Gokstad Faering*, 1974

NICOLAYSEN, N. *Viking Ship discovered at Gokstad in Norway*, 1882

OLSEN, O. and CRUMLIN-PEDERSEN, O. 'Skuldelev Ships', 1967

ROSENBERG, G. 'Hjortspringfunnet', 1937

SAWYER, P. H. *Age of the Vikings*, 1971

SJØVOLD, T. *Oseberg Find*, 1969

STENTON, F. M. *Bayeux Tapestry*, 1957

THORVILDSEN, K. *Ladby-Skibet*, 1957

Chapter 15

Further Aspects of Viking Age Boatbuilding

by Sean McGrail, Chief Archaeologist, National Maritime Museum

The characteristic features of Viking Age boats and ships evolved over centuries, and there were variant forms in different regions of Northern Europe, as described in Chapter 14. Function, too, had its effect on form, so that for example, a longship would necessarily have a different midship cross section from a cargo vessel, and an ocean trader would be of sturdier construction than a coastal ship. Nevertheless, the evidence from a number of well recorded finds from those parts of Northern Europe associated with Viking settlement and influence, is that these sea-going boats, ranging in date from about AD800–1200, had many basic features in common. Evidence from future excavations, and more complex taxonomic studies may change the picture somewhat, but, on the evidence at present available, the general characteristics of these boats and ships, built in what may be called the Viking sea-going tradition, may be summarised in the following way.

They were double-ended with a keel scarfed to stems forward and aft, and had a distinctive sheer line. Their main strength lay in a shell of thin planking which was edge-joined, clenched with iron nails. Symmetrical ribs or frames were lashed or fastened by trenails to the strakes but not to the keel, and over most ribs was a characteristically slender crossbeam and later, a thwart, giving added support and stability to the shell. They were propelled by oars and by a sail on a mast stepped near amidships, and were steered by means of a side rudder.

Another characteristic feature of Viking boatbuilding was the use of short vertical keel/stem scarfs, Figure 158. By 20th century British boatbuilding standards these scarfs are too weak and short, the Gokstad *faering*, for example, having keel/stem scarfs with a slope of 1:4 compared with today's recommended range of 1:7 to 1:12. Modern boatbuilders would also prefer to use horizontal, hooked scarfs, both clenched and glued. The position of the plank scarfs in some Viking Age ships and boats has also been criticised in the light of modern methods. The *faering* plank/stem scarfs and plank scarfs in adjoining strakes, are probably too close together to

234

National Maritime Museum

Figure 158   A keel/stem scarf on the Gokstad *faering* replica built at Greenwich in 1972.

conform with current practice. This criticism of keel scarfs and of plank scarfs overlooks the fact that Viking Age boatbuilders produced an interdependent structure—the 'weak' keel scarfs and the 'too close together' plank scarfs being supported, and their strength reinforced by the whole shell of planking, keel and stems.

This flexible supple construction, combining strength with minimum weight, evidently enabled a ship to 'ride the punch' of the sea rather than rigidly battling against it. Captain Magnus Andersen sailed a replica of the Gokstad ship across the Atlantic in 1893. It is not clear now how authentic were the methods used to build this replica, and thus how valid are the results of the sea trials, but Andersen records in his book about the voyage, that

> '... the bottom together with the keel followed the movements of the ship, and with a strong head-sea the vertical movement of the keel could be as much as $\frac{3}{4}$ inch, but strangely enough, the ship was no less watertight for that. Her great elasticity was apparent also in other ways; in heavy seas, for instance, the gunwales would writhe by anything up to six inches.'[1]

Thus this lightweight, supple structure may well have been more successful than a more rigid one, which with the materials and technology of those days would probably have had to be more massive. Further experimental work, including extensive sea trials, is required to substantiate this theory.

Other important aspects of Viking Age boatbuilding remain to be considered: the selection and conversion of timber, and the use of tools and design aids. These are

[1] Quoted by A. E. Christensen in *Boats of the North*, pp. 39–40.

topics to which boat archaeologists now give more attention than has been the case in the past. Ole Crumlin-Pedersen[2] and Arne Emil Christensen[3] have contributed most to the understanding of these matters, and some of their findings are here integrated with experience gained at Greenwich during the building of the *faering* replica in 1972. The questions posed are relevant to all types of boatbuilding: here they are discussed within the Viking context, but as there was a certain homogeneity of culture throughout the North Sea littoral, some of the discussion may also be relevant to the Sutton Hoo ship and the Graveney boat of Saxon England, and to other Early Medieval vessels of Northern Europe. As this type of research is in the process of development, definitive generalised statements cannot always be made; the available evidence often only permitting a range of possibilities to be suggested.

Which type of timber was used?

In general, oak seems to have been preferred for boatbuilding wherever it was available. Archaeological evidence may be biased in that oak has a greater chance of survival than many types of wood, but this apparent preference for oak is confirmed by several literary sources. To a degree, ash was used—witness the Old English term '*Aesc*'—ash, used by contemporary writers to describe the boats of the Norsemen. Pine, readily available in much of Northern Europe, was also used for strakes, masts and oars, whilst beech, alder, birch, lime and willow were used in the Skuldelev ships for ribs, trenails and similar fittings.

The preference for oak may best be explained in the words of John Evelyn, the 17th century diarist, oak is 'tough, bending well, strong and not too heavy, nor easily admitting water', for this preference persisted in England until the eclipse of wooden ships. The properties of European oak given in the Department of the Environment's *Handbook of Hardwoods*, more than bear out Evelyn's description. Oak has been taken as the standard of comparison for the strength properties of many of the hardwoods; it has 'very good' bending properties, and it is in the second of five groups when classified for durability. Tall forest oak, usually of straight grain and without low branches provided wood for the keels and the long runs of planking; more isolated oaks produced the naturally curved timber required for the ribs and similar parts of the boat. It was considered most important to select individual trees with the timber to match the job in hand. As Snorri Sturluson, the early 13th century Icelandic historian, wrote in the *Heimskringla*: 'all (timber) that was used was selected very carefully'.

When were the trees felled?

It has long been believed that there was a right time and a right season for felling timber. Some of these beliefs were superstitions connected, for example, with the phases of the moon, but others indicated that winter was the best time, and there are

[2] 'Skuldelev Ships II', *Acta Archaeologica*, 38, pp. 73–174, 1967.
[3] Hasslöf, O. (ed), *Ships and Shipyards, Sailors and Fishermen*, pp. 235–59, 1972

sound reasons why this could be so. Firstly, this time of year fitted the cyclic nature of medieval and pre-medieval life. Winter felling also meant that autumnal crops such as acorns could be used, and after the leaves had fallen deciduous trees were easier to investigate and prepare. Extraction of the log is easier over the hard ground of winter, and logs may subsequently be floated downstream in maximum water, where this is necessary. Logs left lying in winter are less liable to rot as the temperature is often too low for insect and fungi propagation. And the air-drying of logs can be done in winter at a slower and therefore a safer speed. Thus the winter season has many advantages.

Some of these considerations certainly applied during the Viking Age, and there is literary evidence for the winter felling of trees—the building of the *Long Serpent* by Olaf Tryggvason as recorded in *Heimskringla* saga, for example. Winter therefore was evidently the preferred time, but it is possible that, in times of stress, trees were felled at any season to meet an urgent requirement for boats.

Was the timber seasoned?

If timber was used immediately after felling, then considerations of rot and air-drying discussed in the preceding section are not relevant. But was wood used green in medieval boatbuilding or was it seasoned before use? The evidence for this may be analysed under six headings:

(1) Archaeological evidence

Several partly worked pieces of timber obviously destined for boatbuilding have been found in bogs in Scandinavia and in Britain (for example, the two stems found in a moss on the Isle of Eigg in 1878). Two different and somewhat conflicting reasons may be advanced to explain why timber should be stored in this way:

(a) The oak was temporarily stored in incipient bogs so that the anaerobic conditions obtaining there would prevent decay. For a time this timber would also be kept moist and fresh and thus easier to work than seasoned oak.

(b) The oak was temporarily stored in water to keep it fresh and moist so that it could be worked relatively easily in future boatbuilding. There would also be a degree of protection against decay. The water subsequently turned to bog.

Time immersed in bog or water would determine the equilibrium state reached by the oak. Long exposure to the acidic conditions in a bog would result in mineral formation within the oak, and it is the experience of the Jodrell Laboratory at the Royal Botanic Gardens, Kew, that oak recovered after many years in this environment is invariably harder to work than fresh or even seasoned oak. Oak stored for many years underwater, would, on the other hand, become waterlogged and thus unsuitable for boat building.

If it is accepted that Viking Age boatbuilders intended to store worked oak for a year or two at most, then it must be concluded that they did so for preserving reasons and to keep it moist: the hardening effect of bog and the waterlogging effect of underwater storage not having time to make a significant impact. Whether bog or water was used for storage may be determined by future research. MacPherson, who recorded the finding of the two stems on Eigg, mentions the belief that the moss was formerly a lake used by the Norsemen. Contemporary west Norwegian practice, described below, may indicate that Viking Age boatbuilders did in fact use water storage.

(2) Textual evidence

References to the building of boats immediately after the felling of trees are found in medieval literature from several North European countries: the saga description of the building of the *Long Serpent* illustrates this point.

(3) Recent practice

A description of the building of *sixerns* in early 20th century Shetland states that 'large trees free from knots were used, cut into planks of the required thickness just before use. In this state they were much more pliable than seasoned boards would have been and steaming was not required'. And Christensen has described how A. N. Søvik who builds Oselver boats, and his neighbours in the Bergen area of west Norway keep their oak in water. Søvik's boatshed is built out over the sea and oak 'blanks' for the keels are kept under the house for several years; they are taken direct to the building shed when required for a boat. No similar storage methods for strake material is known, however.

In a survey of British wooden boatbuilding practices carried out for the Forest Products Research Laboratory in 1963, A. V. Thomas reported that the 'keels of large cruisers and fishing boats are often laid down in a green condition and, as far as possible, are kept damp during the construction of the boat'. He adds, however, that logs converted into boards for later use as frames and planking are air-seasoned for twelve months or more until their moisture content is below 20%m when danger from decay is very much reduced.

(4) Dangers of timber decay

From the early 17th century, accounts of British shipbuilding emphasise the destructive effect of dry rot. The long search for methods to combat this has been described by Moll and by Albion in articles in the *Mariners' Mirror* for 1926 and 1952. The solution gradually evolved was to insist on the use of well-seasoned timber: it was believed that to build ships of fresh green timber was to court disaster. We now know that the fungi causing dry rot require four conditions for growth:

(a)   food—wood, in this case.

(b)   moisture—they can only grow in timber of more than 20% moisture content.

(c)   oxygen—those parts of a boat permanently submerged, especially in sea water which is mildly antiseptic, will experience little serious decay because of the relatively anaerobic conditions.

(d)   optimum range of ambient temperature—growth is very slow below 10° and above 40°C: the most dangerous range is 27°C–32°C.

By using well-dried timber, 17th century and later shipbuilders using sawn planks, many of which were probably tangential, were attempting to avoid dry rot by keeping below the critical moisture content of 20%.

Timber research workers have recently established that fungi can penetrate the tangential faces of pine test blocks more readily than radial faces, although there is a greater degree of decay of the superficial layers in the latter case. Dr John Levy of Imperial College, London University, considers that this differential rate of penetration also occurs in oak heart wood, and that although a radial oak plank may have a thin layer of decay at the surface, the rate of decay buildup through the thicknesses of the plank will be slow. Tangentially cut oak planks, on the other hand, are likely to decay relatively quickly through the plank thickness.

The wood most susceptible to attack in boats is thus those parts not permanently submerged, especially where there is no ventilation. Open boats, which are well ventilated, are therefore less liable to attack, and those built from radially cut or cleft timber are probably more resistant to infection. Oak has a good degreee of natural resistance to fungal decay and, in addition, the use of pine tar (Stockholm tar) impregnates the wood with a substance toxic to fungi. Evidence for the use of tar may well extend back to Biblical times (Genesis 6, v 14) and it is well attested in the historical record from Roman times onwards and especially in the Viking Age. Oak is resistant to impregnation, but a surface layer of tar will act as a barrier against infection.

Thus the Viking Age open boat built from radially cleft oak and treated with pine tar was well placed to resist dry rot. Boats and ships with closed unventilated spaces, built from tangentially cut planks, are, on the other hand, more susceptible to attack and this fact makes modern boatbuilders insist on well-seasoned timber.

(5)   Dangers during the drying process

Moisture is present in fresh wood in two forms: free water in the cell cavities, and absorbed water in the cell walls. As the wood dries it first loses a large proportion of the free water: only after this is moisture lost from the cell walls. Down to the point where most of the water has evaporated from within the cells but the cell walls are still saturated, the wood undergoes little if any change in shape or physical appearance. Drying beyond this fibre saturation point causes the wood to shrink. The dimensional changes are not the same in all directions (they are of the order: longitudinal 1: radial 12: tangential 24) and this differential shrinkage causes stresses in the timber and distortion. In addition, the various layers of the wood dry at unequal speed, the outer layers drying more quickly than the inner layers can diffuse moisture to the surface, and this moisture gradient results in checks and splitting of the wood—this is very true of the end surfaces, and oak especially has marked tendencies to split and check. These tendencies may be reduced by the use of special drying schedules to dry the wood below fibre saturation point until it is in equilibrium with its environment: for example at 90% relative humidity the wood will have a moisture content of about 20%; at 60% relative humidity, moisture content will be about 12%.

An alternative treatment would be to keep the wood *above* fibre saturation point—for oak this means a moisture content of $\geqslant 27\%$. In this state the wood will be dimensionally stable and there will be little risk of checks or distortions. By using unseasoned 'green' timber, and building it quickly into a boat, the moisture content can be maintained at a high level until the boat becomes stabilised in water afloat at a moisture content around fibre saturation point. Those parts of a boat permanently in water should thus remain stable. Parts out of water will probably dry to somewhat below fibre saturation point, but those sections which are exposed to a salt-laden atmosphere may accumulate a fine layer of salt which is hygroscopic and will provide a buffer to environmental changes, keeping the moisture content high. This theory has not—so far as is known—been subjected to a controlled test. This will be done in future research work by the National Maritime Museum.

(6) The strength characteristics of timber

During the drying process the reduction in moisture content affects the various strength properties. Hardness and stiffness, compressive strength and bending strength are increased: resistance to shock and toughness are reduced. Thus fresh green oak is considerably easier to work than seasoned oak, and Ole Crumlin-Pedersen has heard Scandinavian boatbuilders describe green oak as 'butter' oak and praise it for its softness, favourably contrasting it with dry oak which is called 'bone' oak. Again, fresh oak is bent more easily—its supple resistance depends upon high moisture content, and this is especially important for strakes—best results are obtained at about 25% moisture content. Oak of a higher moisture content is however, apt to rupture on the inner face when bent. This indicates that strake planks should be somewhat less green than unbent members of a boat's structure—this would occur naturally if planks were split from the log at the same time as, or even before, the keel and stems were being worked.

The evidence considered above suggests that, for open boats, the advantages of using green timber especially for those parts below the waterline, outweigh the disadvantages. The textual and ethnographic evidence indicates that green oak was used until recent times in some parts of North Europe where the influence of big shipbuilding methods had not penetrated. Viking Age boats may also have been built of green timber, and stabilised in their natural element, the sea, at relatively high moisture contents. Careful treatment must have been essential when boats were hauled out over winter: a *naust* or boathouse close to the sea, and further applications of Stockholm tar would minimise the problems of drying out.

During the building of the *faering* replica the seasoned oak did develop cracks, shakes and distortion; especially was this true of the stem which had to be worked to a feather edge. The use of suitable green oak would, on the evidence now available, have been structurally sound and probably authentic. The National Maritime Museum plans to test this theory during future boatbuilding projects, due weight being given to environmental factors, for what may be appropriate to western Scandinavia is not necessarily directly applicable to southern Britain.

How were logs converted into planks?

There are two basic methods of converting a log into boards, known today as *plain* or *flat sawn*, and *quarter* or *rift sawn*. They might be more graphically described as *tangential* and *radial* for in the former method timber is cut in a plane roughly tangential to the growth rings, whilst in quarter sawing, the cutting plane is approximately at right angles to the growth rings, i.e. parallel with the rays. Efficient use of saws, especially power saws, means that it is more practical nowadays to produce boards cut in planes other than exactly tangential or radial, and the current British Standard (BS 565/1972) allows for this by defining *plain sawn* as timber converted so that the growth rings meet the face in any part at an angle of less than 45°; whilst in *quarter sawn* the angle is greater than or equal to 45°. Some variants of these two methods are illustrated, Figure 159.

Before the days of great saws, trees were converted by splitting, and the easiest way to split an oak is radially because the large rays assist the cleaving. Moisture

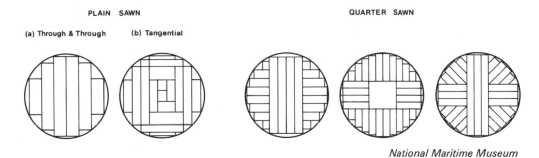

PLAIN SAWN   QUARTER SAWN

(a) Through & Through   (b) Tangential

National Maritime Museum

Figure 159   Twentieth century methods of log conversion.

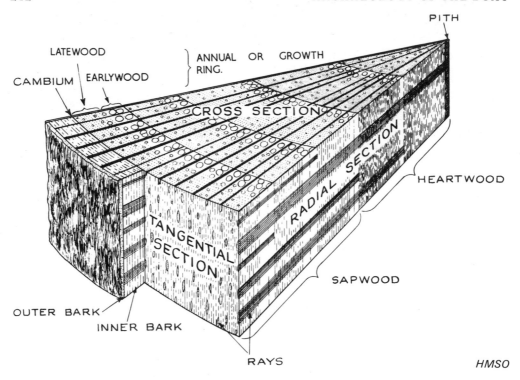

Figure 160   The principal structural features of hardwood.

decreases the adhesion of one cell to another, and therefore green wood splits more easily than seasoned. To get good cleft board or cloveboard, sound straight logs are required; logs with corkscrew grain will not cleave freely and can only result in poor board. A cloven board follows the natural run of the grain, and this results in a stronger board than one in which the grain slopes from one face of a plank towards the other, as can happen with sawn board, which can fail by splitting when subject to heavy loading.

Cleft oak planks thus have several desirable characteristics because they are split. They have other useful attributes because they are radial rather than tangential. The rays run parallel to the radial faces, Figure 160, and thus radial planks are stronger than comparable tangential ones, and will not split across the plank so readily. Knots reduce strength in tension, compression and bending. and in general, a knot in a tangentially cut or sawn log will be present in many of the planks; whereas only those radial planks which lie within the angle of the knot will be affected. Another quality of radial planking is that as it dries out from green timber it is more stable than tangential boards in that it shrinks less in breadth, and is not so liable to warp, check or split. As a percentage of the original dimension the shrinkage of most timbers in the radial plane is approximately half that in the tangential plane. This is because the ray cells have their long axis in the radial plane and so tend to resist shrinkage in that direction. Conversely, the rays are at right angles to the tangential face and in this plane, acting somewhat like wedges, they force the wood apart into checks and shakes. This shrinkage phenomenon occurs only below the fibre saturation point, and thus green timber kept above this level will not be so degraded whether it is tangential or radial cut. Another advantage which radial planks have over tangential ones is, as mentioned in the section on *Decay*, that fungi penetrates more readily into tangential faces.

In addition to these general qualities clove boards have two distinct advantages in clinker work. Firstly, dimensional movements due to reaction to changing environmental relative humidity are greatest, when expressed as a percentage, across the thickness of a radial plank, that is its smallest dimension. In absolute terms this is small; it is also a movement in line with the axis of the clenched nails and is, therefore, resisted by them and the effect is cushioned to some degree by the luting in the land. With tangential planks, on the other hand, movement is greatest across the breadth of a plank, at right angles to the axis of the clench nails. This is a larger movement in absolute terms, and clinker work is not so well able to resist or cushion the effects. The second advantage is that nails are driven into a radial plank at right angles to the plane of weakness, whereas with a tangential plank, the nails are driven in parallel to this radial plane and thus have a greater tendency to split the plank.

Until relatively recently, timber from excavated ships was not examined thoroughly, but when this has been done oak from Viking Age wrecks has almost invariably been found to be split radially. Crumlin-Pedersen found only one tangentially split oak plank in the Skuldelev ships. Possibly these rare tangential splits were made when oak logs were not available of sufficient diameter to give radial planks of the required breadth. Splitting a tree by cleaving it into a series of diminishing halves produces radial planks of a uniform breadth and of triangular or wedge-shaped cross sections, Figure 161. This shape can readily be used in clinker work and also in housebuilding, where it is known as clapboard or cloboard. The Skuldelev ships' planks had a wedge angle of *c*.11°, corresponding to splitting a log into thirty-two sections. Experiments at Moesgård in Denmark have shown that on average twenty sound radial splits can be obtained from each log. The experienced Viking Age timber worker, with probably a better range of trees to chose from, may well have had a higher success rate. To obtain planks of a given breadth, logs of diameter greater than three times this breadth must be chosen, Figure 161.

The use of cleft oak persisted in English shipbuilding well into the 16th century. Craftsmen in other trades have also long recognised the superiority of cleft oak and value it for its strength and reliability. It has many advantages over planks that are sawn or are tangential.

Scots pine, the other timber frequently found in Viking Age ships, has different cleavage and strength characteristics from oak. In addition, at maturity pine trees are generally only half the diameter of oak, 2–3 ft (60–90 cm) as against 4–6 ft (1·20–1·80 m). Radially split planks of pine do not, therefore, have all the

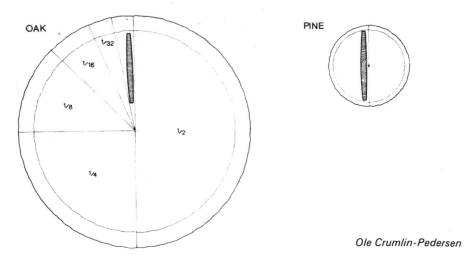

Figure 161   Wood splitting techniques.

advantages of similar ones of oak and they may be of insufficient breadth over the required lengths. It is not now possible to be certain whether the Gokstad *faering* pine sheer strakes were radially or tangentially split. The pine planks in the Skuldelev ships have however been examined in detail and it is clear that they are not true radials but are more nearly 'diameters' of the log close to the pith, Figure 161, each log producing only two, or at the most four, such planks. Crumlin-Pedersen calls this 'tangentially orientated', but by BS 565/1972 these would be 'quarter-sawn' timber in that over most of their breadth the growth rings meet the face at an angle of not less than 45°. It may be deduced that these planks have the properties of radial splits, at least to some degree.

It may thus be claimed that Viking Age craftsmen evolved the best method of converting each type of timber for the particular job in hand.

How were boats 'designed'?

How did the Viking boatbuilder translate the idea of a boat into reality? He may have wanted to repeat a previous design—a more or less exact copy within the limitations of the stock of timber available to him, or he may have been asked to modify one—'build me a boat like the one you built for Ola last year, but two feet longer and with rather more beam aft' as Christensen says. Or he may have been a daring innovator.

If the boatbuilder had the original boat to hand he could make a direct copy, modified where necessary to suit a somewhat different requirement. There must have been occasions, however, when he wanted to record the principal measurements of some boat for future use. Christensen has identified two aids, the boat ell and the boat level, which have a long history of use in Scandinavia. These aids enable a man unable to read or write, to record a boat's main scantlings and to use them at a later date. The boat ell records a number of important measurements from a base line stretched between the stems, and some significant breadths: in essence a table of offsets with marked lengths instead of figures. The boat level records the angle of slope of each strake; this, together with the breadth of each plank, determines the essential form of a boat. It cannot yet be said that either of these aids was, in fact, available in the Viking Age, but the possibility may be borne in mind.

Alternatively, it is possible that boats were built by eye. Christensen claims that the boat of traditional Northern European shell-construction 'may be pure sculptural work, for the builder shapes the hull in the course of his work'. As he sees the shape emerging before his eyes, the builder can alter the angle of the garboards slightly, increase the breadth of the next pair of strakes, alter the sheer line aft and so on. As he builds he judges the shape necessary to produce a boat for the work specified. Some changes may be due to experience gained in previous boats—to cure a defect such as taking water over the bows—and some may be intended to enhance a quality such as the cargo capacity. There is a living tradition of boatbuilding by eye in Scandinavia, but again, there is no direct evidence for use in antiquity, unless Thorberg's action in altering the planking of Olaf Tryggvason's *Long Serpent* by eye can be so interpreted. Thorberg, the stem smith, 'had gone from stem to stem, and cut one deep notch after the other down one side of the planking. . . . Then Thorberg went and smoothed the ship's side until the deep notches had all disappeared. Then the king and all present declared that the ship was much handsomer on the side which Thorberg had cut, and the king asked him to shape it so on both sides and gave him great thanks for the improvement.'[4] Thorberg was subsequently made master boatbuilder.

It is possible too, that there were traditional rules of thumb, similar to the length/breadth/depth ratios of 6·6:2·3:1 recommended in 17th century England. Such rules would set the parameters within which individual craftsmen would build to their own design.

As described in Chapter 3, one of the strands of recent British clinker tradition has been the use of the passive mould as an aid to obtaining the required shape. Moulds may be full or half moulds, and they may be used at every frame or station or restricted to a single midship mould. The shape they convey does not have to be followed exactly—for example the boat may be built broader at certain stations, or the moulds may be spaced out at different intervals. A certain element of building by eye is in use here, with the moulds as a general control. It is uncertain, however, when this method became established in Britain, and it is possible that it has been adapted from a non edge-joined skeleton building tradition.

Shetland boats were built by 'rule of thumb' and 'by eye', and these boats and the living tradition of this method in western Norway, may be modern survivals of Viking Age techniques, but we have no direct evidence. Indeed, none of the possible

[4] quoted by Foote, P. G. and Wilson, D. M., in *Viking Achievement* pp. 250–1, 1970.

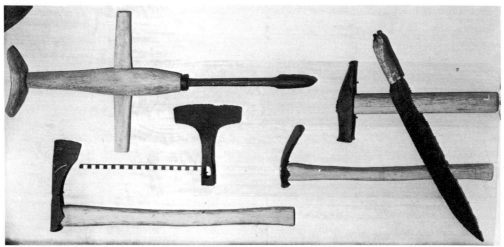

Statens Historiska Museum, Stockholm

Figure 162   Tools from Mastermyr, Gotland, dated to about AD 1000: axe, adzes, hafted wedge, auger with spoon bit, and saw.

methods described can as yet be shown to have been used in Early Medieval times and more research and experiment is required into this matter before a firm hypothesis can be formulated.

Which tools were used?

Boatbuilding tools have been recovered from Viking Age graves and other sites in Scandinavia, including the well-known Swedish find from Mastermyr in Gotland, Figure 162.

Tools are also depicted by several Early Medieval artists, as for example on the Bayeux Tapestry, Figure 163. A study of these finds and the illustrations, and the tool marks left on ancient boat finds, leads to the conclusion that many boatbuilder's hand tools have changed but little over the last thousand years. Thus axe, adze, auger with a spoon bit, profile or moulding iron, draw knife and hafted wedge are essentially the same in form.

Some authors do not believe that the plane was available in Early Medieval Europe, but a 5th century plane has been found in Vimose, Denmark, and a small 6th century plane of antler at Sarre in Kent and these finds, together with the recognition of plane marks on the Skuldelev ships by Crumlin-Pedersen, show that planes were known and used. It has also been said that only axe marks are found on ships and boats of this period and that thus adzes were not used. But it is almost certain that an adze must have been used to shape certain curved surfaces in the Skuldelev ships. Two small saws have been found in Anglo-Saxon contexts and the tool chest from Mastermyr contained three saws. The Saxon saws are too small for serious boatbuilding work and were probably used when making bone combs. The

from *Bayeux Tapestry* by F. Stenton, Phaidon Press

Figure 163   Building William's invasion fleet.

Swedish saws are bigger and could possibly be used by a boatbuilder, but the lack of saw marks on boat finds of this period means that their use cannot so far be directly proved.

The preceding discussion indicates that the modern builder of Viking boat replicas can include the following hand tools in his kit with certainty of authenticity, on the evidence of tool marks:

> axe, draw knife, profile or moulding iron, auger and spoon bits, plane and awl.

Using the evidence of archaeological finds of contemporary date, he can include the following, with only a little less certainty:

> adze, rasp, wedges, anvil, cold chisel, punch, hammer, tongs, metal shears, draw plate, files, gouges, chisels and knife.

And it is probably reasonable to accept that the following basic aids can also be used:

> block and tackle, rollers, sheerlegs, Spanish windlass, cramps, shores, spalls, measuring rods, plumb bob, dividers, squares and mallets.

They are simple aids and have been used over much of Europe from at least Roman times.

The form of individual tools appears to have altered little between AD 900 and AD 1900, with one exception: the type of adze found at Mastermyr with a very long cutting edge, Figure 162, does not seem to have been used in post-Medieval times. 20th century tools probably have many of the characteristics of their Viking Age equivalents, but modern steel tools almost certainly retain an efficient cutting edge for longer. In general, present day methods of holding these tools also seem to be those used a thousand years ago. The axe, however, was probably held close to the blade for fine work—not known to be used in this way in 20th century British boatbuilding, but a method still in use in Norway.

As pointed out in Chapter 1, boat archaeology is only just emerging as a scientific discipline: much research and experimental work must be undertaken before definitive answers can be given to the questions posed in this chapter. Nevertheless the archaeological and technological evidence considered here points towards the formation of the following hypothesis. Without modern methods of analysis and of testing materials, boatbuilders of the Viking Age evolved techniques of choosing the right tree, converting it at the right time and in the right manner to produce the best timber for building the types of boat which best suited their environment and economy.

Research today can point out technical and scientific reasons why some of these techniques best satisfied the Vikings' operational requirements, but it is doubtful whether the Viking boatbuilders were fully aware of these. By trial and error methods, and by acute observation of the effects of varying certain factors, they could reject sub-optimal methods and materials and perfect those which gave their boats desirable characteristics.

Bibliography

ALBION, R. G.   'Timber Problems of the Royal Navy 1652–1862', 1952
BASCH, L.   'Ancient Wrecks and the Archaeology of Ships', 1972
BRØGGER, A. W. and SHETELIG, H.   *Viking Ships, their Ancestry and Evolution*, 1951
BRUCE, R. S.   'More about sixerns', 1934
CARR-LAUGHTON, L. G.   'Clove-board', 1957
CHRISTENSEN, A. E.   *Boats of the North*, 1968
CHRISTENSEN, A. E.   'Boatbuilding Tools and the Process of Learning', 1972
CORBETT, N. H.   'Micro-morphological studies on the degradation of lignified cell walls by ascomycetes and fungi imperfecti', 1965
FOOTE, P. G. and WILSON, D. M.   *Viking Achievement*, 1970
GJELLESTAD, A. J.   'Litt om Oselverbäter', 1969
GOODMAN, W. L.   *History of Woodworking Tools*, 1964
Handbook of Hardwoods, 1969
Handbook of Softwoods, 1968
HASSLÖF, O.   'Main Principles in the Technology of Shipbuilding', 1972
HORNELL, J.   'Fishing luggers of Hastings', 1938
JANE, F. W.   *Structure of Wood*, 1970
LAVERS, G. M.   *Strength Properties of Timbers*, 1969
MCGRAIL, S. and MCKEE, J. E. G.   *Building and Trials of the Replica of an Ancient Boat: The Gokstad Faering*, 1974

MACPHERSON, N.   'Notes on antiquities from the Isle of Eigg', 1877/8
MOLL, F.   'History of Wood Preserving in shipbuilding', 1926
NICOLAYSEN, N.   *Viking Ship discovered at Gokstad in Norway*, 1882
OLSEN, O. and CRUMLIN-PEDERSEN, O.   'Skuldelev Ships', 1967
PETERSEN, J.   'Vikingetidens Redskaper', 1951
SALISBURY, W. (ed)   *Treatise on Shipbuilding*, 1958
SANDISON, C.   *Sixareen and her racing descendants*, 1954
SAVORY, J. G.   *Prevention of decay of wood in boats*, 1966
THOMAS, A. V.   *Timbers used in the Boatbuilding Industry*, 1964
WILSON, D. M.   'Anglo Saxon Carpenters' Tools', 1968

Chapter 16

The Clinker-built Boat after the Viking Period

WITH THE GENERAL development of Europe in the 11th and 12th centuries the Viking Age passed away, but the Scandinavians during this period had given great impetus to the development of the clinker-built boat. There is a good deal of evidence about the development of ship and boat building in the 12th, 13th and 14th centuries. This is provided partly by carefully drawn seals of seaport towns which often show contemporary ships in considerable detail, and by medieval wrecks which have been excavated in Sweden, Norway, Germany, Poland, Denmark, Holland and Britain. These show that both keel and keel plank traditions continued to develop and intermingle. This and other evidence suggests that North European boats and ships followed three very broad main lines of development between the 11th century and 15th century when the technique was generally adopted of building large vessels without edge-joining. Meanwhile the older traditions persisted in small vessels and boats. Before this happened the three main lines of development AD 1100–1400 were:

(1)   the improvement and development of the round-hulled clinker-built boat.
(2)   the development of the flat-bottomed boat into the medieval ships called cogs.
(3)   the development of that mysterious vessel, the hulk.

As the Viking Age drew to a close clinker-built ships became bigger and more complicated. They acquired three lines of beams above the floor timbers, grew broader and deeper and the planks of their shells and their timbers became bigger and heavier. Remains found in Bergen in 1960 show a merchant vessel of about AD 1250 which was 85 ft (25·9 m) long and nearly 30 ft (9·14 m) wide. British seals of the same period illustrate similar large clinker-built vessels. The long overhanging stem and stern of the Saxon/Scandinavian tradition gave way in many larger vessels to a relatively straight, much more upright stem and stern post. An important find made at Kalmar in Sweden shows several small clinker-built merchant ships of the

National Maritime Museum

Figure 164   The Seal of Paris.

National Maritime Museum

Figure 165 The second Seal of Winchelsea.

Arne Emil Christensen, Jnr

Figure 166   A *holrikjekta*.

13th century. Some of their beams projected through the sides of the vessel in the manner shown on contemporary seals. They had short fore and after decks and were equipped with windlasses, stern rudders hanging from a straight stern post and upright stems. Their general proportions suggest the traditions of the Skuldelev big cargo ship rather than the other Viking ship finds.

The seal of the City of Paris, Figure 164, dated about AD 1200, shows a development of the double-ended clinker-built ship, while the Second Seal of the Corporation of Winchelsea, Figure 165, dated AD 1274, shows a double-ended ship with a quarter rudder. Some of the beams project through the sides of the hull, as they do in the Kalmar ships.

The tradition is carried on even into the 20th century in the Norwegian Nordlands *jegt*. A *holrikjekta* in Nord-fjord, Figure 166, shows a great single-masted clinker-built merchant vessel, now preserved in Norway, of a type which existed in great numbers in the 19th century, carrying on an extensive trade between north and south Norway and further afield. Some of these vessels even crossed the Atlantic in the late 19th century. Figure 167 shows one of them discharging firewood at one of the old quays at Bergen.

Warships also continued to be constructed as round-hulled, clinker-built vessels, but they suffered from a peculiar disadvantage in that a new type of ship, the cog, which was coming into use, was much higher-sided and this gave a great advantage to her fighting men, who could rain arrows and spears down on the decks of the old longships. To overcome this longships were fitted with 'castles', fore and aft—this can be seen in some of the seals like that of Winchelsea, Figure 165. But the cogs also

Bergen Sjøfartsmuseum

Figure 167   A 19th century photograph of a *jekt* at Bergen.

National Maritime Museum

Figure 168   A model of a coble from the North East coast of England.

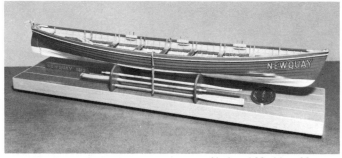

National Maritime Museum

Figure 169   A model of a Cornish gig.

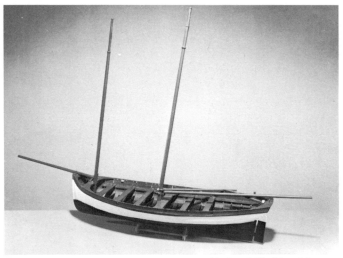

National Maritime Museum

Figure 170   A model of the Manx schooner *Peggy* of 1791.

had castles built onto them and the use of the old type of clinker-built ships for war purposes really came to an end in the 1300s.

But although clinker building for large vessels went out of use, it persisted for boats and small ships down to the end of wooden boatbuilding and remained the principal tradition in Britain and Scandinavia and parts of North America. A number of examples of clinker-built boats built in different parts of Britain and North America for different purposes are illustrated here. All carry on the ancient tradition developed long before the Graveney boat was built, more than a thousand years ago, of shell-construction, edge-joined with inserted frames.

The coble, Figure 168, is a very distinctive boat type from the north-east coast of England. She was normally equipped with a tall narrow dipping lug sail and oars worked over a single thole pin. Her deep sharp forefoot and long rudder enabled her to work to windward despite her flat run. In some aspects her hull anticipates modern motorboat practices. Bob Strongman's lobster boat (see Chapter 2) is in some ways a big smooth-skinned coble. The long narrow Cornish gig, Figure 169, was used as a pilot boat and for general work all around the Cornish coast in the 18th and 19th centuries. Gigs are still used for rowing races on the North Cornish coast and among the Scilly Isles and new ones were built in the 1970s. The clinker-built schooner *Peggy*, Figure 170, was built in 1791 in the Isle of Man as a working boat. She carried out the maritime equivalent of the combined role of a cart and a small carriage for the family who owned her. She is still in existence and is displayed in the Nautical Museum of the Manx Museum at Castletown, Isle of Man. The *Peggy* is remarkably similar in shape, size and sailplan to the Chebacco boats, the small schooners in which the fisheries of New England and Nova Scotia were carried on in the years immediately after the American Revolution. These have their descendants today in the Gaspé schooners of Quebec, clinker-built vessels almost unaltered from the schooners of two centuries ago, Figure 171. In Prince Edward Island, Canada, miniatures of these little schooners, tiny shallops only 14 ft (4·27 m) or 16 ft (4·88 m) long and lapstrake-built, were used in the lobster fishery until the first motorboats came into common use after the First World War, Figure 172. Today clinker or lapstrake boats are still being used in the fishery off the north shore of Cape Breton in Canada. The famous Block Island boats of southern Massachusetts were also lapstrake built, Figure 173.

The model of the beach boat *Boy Albert* from Yarmouth, England, Figure 174, shows the type of flat-floored, full-bowed, transom stern clinker-built beach boat which, with local variations in design, was to be found all round the coast of southern Britain until very recent years. At the time of writing, because they are so long lasting and despite the advantages of glass-reinforced plastic, there are still thousands of them, like the *Nugget* in Chapter 2, in use.

In these British boats, particularly of the type represented by *Boy Albert*, in all its multitudinous variations, the frames were steamed and bent and were more numerous than the stronger grown timbers of Scandinavian boats and the earlier British boats. This steamed frame technique was developed perhaps as late, in fact, as the middle 19th century.

Basil Greenhill

Figure 171 Gaspé schooners near Bonaventure, Quebec. Note that they are lapstrake-built and very similar to the *Peggy* in general form.

National Maritime Museum

Figure 172 Lapstrake shallop-rigged boat used in the lobster fishing from Tignish, Prince Edward Island, Canada, until the 1920s.

Basil Greenhill

Figure 173 A lapstrake-built Block Island boat preserved at Mystic Seaport, Connecticut.

In Scandinavia and northern Britain the oldest traditions of boatbuilding have been followed down to very recent years. Big clinker-built boats were used in the northern fisheries of Norway and the Shetland Isles until well into the present century. A number of examples of these Norwegian clinker-built boats are preserved in the boat hall of the Maritime Museum in Oslo, including a superb *femboring*, a type of single squaresail boat in which deep sea fishing was carried out until the latter part of the last century, and even into the present. A smaller example of the same general type, the Nordlands boat, in the possession of the Danish National Museum was referred to and illustrated in the last chapter, Figure 157. There is a fine model of the type in the National Maritime Museum which probably dates from the very early 19th century. In Shetland very similar boats were used until the present century. A long-range fishery, operating ninety miles offshore, was carried on in six-oared boats using squaresails, very similar to those of the Nordlands boat.

National Maritime Museum

Figure 174   Model of the British beach boat *Boy Albert.*

Bibliography

ÅKERLUND, H.   *Fartygsfynden i den forna hamnen i Kalmar*, 1951
ANDERSON, R. C.   'The Bursledon Ship', 1934
BRINDLEY, H. H.   *Impressions and casts of seals, coins, tokens, medals and other objects of Art exhibited in the Seal Room of the National Maritime Museum*, 1938
BURWASH, D.   *English Merchant Shipping 1460–1540*, 1947
CHRISTENSEN, A. E.   *Boats of the North*, 1968
DADE, E.   *Sail and Oar*, 1933
DADE, E.   'The Cobles', 1934
EWE, H.   *Schiffe auf Siegeln*, 1972
GILLIS, R. H. C.   'Pilot gigs of Cornwall and the Isles of Scilly', 1969
MARCH, E. J.   *Inshore Craft of Britain*, 1970
MOORE, A.   *Last Days of Mast and Sail*, 1925
PRYNNE, M.   'Some general considerations applying to the examination of the remains of old ships', 1973
WARINGTON-SMYTH, H.   *Mast and Sail in Europe and Asia*, 1906
WHITE, E. W.   *British Fishing Boats and Coastal Craft*, 1950

Chapter 17

The Cog and the Flat-bottomed Boat after the Vikings

THE VESSEL WHICH proved such a formidable rival to the northern round-hulled clinker-built vessel in the 1200s was the cog. She was particularly associated with the towns of the north German Hanseatic League. She appears to have been developed from the flat-bottomed plank-built boat traditions of West Germany and the Low Countries, being a flat-bottomed vessel usually with clinker-built sides. Sometimes the planks of the sides appear to have been laid with the upper edges of the lower planks outboard instead of inboard, Figure 175, as in the main North European clinker-building tradition.

She was a totally different shape from the northern round-hulled clinker-built boat, with high sides, little flare, a straight stem and stern post and a stern rudder—a development, perhaps, of the tradition which produced the Bruges boat. In modern terms she was something like a gigantic Banks dory. The cog was a high-sided, deep draughted sailing vessel, probably able to carry more cargo than the round-hulled types in the same overall length and draught and more suited to shallow tidal waters, if less seaworthy, and because of her high sides, she was able to defend herself against attack in an age of perpetual piracy. She was also, for reasons which will now be obvious to the reader of this book, easier and cheaper to build than boats and vessels in the northern round-hull clinker tradition and she could be built by less skilled people.

In the 13th century the cog grew from its Frisian origins to be the leading merchant ship of North Europe and spread down to the Mediterranean. A Florentine wrote in 1304,

> 'At this time people came from Bayonne in Gascony in their ships, which in Bayonne they call cogs, through the Straits of Gibraltar, on bucaneering expeditions in the Mediterranean, where they inflicted much damage. After that time people from Genoa, Venice and Catalonia

259

National Maritime Museum

Figure 175   The Seal of
Kiel.

National Maritime Museum

Figure 176   The Seal of
Elbing.

began to employ cogs for their seafaring and abandon the use of their own large ships owing to the seaworthiness and lower cost of cogs. Thus great changes were wrought in the ship form of our fleet.'

The reign of the cog seems to have lasted until about the year 1400.

She is shown most clearly in contemporary illustration in the two seals of Kiel and Elbing. The Kiel seal dated from about AD 1365 and the Elbing seal some fifteen years earlier, Figures 175 and 176. But conclusive evidence as to the shape and structure of the cog was obtained by the excavation of a very large part of the hull of one in the harbour of Bremen, Germany in 1962. Like the Graveney boat she has been subjected to a long process of recording which has revealed her to be 77 ft (23·5 m) long and 23 ft (7 m) in breadth. She has been dated at about the year 1400. The Bremen cog has high clinker-built sides, a straight sloping stem and a stern post. She is in fact pretty well what was expected from contemporary illustrations. As might be expected from her late date, she demonstrates a tendency towards a refinement of form which is a constantly recurring factor in the history of different kinds of flat-bottomed boats. The flat smooth plank bottom has been reduced to a relatively small area, the ends sharpened, a small keel added. She had an after castle which is not part of the permanent structure of the vessel herself. Altogether she looks remarkably like the cogs of medieval seals, and Figure 177, a photograph of a reconstruction model taken from the starboard beam, shows the type very well. What it does not show is that the planks of her flat bottom were not edge joined, but fastened only to the floor timbers with trenails. It could therefore be that she and her numerous sisters represent a development of a different strand in boatbuilding traditions from some of the other flat-bottomed vessels which have been examined here—see Chapter 3. The vessel is now on public display in the new Maritime Museum at Bremerhaven.

Abel, *Die Bremmer Hanse Kogge*

Figure 177   A reconstruction model of the Bremen cog.

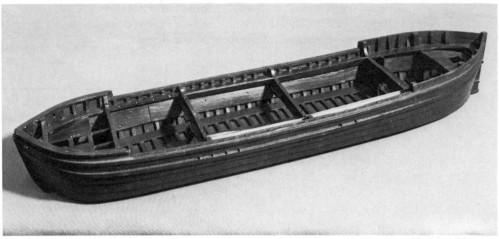

National Maritime Museum

Figure 178   A model of the Rother barge.

National Maritime Museum

Figure 179   A model of
a *schokker.*

National Maritime Museum

Figure 180 A model of a *pavilionpoon*.

National Maritime Museum

Figure 181 A model of a *botter*.

Figure 182   Excavation
in the North-East Pol-
der.

G. D. van der Heide

The family of the cog and her close relatives was an extensive one with many descendants, some of them no doubt in different branches of the family tree. For instance, in the early 19th century a large boat was found in Kent which appears to have been of the cog group. Figure 178 shows a model of her. She was discovered under an old bed of the River Rother in 1824, and was some 64 ft (19·5 m) long, flat-bottomed and clinker-built on the sides with iron rivets and moss luting. Her timbers were secured to the strakes by oak trenails. She had fittings for a mainmast and possibly a bowsprit. No remains of her survive, but from her position in the old river bed it was thought that she must have been wrecked before 1623, and that in fact she may have been abandoned as early as the 13th century.

There have been other fragmentary finds in Germany and Denmark of parts from vessels which were probably of the cog family, but it is not surprising that it is in the

Netherlands, in the conditions which may have given rise to this European building tradition, that its influence has been the strongest and can still be seen in some of the classic Netherlands flat-bottomed boat types which are now carefully registered and preserved as pleasure craft. The three models, Figures 179, 180 and 181, of 19th century Dutch pleasure and working vessels illustrate very clearly the round and flat-bottomed types into which most of the numerous variety of vessels of the Low Countries can be divided. The flat-bottomed *schokker* is in the tradition of the cog. The *pavilionpoon* is a full bodied, round-hulled, non edge-joined inland waterways vessel for freight and passengers, while the *botter* is an intermediate type.

The draining of the polders in the Netherlands has revealed the remains of many vessels which had sunk to the floor of the shallow sea. Wrecks have been found, of very varying sizes, which have been dated from the 11th to the end of the 17th centuries and which show the general characteristics of construction of the cog. Figure 182 shows an 11th century shipwreck being excavated from section Q75 of the North East Polder. The bottom of this ship is flat, the sides are clinker—she is an early example of the family of the cog.

But it is not only in Holland that there have been survivals of the great North European flat-bottomed clinker-sided boatbuilding tradition. Recent research by Eric McKee has shown that until very recent years a series of boat types existed in Somerset which suggest the possible evolution in some local circumstances of sophisticated boats even as large as small cogs from a simple flat-bottomed boat of the type of the turf boat, page 36.

For fishing off the adjacent coast and in the estuary of the river Parret near the home of the turf boat on the Somerset levels a larger more seaworthy boat of very similar construction, locally known as the flatner, was used. She had both fore and aft and athwartships rockers to make her easy to handle ashore on the extremely muddy banks of the Bridgwater river, Figure 183. For lightering and barge work in the Parret estuary and on the river, big double-ended barges with straight stem and stern post, flat bottoms and clinker sides were built, Figure 184. These boats were in the shape of small cogs and were locally known as 'Bridgwater boats'. Perhaps they were the last of the medieval cogs' near relations to survive in commercial use in Britain. It is a reasonable hypothesis that the cog type served on in local places where it was particularly suitable long after its general abandonment as a seagoing type. Very recently, Eric McKee has found boats previously unnoticed but in everyday use, in the lake behind Chesil Beach, which are very similar to the turf boats in general form, and there are other flat-bottomed boats in use on the Dorset coast.

A most striking example of the separate development of a closely similar solution to the problem of building cheaply a shallow draught boat capable of carrying a large cargo and of sailing under a single squaresail, occurred in the state of India now known as Uttar Pradesh. She was the *patalia*. I never saw one myself, but I heard of them from boatmen of the Ganges and it is clear that this obsolescent, if not now completely obsolete, boat type was in some ways structurally parallel with the European cog. She had a flat bottom built of two layers of heavy planking, one running fore and aft and the other athwartships, and fastened with heavy iron

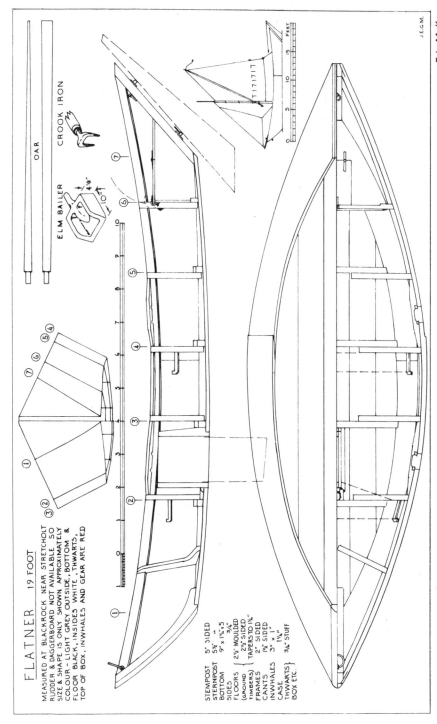

FLATNER 19 FOOT

MEASURED AT BLACKROCK NEAR STRETCHOLT
RUDDER & DAGGERBOARD NOT AVAILABLE SO
SIZE & SHAPE IS ONLY SHOWN APPROXIMATELY
COLOUR - LIGHT GREY OUTSIDE, BOTTOM &
FLOOR BLACK, INSIDES WHITE, THWARTS,
TOP OF BOX, INWHALES AND GEAR ARE RED

OAR

CROOK IRON

ELM BAILER

STEMPOST   5" SIDED
STERNPOST   5½"   "
BOTTOM   9" x 1¼"x.5
SIDES   ¾"
FLOORS   2½" MOULDED
(GROUND   2½" SIDED
TIMBERS)   TAPERS TO 1¼"
FRAMES   2" SIDED
CANTS   1½" SIDED
INWHALES   3" x 1"
CASE   1¼"
THWARTS}   ¾" STUFF
BOX ETC.}

FEET

J.E.G.M.

Eric McKee

Figure 183   Structural and lines drawing of a Bridgwater flatner.

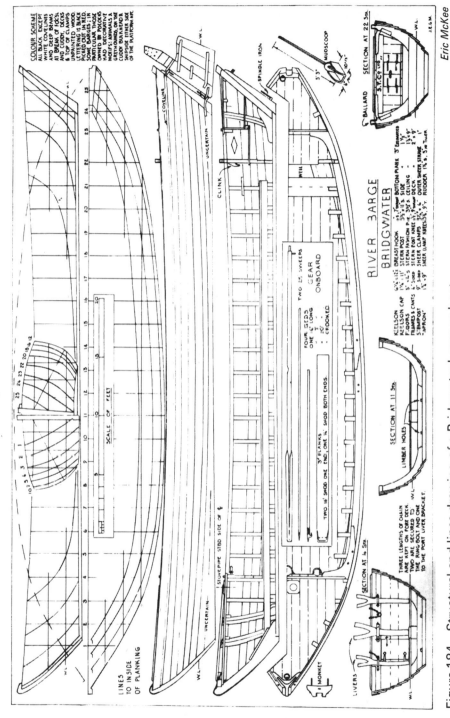

Figure 184   Structural and lines drawing of a Bridgwater barge or boat.

Eric McKee

Basil Greenhill

Figure 185   Flat-bottomed clinker-sided boat from Uttar Pradesh.

spikes. This floor was forced up at bow and stern to give it a pronounced fore and aft rocker and on to it were built sides of very heavy planks laid in ordinary clinker fashion. In the bigger boats, I was told, the overlap of the planks was so deep that the sides were actually three planks thick. The *patalia* had no floor timbers, but she had knees where the sides joined the floor and she had side pieces.

Many smooth-skinned, edge-joined, river sailing vessels of Uttar Pradesh in the 1950s were still equipped with boats about 18 ft (5·49 m) long, flat-bottomed with clinker-built sides in the manner of the *patalia*, Figure 185. Once again the small boats of today represent big vessels now vanished.

The tradition of the simple flat-bottomed boat in many variations—straight sides and curved sides; with bottom rocker fore and aft; and athwartships; with refined bows and sterns; smooth-skinned and clinker-built; double ended and with transom sterns; with straight stems and curved stems; upright and sloping—can be traced through illustration, description and surviving boat types in Europe, from the Southern Baltic to the Mediterranean, from medieval times to the present day. Numerous examples exist today in Denmark, Southern Sweden, Germany, Holland, France and especially in North America.

This is one of the main streams of European boat development, and the long narrow flat-bottomed boat is one of the most widely distributed of all boat forms. Its

Basil Greenhill

Figure 186   Dory-building shop in Friendship, Maine, and one of its products.

presence in Asia probably indicates a separate origin there. It occurs wherever simple, cheap boats, which do not need great skill to build, are needed for use in shallow, rough water. There is always a tendency to refine the bows and broaden the stern to make the boat more seaworthy, easier and safer under sail. In this century with the introduction of motors, this tendency has been demonstrated again and again. In that some of them show in miniature the constructional characteristics of the cog, so again do the last wooden small boats illustrate the designs and practices which gave rise to big ships, long obsolete.

The most numerous and best known in the English speaking world of these small flat-bottomed boats is the Banks dory. The fairly typical north-east coast North American dory shown here, Figure 186, was photographed outside a dory building shop in Friendship, Maine. She represents a very well-known late 19th century manifestation of the flat-bottomed tradition. The dory in this form is the product of an industrial age. Because only one plank in her structure need essentially be of curved shape in the flat (though often the other strakes were shaped a little as well though less so in the mass-produced dories, the hull form of which was conditioned by the method of production), see Figure 31, she is simple to build and can be put together with minimum wastage in quantity by unskilled labour from pre-cut parts made from stock sawn planks. When, in the second half of the 19th century, the

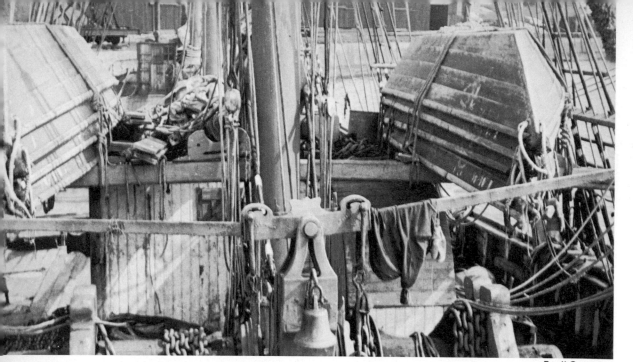

Figure 187 Dories nested on the deck of the French fishing barquentine *Immaculé Conception* in St Malo, fresh in from the North Atlantic banks, in 1939.

increasing demand following on the increase of population in North America led to the expansion of the North American Banks fishery from Massachusetts, from Maine, and from almost every port in Nova Scotia in order to extend the fishing capacity of individual vessels the custom was adopted, (probably from a French practice in vessels from St Pierre) of carrying a number of small boats which were dropped over the sides of the fishing schooners and from which one or two men fished with one kind of gear or another. These boats had to be cheap, partly because the initial capital available was not large, and secondly because they were highly expendable. They were not only lost by the sheer perils of the trade but they were lost also in large numbers by being washed overboard from the decks of hard-driven vessels on their way back from the fishing grounds with the fish for market. Because they did not need the strength of permanent thwarts they could be carried nested inside one another on a vessel's deck, Figure 187. The dory, produced in great numbers in boatbuilding workshops, some using almost mass production methods, was the answer, and, because they became readily available cheaply from this source, dories became almost the standard small fishing boat for beach work all the way down the east coast of North America from Massachusetts to Newfoundland.

The dory has become part of the North American scene and almost the typical flat-bottomed rowing boat of the modern world. She was also used by the French and Portuguese North Atlantic fishermen. Her possible history is therefore worth looking at in a little more detail, especially as in recent years it has been the subject of minor international controversy between Nova Scotia and New England, and

Museum of History and Technology, Washington, DC

Figure 188   The Continental gunboat *Philadelphia*, built and sunk on Lake Champlain in 1776, as she is today on display in Washington.

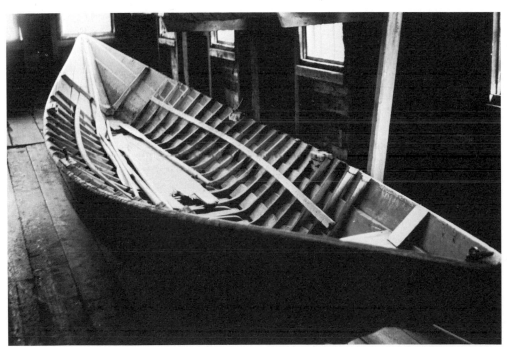

Basil Greenhill

Figure 189   Lumberman's *bateau* in the Maritime Museum at Bath, Maine.

Europe and North America. She is a simple case of a boat developing when required for a very special purpose, suited to that purpose, but adaptable to a very limited range of other purposes, and not to be judged on other grounds than her fitness for the job for which she was designed, see Chapter 1.

Given the age and widespread extent of the flat-bottomed tradition the particular form assumed by the dory could have developed at any time when the need arose. Dories were, and are, or of all sizes from 11 ft (3·35 m) to 28 ft (8·53 m) in overall length. Most had a tall, narrow transom, introduced to enable the boat to be sculled with a single oar, but some were double-ended. The general type existed in numerous forms in North America from the 17th century onwards and played its part in United States history, Figure 188, but the most spectacular form was perhaps the big lumberman's bateau, of which an example from Maine is in Figure 189.

But the local development of the Banks dory seems to have come from another source. Charles de la Morandiere gives an interesting account.[1] When St Pierre and Miquelon were returned to France in 1763 their inhabitants lacked capital to build sophisticated boats. They therefore copied the flat-bottomed, double-ended boats currently in use by the equally poor English fishermen of the south coasts of Newfoundland, who presumably had inherited the flat-bottomed tradition from Britain—and perhaps from the flat-bottomed boats in use on the coast of Dorset, an area with strong Newfoundland connections. One of the factors in the development of these flat-bottomed boats had been the necessity of beaching after each use—easier in general with rockered flat-bottomed boats than with keel boats (see the references to the Jersey skiff types later in this chapter). In St Pierre these boats, locally dubbed wherries, were built in great numbers. Morandiere suggests that it was the wherry which inspired the American and Canadian development of the Banks dory, which appears to have taken place in the 1850s. Innes gives the birth of dory handline fishing as taking place at Southport, Maine, in 1858.[2] By the early 1870s dories, bought from American schooners, were in use at St Pierre. In 1885 more than one thousand dories were bought from the United States. French fishing vessels visiting St Pierre were quick to adopt the new, cheap boats and dory factories were established, notably at St Malo, where exact copies of New England dories were made in great numbers. The type was also adopted by the Portuguese schooner owners.

Because she is relatively easy and cheap to construct, and yet is of an ancient boatbuilding tradition (and, since this is a boat which at its best requires skilful handling, she must be very carefully designed), a well-designed small dory is perhaps the best boat to build to learn something of the problems and skills of an ancient boatbuilding tradition. A number of small dories have been built in the National Maritime Museum boatbuilding shop by youth groups and others.

---

[1] *The History of the French Cod Fishing Industry in North America*, G-P Maisonneuve et Larose, vol 3, pp. 1041–2, Paris, 1966.

[2] *The Cod Fisheries*, Toronto University Press, 1954.

The development of the transom-sterned, flat-bottomed boat in the 19th century was particularly associated with the east coast of North America and in general, in contrast with European practice, flat-bottomed craft were the most widely used of North American boat types in the days before the introduction of small gasoline and diesel marine engines and outboards. In Chapter 2 of this book we saw George Adams at work on building skiffs, vessels built the other way round from the dory, which begins with its bottom, planked fore and aft, and has the sides added, while George Adams started with the sides and fastened the bottom planks athwartships, cutting off the ends to shape. Variations of George Adams' skiffs are still to be found all the way from Georgia to Newfoundland. Some reached a high degree of development and size, like the Newhaven sharpie, developed for oyster fishing in Long Island Sound in the middle of the 19th century. She was, of course, very economical to build for her size, easy to handle, and, in the words of Howard I. Chapelle, she was 'manoeuvrable, fast and seaworthy, the type was soon adopted for fishing along the eastern and south eastern coasts of the United States and in other areas. Later, because of its speed, the sharpie became popular for racing and

Basil Greenhill

Figure 190   A Newhaven sharpie.

Figure 191   'Cape Fear' skiff from Georgia.

yachting . . . The Newhaven sharpie proved that a long, narrow hull is most efficient in a flat-bottomed boat'.[3]

Figure 190 shows the hull of a Newhaven sharpie preserved at the Mariners' Museum at Newport News. Some of the biggest of the sharpies, notably those in the oyster fishery of the North Carolina Sounds were schooner rigged.

By way of contrast with the sharpie, two other types are illustrated. Figure 191 is a brand new version of the skiff, all-plywood built with the stern widened for an outboard motor mounted in a well, photographed on sale outside Savannah, Georgia, in 1973. Figure 192 is a rowing and sailing skiff from Maine, equipped with a wheel and handles for easier launching and pulling out. The type is common in the Eastern States and obviates the necessity for a launching trolley. This particular variation was developed at Seal Cove, south of Portland, Maine, in the second half of the last century as a tender for large sailing lobster boats. A replica built by Alan Hinks at Appledore from drawings by Howard I. Chapelle has been subjected to extensive sea trials by the National Maritime Museum, and has proved an ideal pulling boat for use in a swift flowing tidal river and its estuary. She was pulled up a slipway after use.

There are two further variations on the flat-bottomed boat, both particularly associated with North America, which should be described here. These are the skiff with curved plank-built sides above a narrow flat rockered bottom and the 'V'-bottomed boat.

The first form occurs among other places in Denmark and in Britain, where it was built at Weston-super-Mare and at Clevedon in Somerset. Eric McKee's drawing in Figure 193 shows the Weston version. But it was in the United States and Canada, in

[3] Chapelle, 'The Migrations of an American Boat Type', *Contributions from the Museum of History and Technology, Paper 25*, Washington, 1961.

the Sea Bright skiffs of the New Jersey shore, the Staten Island skiffs and the oyster skiffs of the Virginia shore of the Chesapeake, Figure 194, and the skiffs of the Magdalen Islands and the south shore of the Gaspé Peninsula, Figure 195, that the type was developed most highly.

These boats, as Figure 195 shows, could be beached easily on sand, shingle or pebbles and once beached could be moved around without difficulty. They were at the same time safe and handy in the water, particularly in surf, and they were cheaper and easier to build then keel boats. It is just possible (bearing in mind the geographical proximity) that the skiffs of the Magdalen Islands and the south shore

National Maritime Museum

Figure 192   'Farmer's Daughter' skiff from Maine.

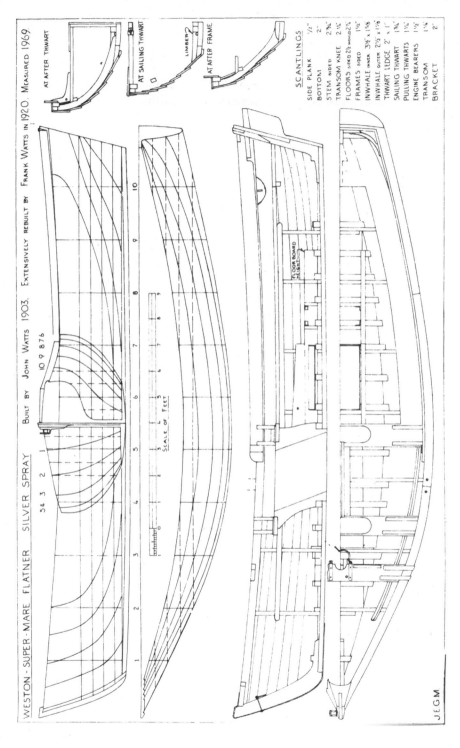

Figure 193   Weston-super-Mare flatner.

Basil Greenhill

Figure 194   Chesapeake oyster skiff at the Mariners' Museum at Newport News. Note that she is lapstrake-built.

Basil Greenhill

Figure 195   A Gaspé skiff (also lapstrake-built). Because of her narrow flat bottom, she can be towed by a tractor across the shingle to the water for launching.

of the Gaspé, like that illustrated here, are the descendants of the wherries of southern Newfoundland and St Pierre which in turn, according to Morandiere's theory, gave rise to the dory. There were dozens of variations of the type in use in eastern North America a century ago and less, some of them 'improved' dories rather than developments of the original form.

But the most spectacular of these round-hulled, flat-bottomed vessels in use in recent years, and the large modern descendant of the family of the cog (though built very differently from the medieval cog), was the St Lawrence *goelette*. These big wooden vessels, latterly motor driven, carrying perhaps one hundred tons of cargo, worked around the small ports of the great estuary of the St Lawrence and in the western part of the Gulf. Seen at sea they appeared to be ordinary small wooden motorships. Lying dried out on the shore they were seen for what they were, completely flat-bottomed and in effect gigantic forms of the Gaspé skiff, Figure 196. The last to be built was launched in the late 1950s. Very fortunately, the National Film Board of Canada recorded her construction in a most valuable documentary film *The Jean Richard*.

The 'V'-bottomed boat (the name is self descriptive) was the last of the classic boatbuilding traditions to develop—probably in North America in the 18th century. It was not until a hundred years later that it began to come into general use

Figure 196 A St Lawrence *goelette*, hauled ashore to make an exhibition, demonstrates her flat bottom by sitting bolt upright on the grass without shores or cradle.

Basil Greenhill

Figure 197   The long lean hull of a Prince Edward Island-built V-bottomed lobster boat hauled out at Georgetown in 1974.

when a boat with better sea keeping abilities than those of the flat-bottomed boat was required, but building costs called for simpler construction than that of the normal round-hulled, non edge-joined, fully skeleton-built vessel. Great development of the 'V'-bottom took place on Chesapeake Bay where it was used in a number of forms and sizes of boat and vessel, the largest of which was the oyster-dredging skipjack, which took over from the bugeyes described in Chapter 8 when the construction costs of the latter became prohibitive, as the principal vessel of the great oyster fisheries of Maryland.

The 'V'-bottom has, of course, been greatly developed in high speed motor pleasure craft, but it also has its modern commercial applications, of which a very handsome example is the 'V'-bottomed lobster boat—a variation of Bob Strongman's boat—of which an example, photographed at Georgetown, Prince Edward Island, in 1974, appears in Figure 197.

But, of course, the flat-bottomed boat has evolved in many other forms, some of which are inter-related. There still exist in the world today examples of all the stages in the evolution of the dugout, punt or scow shown in Figure 198, which illustrates a probable sequence of development from the prehistoric dugout canoe into the punt or scow. The first stage is a simple dugout, then planks are added to increase stability; two dugouts are then joined together and as a further refinement two half dugouts to give a broad-beamed hull. Finally the punt or scow with a plank keel between two half dugouts anticipates the fully-planked boat of the same general shape.

From this root comes the punt with transoms at both ends and many kinds of scow and broad-beamed flat-bottomed boat. Large cargo vessels derived ultimately from this form are still in use in many parts of the world. Punts and scows of all kinds are in use as pleasure boats; many made in fibre-glass are capable of very high speeds with

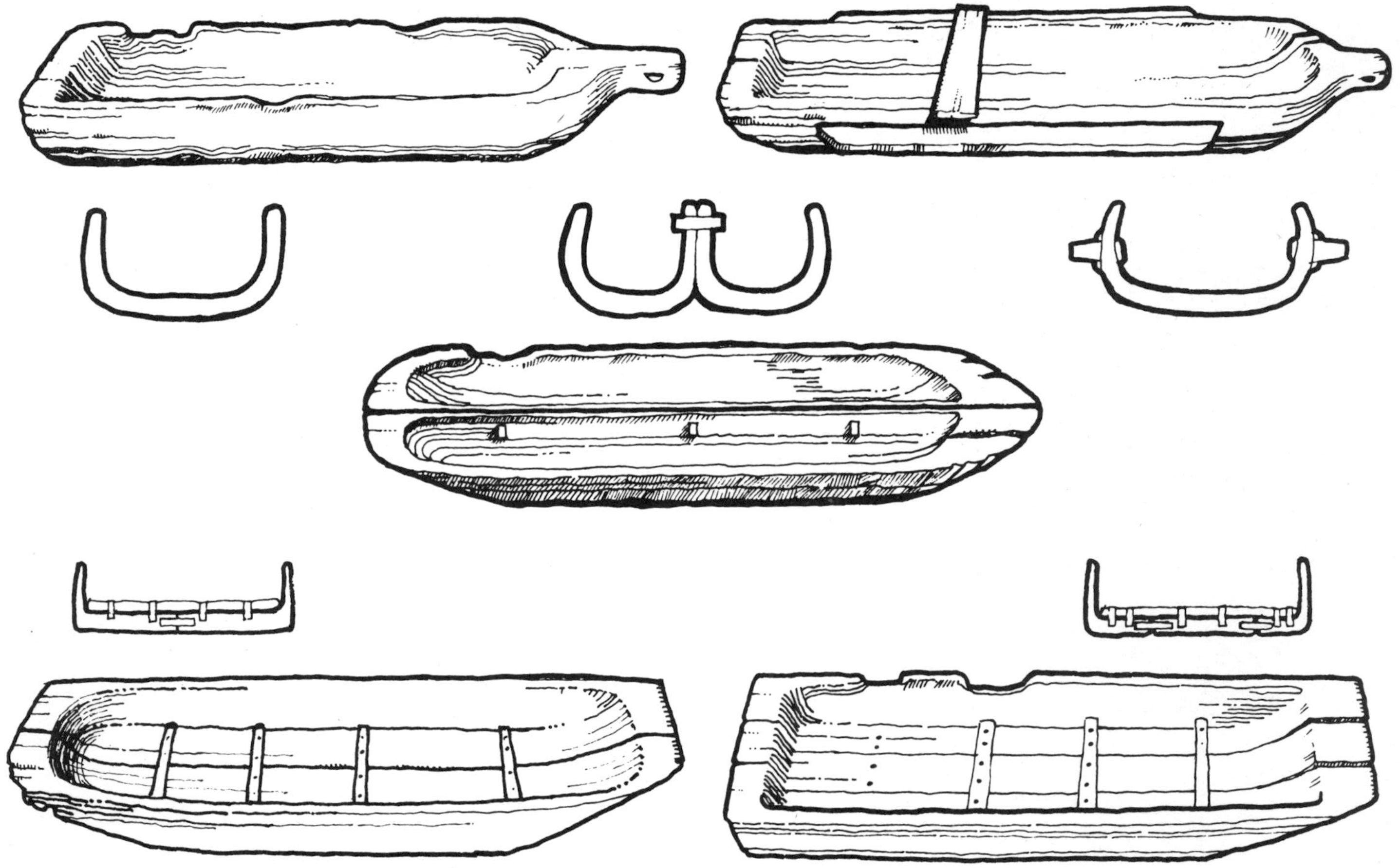

Figure 198 Dugout to scow.

Landström, *The Ship*

Figure 199   Bows of the New Zealand ketch-rigged scow *Owhiti* on the slip under repair. Note the change in the run of planking where the built-on bow section is joined to the true scow hull.

powerful outboards. Thus, again, the small boat of today illustrates the big ship practices of the past.

Just as the Thames barge represents the ultimate development of the flat-bottomed boat in Britain in recent years, so the New Zealand scow shows the same ultimate development on the other side of the earth. Figure 199 shows a very developed form of sailing scow which was built in New Zealand in the late 19th century for service in the extremely rough waters around North Island. Many of these scows, equipped with big drop keels and rigged as ketches (as illustrated), or schooners, survived years of sailing. They carried their cargo on deck and can be regarded, if you like, as gigantic hollow sailing rafts. A few are still in use as motor vessels.

Scows also developed on both coasts of the North American continent. Scow sloops were used in the coastal trade of New England, scow schooners in the Carolina Sounds and on the west coast around San Francisco. One of the latter is now preserved at the San Francisco Maritime State Park, and her photograph, Figure 200, illustrates well the ultimate development of this type.

Bibliography

ABEL, H. (ed)   *Die Bremer Hanse-Kogge*, 1969

BRINDLEY, H. H.   *Impressions and casts of seals, coins, tokens, medals and other objects of Art exhibited in the Seal Room of the National Maritime Museum*, 1938

BURWASH, D.   *English Merchant Shipping 1460–1540*, 1947

CHAPELLE, H. I.   *Boatbuilding*, 1947

CHAPELLE, H. I.   *American Small Sailing Craft*, 1951

CHAPELLE, H. I.   'The Migrations of an American boat-type', 1961

CRUMLIN-PEDERSEN, O.   'Cog-Kogge-Kaage', 1965

DADE, E.   *Sail and Oar*, 1933

de la MORANDIERE, C.   *History of the French Cod Fishing Industry in North America*, 1966

EWE, H.   *Schiffe auf Siegeln*, 1972

FLIEDNER, S.   'Kogge und Hulk', 1969

INNES, H. A.   *Cod Fisheries, the History of an International Economy*, 1954

McKEE, J. E. G.   Unpublished study of East Sussex and Chesil Bank beach boats, undated

McKEE, J. E. G.   'Flatners', 1970

McKEE, J. E. G.   'Weston-super-Mare Flatners', 1971

MacPHERSON RICE, W.   'Account of an Ancient vessel recently found under the old bed of the River Rother, Kent', 1824

MARCH, E. J.   *Inshore Craft of Britain*, 1970

MESSENGER, A. H.   'Notes on the New Zealand Scow', 1969

MOORE, A.   *Last Days of Mast and Sail*, 1925

SHAW, A.   'Bridgwater Flatner', 1969

van der HEIDE, G. D.   'Ship Archaeological Investigations in the Netherlands', 1970

WARINGTON-SMYTH, H.   *Mast and Sail in Europe and Asia*, 1906

WHITE, E. W.   *British Fishing Boats and Coastal Craft*, 1950

Figure 200   Scow schooner *Alma* at San Francisco.   *Dr John H. Harland*

Chapter 18

The Mysterious Hulk

W HILE IN THE years before AD 800 the northern clinker-built ship was developing in Scandinavia and north Germany and the cog was developing in the Low Countries, another type of vessel must have been evolving at the same time in Europe. This was the hulk, or holk, a name derived from an old word for a husk of corn or a peapod, whose shape she closely resembled. I have already referred to her several times and she is illustrated in Chapter 3. Her basic characteristic, the solution adopted by her builders to the problem of the plank ends—to have them all out of the water—is one which, as we have seen, occurs elsewhere in the world, notably in modern Bangladesh. The evidence is much less complete for the development of the hulk than for the clinker-built boat and there is even less evidence than there is for the story of the cog. No recognised and identified remains of a hulk have yet been found. Somewhere in the mud of an estuary or buried in saltings, this most important discovery in the archaeology of boats and ships is waiting to be made. In the meantime, we are dependent for our knowledge of her entirely on pictures, seals and representations on coins.

From these sources it is known that the hulk was quite different in shape from either a cog or a Scandinavian or Frisian clinker-built boat. She was curved both longitudinally and transversely, sometimes, probably, with a long narrow flat bottom curved up at the ends and without a stem or a stern post, her general form determined at least to a degree by the treatment of the plank ends. The type is illustrated on the font of Winchester Cathedral, Figure 40, in clay models, and, among many other seals, on the seal of New Shoreham, Figure 201, where the illustration is quite specifically described as being of a hulk.

Most of these illustrations suggest clinker-laid planking. Although the evidence is so scanty it suggests that the hulk developed to a point at which in the late 1300s it began to replace the cog, as the cog had replaced the round-hulled clinker-built ship. This was perhaps because it was more seaworthy and trade was expanding, and

National Maritime Museum

Figure 201 Hulk on the Seal of New Shoreham.

National Maritime Museum

Figure 202 Hulk on a coin of 1473–4.

because the type was susceptible to development into larger vessels than the cog, a form which has definite size limits. At this stage, with the development of commerce, vessels with greater cargo-carrying capacity were beginning to be needed.

The origins of the hulk are at present unknown. As I pointed out in Chapter 8, a factor in her origin could be the hewn log-built vessel of the type of the Chesapeake log canoe. The Utrecht ship could represent one strand in her ancestry. Given the logical nature of the basic solution to the planking problem, it is not surprising that there are shadowy indications of a similar building tradition in the Mediterranean in the 3rd century AD and later in the Iberian Peninsula. However it began, and from whatever root it sprang into prominence in the late 14th century, its supremacy lasted for about a hundred years before it was replaced by the general development of the skeleton-built non edge-joined ship. But the treatment of the planking persisted in various forms in Europe, see Figure 25. Small vessels continued to be planked in variation of the hulk pattern into the 19th century. This appears to have occurred at Appledore and Bideford in north Devon, an area considered in the early 19th century to be behind the times in many ways.

The 15th century gold coin illustrated here is from a hoard showing representations of hulks which was found on the site of the Palace of Placentia in the grounds of the Royal Naval College, Greenwich in 1971. The coin is an angel of Edward IV, 1473–4. Although it is so late it shows an unmistakable hulk. The hulk by the late 1400s was obsolescent if not obsolete and as so often with designs of coins, etc, the designer seems deliberately to have chosen an anachronistic form to illustrate.

Bibliography

BRINDLEY, H. H.   *Impressions and casts of seals, coins, tokens, medals and other objects of Art exhibited in the Seal Room of the National Maritime Museum*, 1938

BURWASH, D.   *English Merchant Shipping 1460–1540*, 1947

CRUMLIN-PEDERSEN, O.   'Das Haithabuschiff', 1969

EWE, H.   *Schiffe auf Siegeln*, 1972

FLIEDNER, S.   'Kogge und Hulk', 1969

WASKONIG, D.   'Bidliche Darstellungen des Hulk', 1969

Chapter 19

Skeletons everywhere

THE COG, THE hulk and the clinker-built ship of the north influenced one another. Cogs were evidently built in which the flat bottom became almost vestigial, as in the Bremen cog, and they were fitted with keels. The terms cog and hulk became confused and interchangeable and ship types appear to have become even less clearly defined in contemporary usage—at least the usage of the officials who kept the records—than before. In the early 15th century the same ship may have been called a cog in one port and a hulk in the next one she visited. Many other names were used with reference to ships: thus we read of the barge, balinger, crayer, navis, neif or nef, scoute, dogger, farcost, spinece, hoy, hayne, topship, foucet, galley and batella (which term is still used in Pakistan). Sometimes these terms seem to have been used almost indiscriminately, and differently from port to port. Only rarely do we have any information about the structure of the vessels concerned.

But a great change which was to sweep away much that was traditional was already under way, and the roots of some of it lay in the stresses to which every boat and vessel is subjected. There was of course a limit to the size to which a vessel dependent for the greater part of its strength on edge-joining could be built, if it were to be strong enough for sea service with heavy loads. However massive the planks of which she was constructed and however many of them were used (in clinker construction overlapping and overlapping again), still the shell of a big edge-joined vessel without very heavy frames was weak in relation to its size and the great stresses to which it was subjected, deep laden with guns, stores and cargo in a rough sea. The remains of the probable hull of the *Grace Dieu*, Henry V's great clinker-built warship launched in 1418 and of a size comparable with that of HMS *Victory*, as they lie in the Hamble river today show her to have been massively constructed.

The alternative method of construction involved a great and complex technical revolution with roots and implications reaching deep into the structure of the societies in which it took place. For reasons already explained, the technique of non edge-joined construction on a pre-erected skeleton was completely different from the old and very widespread traditions of edge-joined boat and shipbuilding. The builder could no longer shape the vessel according to tradition, use and available material as she grew on the slipway, she had to be conceived as a whole before she could be built. The parts that determined her shape ceased to be the strakes, shaped to fit as she grew, but became her frames, which had to be shaped according to a pre-determined design unless the method of building on one frame and the natural curve of the batten, described in Chapter 3, was used. Even then it was still the frames which determined the shape of the vessel, however their shapes were derived. It was a fundamental change in the whole approach to building vessels.

The origin and antiquity of non edge-joined construction is still unknown and unclear. For generations it was assumed that the technique began in the Mediterranean and was ancient. But this assumption appears often to have been based largely on the confusion described in Chapter 3, that is, that as the smooth-skinned vessels with which late 19th and early 20th century European scholars were familiar were (on the whole) non edge-joined and fully skeleton built, and edge-joining was associated with obviously overlapping planks; therefore the existence of strakes which did not obviously overlap it was assumed, meant, throughout the world and the history of man, necessarily non edge-joined skeleton construction. Since Southern European vessels were smooth skinned, the thinking ran, then they must have been built like big 19th century wooden ships. But John Morrison's chapter in this book has shown that in fact edge-joined construction, one small possible hint from Herodotus apart, was the standard method of building vessels in Graeco-Roman times. The systems used were perhaps very different from those of later North European edge-joined traditions. Edge-joining in some Southern European traditions may have played a smaller part in the total strength of the vessel than it did in North Europe, the larger part of the strength may have come from wales, massive strakes relatively high in the structure. But the edge-joining was essential for the construction of the vessel as a shell into which the frames, shaped to fit, were inserted.

We have seen that some intermediate forms, including the use of some non edge-joined planks, developed in different parts of the world, as in the different parts of the Indus watershed, and that evidence, including the earliest finds found in the City of London, indicate that something rather similar may have existed in Britain and in Europe from very early in the present era. These particular traditions, however, appear to be associated with river and sheltered water vessels and the nature of construction does not appear to be suited to meeting the stresses of prolonged seafaring. I have suggested that it is just possible that some boats of these types represent the ultimate development of raft traditions, though others may well have had an ultimate origin in dugouts.

However, one development which may have come out of these traditions, the cog, was very successful as a seagoing vessel. The archaeological evidence, such as it is, shows that some cogs had the planks of the flat, or near flat, bottom not joined edge to edge. But other than in some of these flat bottomed boats there appears to be little firm evidence at present of non edge-joined construction in Europe between Biscay France and Scandinavia or in the Mediterranean in the 1st millennium AD. There is little or none in Scandinavia, where good fortune has left us more evidence than anywhere else, so that we really do know a little about the development of boat and shipbuilding over a limited period and area. All this evidence indicates highly developed edge-joined techniques.

Where, when and why then did non edge-joined fully skeleton-construction evolve? The where and when are very difficult, and as I have already said, as with many aspects of the development of the boat at this stage, we just do not have the evidence, the material, on which to base hypotheses. We will do best to concentrate on the thorough excavation, examination and publication of archaeological material, on documentary research and the examination with professional specialist knowledge of the evidence provided by carvings, drawings and pictures, rather than on building up theories about this most important aspect of the history of ships on the basis of present knowledge. But the development of non edge-joined fully skeleton shipbuilding with all its possibilities for extended seafaring, trading and the establishment of authority, is one of the great technical achievements in the history of European (and, at one remove, of North American) man. It is to be hoped therefore that research into this important subject can in due course be pursued further from the several possible angles and through the separate disciplines involved.

The question why is another matter and I suggest that examination of possible answers, in very general terms, may throw some light on where it may be possible to look for answers to the questions when and where. The ultimate result of the great change was the building of ships which were strong and big enough to carry adequate supplies, cargo and men (and women) at a time when the wastage of human life of more than fifty per cent was normal, and, perhaps most important of all initially, sufficient heavy guns to make long ocean voyages with profitable results to the sponsors. The vessels were strong enough to survive the stresses imposed on them for months, sometimes years, on end without needing repairs greater than could be done on some remote beach by their own skilled people. In other words, the result was ships in which it was possible for European man, given many other factors in his favour, to make his travels, and eventually his domination, world wide. And in due course non edge-joined fully skeleton-built ships could be regularly constructed which were far larger than was really possible with edge-joined inserted frame techniques.

This does not imply that the right ship was necessarily developed to meet the demands of profitable world travel with the authority established by shipborne guns. The cause may have been largely other, and the world travel may have followed upon the possession of the right vehicle, initially brought into existence, or partly brought into existence, for other purposes, and the travel may have encouraged its further development. Indeed, given the extreme difficulty and slowness of the innovation, clearly demonstrated by the history of its very slow spread over the next five hundred or so years, this is likely to have been the order of events. We must look therefore before the development of ocean voyaging for traces of the early development of the non edge-joined skeleton-built vessels and, as with so many other things in the history of shipbuilding and navigation, the innovation probably began earlier than has been thought. It may have happened more than once, in different places in different ways.

Ocean voyaging, in the sense in which we are considering it now, perhaps began in the shadows of the early 15th century from the west coast of Europe, that is the Iberian Peninsula, Biscay France and Britain. It is in these areas that we might look for evidence of the beginnings of the great but prolonged revolution, say between 1200 and about 1400, stretching back well into, and even before, the era of the cog, hulk and the great clinker-built ship. The evidence may take a number of forms. In so far as the material exists it could be useful, for instance, to examine in this context the development of the trades of the areas concerned in the 13th and 14th centuries from the point of view of the demands that changes may have made for larger and stronger vessels.

There is one factor which has perhaps been rather overlooked. It is very widely known that the scant evidence shows that between the late 14th century and the late 15th century the European sailing ship, north and south, underwent dramatic development in matters of sails and rigging. In those years the sailing ship appears to have grown suddenly in matters of rig from a single master with a single squaresail to a three-masted vessel with squaresails on each mast, topsails and even topgallants, Figures 203 and 204. There are few contemporary illustrations and even fewer descriptions, and a great deal of work needs to be done to determine what further unrecognised evidence exists for this great development in the sailing ship.

So the tool of European expansion, the three-masted non-edged joined skeleton-built sailing ship was born. She was the vehicle of achievement at an almost explosive rate. Just as she herself seems to have developed at a pace which can almost be compared with that of the aeroplane in the 20th century, so the discovery of the sea and of the true extent of the world which she made possible, took place in less than a century. But the critical century of her origin, as far as the development of the ship is concerned, remains largely shrouded in mystery. There has long been interest in the matter of her origin. For instance R. C. Anderson and R. Morton Nance in Britain drew attention many years ago in articles in *Mariner's Mirror* to contemporary source material of the 15th and 16th centuries.

Most histories of the ship draw attention to this period of development. There may have been many and complex causes, but a contributing factor may well have been developments occurring, again rather earlier than has been thought, in non edge-joined skeleton construction, the results being stronger, more burdensome vessels, able to carry the three-masted rig really essential for prolonged ocean voyaging in all conditions. Major General Michael Prynne has suggested to me in a private communication that ship construction on the basis of frames of calculated form could have had its origins in the highly competitive field of galley building in the Mediterranean. He has pointed out that Venetian accounts of the 15th century show that the order of building was the keel and posts, the calculated frames, the

Figure 203   Model of the Mataro ship, a one- or two-masted vessel of the early 15th century.

National Maritime Museum

Figure 204   Three-masted ship of the period 1470–1480. This Italian engraving, acquired by the National Maritime Museum in 1975, is one of the few closely dated depictions of a three-masted square-rigged ship of the 15th century.

wales, and then the rest of the frames and the planking—a sophisticated version of building on one frame and a natural curve of the batten. It is possible also that the non-edge joined tradition inherent in the bottom of the cog could have played some part in the development of fully non-edge joined construction.

An important contribution has been made in recent years by the Swedish Maritime Historian, Dr Olof Hasslöf,[1] formerly Professor of Maritime Ethnology at the University of Copenhagen. There is, of course, always the danger in this kind of research that the discussion will in the end be about a word rather than about the realities behind it. Bearing this in mind, and bearing in mind also that we do not know what the word meant at the time, it is nevertheless interesting that the earliest appearance of the term *carvel*, in one form or another, which Hasslöf quotes is a Portuguese one of 1255, in which *caravela* refers to small fishing boats along the Portuguese coast. The term is used later of larger vessels and the history of both the term and of shipbuilding in the next two centuries is very obscure. In Mediterranean countries it has been difficult to associate the term carvel with a method of shipbuilding because all vessels, whether edge-joined or not, were smooth-skinned. In Northern and Western Europe, however, the distinction was clearer because edge-joined vessels were usually clinker-built. It is in this area, therefore, that the word carvel can first be associated with a method of building distinct from the old traditions. At the end of the 15th century hard evidence perhaps begins to appear in English written records. Hasslöf points out that in English shipyard ledgers of the 13th, 14th and 15th centuries the terms 'spiknayl', 'clinch-nayl' and 'rivetts' are frequently used and would appear to refer to fastenings used in clinker building. But in the 1490s items begin to appear which refer to 'carvell nayles'. Early in the 1500s the Great Galley, clinker-built in 1515, was ordered to be broken up and rebuilt carvel. A State Paper of 1545 records that clinker-built vessels were 'both feeble, olde and out of fashion'.

There is German evidence suggesting much the same development at a slightly earlier period and under Western European influence. The Chronicle of Zeeland by Jan Reygersbergen which dates from the mid-16th century, contains the following passage:

> 'about 1459, at first in Zierikzee, following the example of a Breton named Julian, carvel built ships began to be built instead of the hulks and craiers up to then solely in use. Velius, the Chronicler, who however wrote about three-quarters of a century later, supplements this information to the effect that the older ship type has been ... the old clinker built type with the planks overlapping. Which kind of work was changed about this time and hence carvel-built types began to be made ...[2]

[1] In English in articles in Volumes 49 and 52 of *Mariner's Mirror* and very conveniently in his long contributions to *Ships and Shipyards, Sailors and Fishermen*—see previous references.

[2] Walther Vogel, *Geschichte der Deutschen Seeschiffahrt*, Berlin, 1915.

Figure 205   Jack Tregaskes at Tregaskes' Yard, Par, Cornwall in 1932, renewing caulking in the three-masted schooner *Jane Banks*, formerly the *Frau Minna Petersen*, built at Portmadoc in 1878.

Clearly, much more research and much more evidence are needed before statements can be made with any confidence on the questions of when, where and why non edge-joined, fully skeleton construction, began to be developed seriously. But there are some obvious difficulties which faced the early builders. Beyond a certain general size the edge-joined shell-constructed vessel did not really work for a number of reasons, not the least of which must have been the sheer difficulty of building large structures by this method with the resources available. But up to a certain point in size she was almost ideally suited to face the alternating tension and compression strains imposed at sea. The numerous fastenings of the plank edges resisted both the forces pulling them apart and those pushing them apart. In some southern traditions heavy wales gave great strength. To replace this tough strength, massive internal support was needed in the form of very strong and large continuous frames. But something else was needed as well to replace the loss of the strength provided by the edge-joining, or else the working of the vessel would result in heavy leaking, if not weakening of the whole structure. The answer, of course, was to provide an inner lining of planks, the ceiling, and to jam the outside planks as closely together as possible and then to ram caulking between them, not only to produce a watertight vessel, but also to seek to make the whole structure as near as possible a unity, so that it could withstand best the continually varying stresses to which it was subjected. This caulking had to be properly done or else it was spewed out between the planks by the compression, or it dropped out when the planks were forced apart. It had often to be re-done, and at its best was always a compromise. In old vessels it became more and more difficult to caulk them satisfactorily and so an old non edge-joined wooden ship rapidly deteriorated once a certain stage in her wearing out was passed. The caulking was a skilled business, even a full-time occupation for some men. The plank edges were slightly bevelled for the outer half and oakum driven in with shaped irons and caulking mallets, which were specially made for the job. The seam was then sealed off with pitch, Figure 205. Examples of the tools can be seen on display in the National Maritime Museum, in a number of museums in the United States and at Port Hill in Prince Edward Island, Canada.

The builders who developed the new non edge-joined construction, wherever and whenever it was that they did so, had many problems to face. As I have already said in Chapter 3, it is not certain whether the various intermediate forms of construction, such as starting with the shell-construction of the lower part of the vessel and then fitting shaped frames, ending with non edge-joined strakes in the upper structure and so forth, Figure 206, may be taken to give evidence of how non edge-joined construction evolved from edge-joined, or whether they represent borrowings from already developed non edge-joined traditions. Certainly in some cases the latter is undoubtedly true. In Japan, as was explained in Chapter 8, Government pressure was brought to bear to bring about the adoption of non edge-joined construction. In the late 1950s many small vessels were still being constructed partly by the traditional methods with borrowings from the new, Figure 207. In Pakistan different combinations of edge-joining with borrowings from non edge-joined constructions have been used for many years, Figure 208. Even in Bangladesh, home of

Figure 206   Edge-joined, clinker-built lower body, non edge-joined top strakes, a galeass (a ketch-rigged merchant vessel) under construction at Kongsviken in Sweden in 1938.

Figure 207   Intermediate construction methods in Japan, 1957. The vessels have been shaped as traditional frameless *Yamato-gata* boats but frames have been added during construction. The standing figure is Captain W. J. Lewis Parker, United States Coastguard.

Figure 208   Non edge-joined planking temporarily joined with cleats and set up to moulds which will in due course be replaced by frames, Karachi, 1954.

pure edge-joined frameless shell construction, intermediate methods are also used.

But whatever was the sequence of events, it was a long time before non edge-joined fully skeleton-built became the universal way of building a large wooden vessel in Britain and in Northern Europe and North America. The method is described in detail in my book *The Merchant Schooners*.[3] It comprised, in outline, first the making of a scale model of one side of the complete vessel, the half model. This could take several forms, but from it the general shape of the finished vessel was ultimately derived. The half model was therefore very important in the development of the design of the vessel.

Measurements taken from the half model were scaled up to full size on the scrieve board or mould loft floor. The shapes of the frames were taken from these full sized drawings and these, of course, determined in large degree the shape of the finished vessel. The frames, once sawn out and made up from their constituent parts, floors, first and second futtocks, etc., were erected on the keel, Figure 210. Either initially, or as the framing developed, the stem and stern posts were erected and fastened. The beam shelves and clamps bound the skeleton together and provided lodging for the ends of the deck beams. Fastening was by thick bolts of galvanised iron. The whole

[3] Newton Abbot, 1968.

structure was bound together with reinforcing knees of wood or iron, by iron straps, and by other means.

The strength of some of these latter day smaller wooden vessels was as great as the limitations of the materials would allow. For example, the schooner *Millom Castle* had a beam shelf of 9 in (23 cm) timber and three stern posts, one inside the other. The framing in the first 25 ft (7·6 m) of her and in the last 25 ft–50 ft (7·6 m–15 m) of her 80 or so ft (24 m) length was almost solid, the frames nearly touching. Her upper frames were 5½ in (14 cm) square and her floors and futtocks 9 in (23 cm) square, and all of oak. The 10 in (25·5 cm) deck beams were of hackmatack.

The complex structure, a skeleton of timber, which now stood on the building slip was ready for planking. The long planks, softened when necessary by soaking with steam, were wrapped around the skeleton structure, shoved, shouldered, wedged, shored and clamped into place. The deck planks presented fewer problems, but the ceiling, the inner lining of the vessel, required nearly as much skilled shaping of the planks as did the outer skin. The vessel was caulked with oakum, driven into the wedge shaped seams between the planks with irons and mallets and the hull was then virtually complete.

Despite the strength and vigour with which European technological development was projected around the world, except to a degree in Japan the style of construction outlined in the last few paragraphs never became the normal method of construction of local vessels over most of the rest of the world. Indeed even in Britain and Northern Europe it spread much more slowly than is generally realised. C. H. Ward Jackson

Figure 209   Presenting a frame to the old shell—the restoration of the coasting ketch *Shamrock*, Cornwall, 1975, by Tom Perkins.

Basil Greenhill

has noted in his studies on behalf of the National Maritime Museum of the ship registration records of the Port of Fowey in Cornwall that it is not until the end of the 18th century and the beginning of the 19th that there was a sudden transition from 'clinker' to 'carvel' in the registered descriptions of the majority of new vessels. Only at this late date was non edge-joined construction generally adopted at this Cornish seafaring centre for smaller vessels, and I think it likely that similar detailed study of shipping registration records will in due course show similar late transitions at some other ports of registration, particularly those remote from centres of population.

In the 1940s I myself talked with elderly men who in the late 1870s had worked in Cornwall on the building of coasting smacks and ketches by the method of moulding on a single frame already described in Chapter 3, 'moulding by the natural run of the batten' as they called the process. From their descriptions, and their whole approach to the subject, non edge-joined skeleton-building was clearly a process which taxed their professional abilities to the utmost and presented a continual challenge. Olof Hasslöf has many examples of the use of the intermediate methods in Scandinavia and indeed Arne Emil Christensen has recorded[4] that after the middle of the 16th century the central governments of all the Scandinavian countries tried to convince shipbuilders and shipowners that non edge-joined skeleton-built vessels were best. Despite continuous government effort the general introduction of this kind of construction was very slow indeed, and only in the 20th century did the use of non edge-joined construction penetrate to the small boats used in coastal fisheries. As late as 1900 in Norway a special 'state travelling teacher of carvel work' was appointed, but it was only the adoption of motor power with the peculiar stresses it imposes that finally led to the general acceptance of non edge-joined construction. Even then, edge-joined construction and intermediate methods have lingered on to the present day, and we know that in Norway, as in Japan, the use of moulds in edge-joined construction was a recent innovation from non edge-joined skeleton building, and not a transitional stage in the development of the latter. As late as the year 1975 the restoration of the coasting ketch *Shamrock* by the National Trust and the National Maritime Museum involved the adoption of intermediate methods. The planking of the vessel being in good repair it was retained and new frames shaped to it and inserted into the shell, Figure 209.

Non edge-joined fully skeleton construction blossomed in an age of big ships and big capital, extensive deep sea seafaring, relatively widespread literacy and the use of half models in the manner described in detail in *The Merchant Schooners*. The use of drawings came slowly and later with the gradual adoption of this technique of communication. Right down to the very end of wooden shipbuilding in the early 20th century drawings were hardly ever used in small shipyards building small merchant vessels in Britain. At its most sophisticated the design stage still took place in the half model, on the mould loft floor and on the slips as the vessel developed.

But in due course and very slowly non edge-joined fully skeleton construction became 'normal' in Britain, Northern Europe and North America and until even

---

[4] In No 1, Volume 2 of *The International Journal of Nautical Archaeology*.

Figure 210   Stern post and midships frames of a wooden dragger rise above the keel at Mahone Bay, Nova Scotia, in 1963. The scrieve board on which the frames are made up is visible in the foreground. The piled timber around is typical of any wood shipbuilding yard anywhere at any period.

Figure 211   Four big schooners under construction at Cobb, Butler and Co's yard, Rockland, Maine, in 1908. The almost complete four-master is the *Jessie A. Bishop*.

Figure 212　The great skeleton of the four-masted schooner *Savannah*, built by David Clark at Kennebunkport, Maine, in 1901.

the 1960s it was still possible to see in Spain, Denmark, Sweden and Norway, in Scotland, Maine and Nova Scotia, Figure 210, the skeletons of wooden vessels rising above the keel blocks in small shipyards.

As late as the first three decades of this century some of the largest wooden vessels ever constructed were being built in New England, Figures 211, 212 and 213. These were the great schooners, four, five and six masters, launched for the coal trade from Virginia to New England ports.

They required prodigious quantities of timber and their frames, posts and deck beams were enormous. Their history has been recorded by Captain W. J. Lewis Parker USCG in *The Great Coal Schooners of New England*[5] and elsewhere. Their huge size, and the special problems created by their efficient sails and rigging which imposed new types of stress on the hull, mark them perhaps as the ultimate development of non edge-joined, fully skeleton-built, wooden vessels. They were the end of a very long and very complex story, about which, despite the length of this book, we still know remarkably little.

[5] The Marine Historical Association Inc, Mystic Seaport, 1948.

Captain W. J. Lewis Parker

Figure 213 The end of the story. The four-masted schooner *Theoline* of Machias, Maine, built by F. Cobb at Rockland, Maine, in 1917, under cargo grabs against a mid-20th century skyline. She was lost in the West Indies in 1942.

Bibliography

ANDERSON, R. C. 'The Bursledon Ship', 1934

BURWASH, D. *English Merchant Shipping 1460–1540*, 1947

CHRISTENSEN, A. E. 'Lucien Basch: Ancient Wrecks and the Archaeology of Ships, A Comment', 1973

GREENHILL, B. *Merchant Schooners*, 1968

HASSLÖF, O. 'Wrecks, Archives and Living Tradition', 1963

HASSLÖF, O. 'Sources of Maritime History and Methods of Research', 1966

HASSLÖF, O. 'Main Principles in the Technology of Shipbuilding', 1972

HIDALGO, M. *Columbus' Ships*, 1966

MORTON NANCE, R. 'The Ship of the Renaissance', 1955

PARKER, W. J. L. *Great Coal Schooners of New England, 1870–1909*, 1948

PARRY, J. H. *The Discovery of the Sea*, 1975

PRYNNE, M. 'Some general considerations applying to the examination of the remains of old ships', 1973

RÅLAMB, Å. C. Skeps Byggerij eller Adelig Öfnings Tionde Tom, 1691

Bibliography

Notes

(1) Place of publication is London unless stated otherwise
(2) *IJNA* = International Journal of Nautical Archaeology
(3) NMM MM + R = National Maritime Museum Maritime Monographs and Reports

ABEL, H. (ed) *Die Bremer Hanse-Kogge*, Bremen, 1969

ABELL, W. *Shipwright's trade*, Cambridge, 1948

ADNEY, E. T. and CHAPELLE, H. I. *Bark Canoes and Skin Boats of North America*, Washington, 1964

ÅKERLUND, H. *Fartygsfynden i den forna hamnen i Kalmar*, Stockholm, 1951

ÅKERLUND, H. *Nydamskeppen*, Goteberg, 1963

ALBION, R. G. 'Timber Problems of the Royal Navy 1652–1862', *Mariner's Mirror*, 38:5–10, 1952

ANDERSON, R. C. 'The Bursledon Ship', *Mariner's Mirror*, 20:158–70, 1934

ARBMAN, H. 'Der Årby-fund', *Acta Archaeologica*, 11:43–102, 1940

ARNOLD, B. 'Gallo-Roman boat from the Bay of Bevaix, Lake Neuchatel, Switzerland', *IJNA*, 4:123–6, 1975

AUDEMARD, L. *Les Jonques Chinoises*, Rotterdam, 1957–69

BARNWELL, E. L. 'Caergwrle Cup', *Archaeologica Cambrensis*, 4th series, 6:268–74, 1875

BASCH, L. 'Ancient Wrecks and the Archaeology of Ships', *IJNA*, 1:1–58, 1972

BASCH, L. 'Another Punic wreck in Sicily: its ram. 1. A typological sketch', *IJNA*, 2:201–19, 1975

302

BASS, G. F. 'Cape Gelydonia, a Bronze Age Shipwreck', *Transactions of the American Philosophical Society*, 57, part 8, 1967

BASS, G. F. *Archaeology Under Water*, 1970

BASS, G. F. 'Byzantine Trading Venture', *Scientific American*, 224:23–33, 1971

BASS, G. F. (ed) *A History of Seafaring based on Underwater Archaeology*, 1972

BEAGLEHOLE, J. C. (ed) *The Endeavour Journal of Joseph Banks, 1760–1771*, Sydney, 1962

BETTS, J. H. 'Ships on Minoan Seals' in BLACKMAN, D. J. (ed) *Marine Archaeology*, pp. 325–36, 1973

BLACKMAN, D. J. 'Further Early Evidence of Hull Sheathing', *IJNA*, 1:117–19, 1972

BREWINGTON, M. V. *Chesapeake Bay Log Canoes and Bugeyes*, Cornell, 1963

BRINDLEY, H. H. *Impressions and casts of seals, coins, tokens, medals and other objects of Art exhibited in the Seal Room of the National Maritime Museum*, 1938

BRØGGER, A. W. and SHETELIG, H. *Viking Ships, their Ancestry and Evolution*, Oslo, 1951

BRØGGER, A. W. et al *Osebergfunnet*, Oslo, 1917–28

BRØNDSTED, J. 'Oldtidsbaden fra Als', *Nationalmuseets Bog*, Copenhagen, 1925

BRUCE, R. S. 'More about sixerns', *Mariner's Mirror*, 20:312–22, 1934

BRUCE-MITFORD, R. L. S. *Sutton Hoo Ship Burial*, British Museum, 1968

BURWASH, D. *English Merchant Shipping 1460–1540*, Toronto, 1947

CARPENTER, A. C. et al *The Cattewater Wreck*, NMM MM + R No. 13, 1974

CARR-LAUGHTON, L. G. 'Clove-board', *Mariner's Mirror*, 43:247–9, 1957

CASSON, L. 'New Light on Ancient Rigging and Boatbuilding', *American Neptune*, 24:86–9, 1964

CASSON, L. *Ships and Seamanship in the Ancient World*, Princeton, 1971

CASSON, L. 'Bronze Age Ships. The evidence of the Thera Wall Paintings', *IJNA*, 4:3–10, 1975

CHAPELLE, H. I. *Boatbuilding*, New York, 1947

CHAPELLE, H. I. *American Small Sailing Craft*, New York, 1951

CHAPELLE, H. I. 'The Migrations of an American boat-type', *US National Museum Bulletin 228*, Washington, 1961

CHRISTENSEN, A. E. *Boats of the North*, Oslo, 1968

CHRISTENSEN, A. E. 'Boatbuilding Tools and the Process of Learning' in HASSLÖF, O. (ed) *Ships and Shipyards, Sailors and Fishermen*, pp. 235–59, Copenhagen, 1972

CHRISTENSEN, A. E. 'Lucien Basch: Ancient Wrecks and the Archaeology of Ships. A comment', *IJNA*, 2:137–45, 1973

CLOWES, L. *History of The Royal Navy VII*, 1923

CORBETT, N. H. 'Micro-morphological studies on the degradation of lignified cell walls by ascomycetes and fungi imperfecti', *Journal of Wood Science*, 14:18–29, 1965

CRUMLIN-PEDERSEN, O. 'Cog-Kogge-Kaage', *Handels og Sjofartsmuseet pa Kronberg Arbog*, pp. 81–144, 1965

CRUMLIN-PEDERSEN, O.   'Gredstedbro Ship', *Acta Archaeologica*, 39:262–7, 1968

CRUMLIN-PEDERSEN, O.   'Das Haithabuschiff'. Berichte über *Ausgrabungen in Haithabu*, 3, Neumünster, 1969

CRUMLIN-PEDERSEN, O.   'Viking Ships of Roskilde', *Aspects of the History of Wooden Shipbuilding*, NMM MM + R No. 1, pp. 7–23, 1970

CRUMLIN-PEDERSEN, O.   'Skin or Wood' in HASSLÖF, O. (ed)   *Ships and Shipyards, Sailors and Fishermen*, pp. 208–34, Copenhagen, 1972

DADE, E.   *Sail and Oar*, 1933

DADE, E.   'The Cobles', *Mariner's Mirror*, 20:199–207, 1934

de la MORANDIERE, C.   *History of the French Cod Fishing Industry in North America*, Paris, 1966

de WEERD, M. D. and HAALEBOS, J. K.   'Schepen voor het Opscheppen', *Spiegel Historiael*, 8:386–97, 1973

DUVAL, P-M.   'La forme des navires romains d'après la mosaïque d'Althibutrus', *Mélanges d'archéologie et d'Histoire de l'Ecole Française de Rome*, 61–62 anée, pp. 119–49, 1949

ELLMERS, D.   'Keltischer Schiffbau', *Jahrbuch des Romische-Germanischen Zentralsmuseums Mainz*, 16:73–122, 1969

ELLMERS, D.   *Frühmittelalterliche Handelsschiffahrt in Mittel-und Nordeuropa*, Neumünster, 1972

ELLMERS, D. and PIRLING, R.   'Ein mittelalterliches Schiff aus dem Rhein', *Die Heimat*, 43:45–8, 1972

ESKERÖD, A.   *Kyrkbåtar och Kyrkbåtsfärder*, Stockholm, 1973

EVANS, A. C.   'The Sutton Hoo Ship' in *Three Major Ancient Boat Finds in Britain*, NMM MM + R No. 6, pp. 26–43, 1972

EVANS, A. J.   'Votive Deposit of Gold Objects', *Archaeologia*, 55:391–408, 1897

EWE, H.   *Schiffe auf Siegeln*, Rostock, 1972

FENWICK, V. H. (ed)   *The Graveney Boat* (in press)

FLIEDNER, S.   'Kogge und Hulk' in ABEL, H. (ed)   *Die Bremer Hanse Kogge*, pp. 39–121, Bremen, 1969

FOOTE, P. G. and WILSON, D. M.   *Viking Achievement*, 1970

FROST, H.   'First season of excavation on the Punic Wreck in Sicily', *IJNA*, 2:33–49, 1973

FROST, H.   'The Punic Wreck in Sicily, second season of excavation', *IJNA*, 3:35–42, 1974A

FROST, H.   'The Third Campaign of Excavation of the Punic Ship, Marsala, Sicily', *Mariner's Mirror*, 60:265–6, 1974B

FROST, H.   'Another Punic wreck in Sicily: its ram. 2. The ram from Marsala', *IJNA*, 4:219–28, 1975

GILLIS, R. H. C.   'Pilot gigs of Cornwall and the Isles of Scilly', *Mariner's Mirror*, 55:117–38, 1969

GILLMER, T. C.   *Working Watercraft*, Camden, Maine, 1972

GJELLESTAD, A. J.   'Litt om Oselverbäter', *Norsk Sjøfartsmuseum Arbok*, pp. 18–29, Oslo, 1969

GJESSING, G.   'Båtfunnene fra Bårset og Øksnes', *Tromsø Museum Årshefter*, 58, 1935

GOODMAN, W. L.   *History of Woodworking Tools*, 1964

GRAY, D.   *Archaeologia Homerica*. Band 1, Kapitel G: *Seewesen*. Mit ein Beitrag: *Das Schiffsfresko von Akrotiri Thera von S. Marinatos*: 140–51, Göttingen, 1974

GREENHILL, B.   *Merchant Schooners*, 2 vols, Newton Abbot, 1968

GREENHILL, B.   *Boats and Boatmen of Pakistan*, Newton Abbot, 1971

HAASUM, S.   'Vikingatidens segling och navigation', *Theses and Papers in North European Archaeology*, 4, The Institute of Archaeology at the University of Stockholm, 1974

HADDON, A. C. and HORNELL, J.   *Canoes of Oceania*, 3 vols, Honolulu, 1936–8

Handbook of Hardwoods, Forest Products Research Laboratory, HMSO, 1969

Handbook of Softwoods, Forest Products Research Laboratory, HMSO, 1968

HASSLÖF, O.   'Wrecks, Archives and Living Tradition', *Mariner's Mirror*, 49.162–77, 1963

HASSLÖF, O.   'Sources of Maritime History and Methods of Research', *Mariner's Mirror*, 52:127–44, 1966

HASSLÖF, O.   'Main Principles in the Technology of Shipbuilding' in HASSLÖF, O. (ed)   *Ships and Shipyards, Sailors and Fishermen*, pp. 27–72, Copenhagen, 1972

HIDALGO, M.   *Columbus' Ships*, Barre, Mass, 1966

HOEKSTRA, T. J.   'A note on the Utrecht boats', *IJNA*, 4:390–2, 1975

HORNELL, J.   'Fishing luggers of Hastings', *Mariner's Mirror*, 24:39–54, 1938

HORNELL, J.   *Water Transport*, Newton Abbot, 1970

HOURANI, G. R.   *Arab Seafaring in the Indian Ocean in Ancient and Early Medieval Times*, Princeton, 1951

HUMBLA, P.   'Om Björkebaten från Hille socken', *Från Gästrikland 1949*, Gävle, 1949

INNES, H. A.   *Cod Fisheries, the History of an International Economy*, Toronto, 1954

JANE, F. W.   *Structure of Wood*, 2nd edition, 1970

JENKINS, J. G.   *Nets and Coracles*, Newton Abbot, 1974

JOHNSTONE, P.   'A Medieval Skin Boat', *Antiquity*, 36:32–7, 1962

JOHNSTONE, P.   'The Bantry Boat', *Antiquity*, 38:277–84, 1964

JOHNSTONE, P.   'Bronze Age Sea Trial', *Antiquity*, 46:269–74, 1972

JOHNSTONE, P.   'Stern first in the Stone Age?', *IJNA*, 2:3–11, 1973

JONES, G.   *A History of the Vikings*, 1968

KRISTJÁNSSON, L.   'Graenlenzki Landnemaflotinn og Breidfirzki Báturinn', *Arbók Hins Islenzka Fornleifafélags*, pp. 20–68, Reykjavik, 1965

LAVERS, G. M.   *Strength Properties of Timbers*, Forest Products Research Laboratory Bulletin No. 50, 1969

LANDSTRÖM, B.   *The Ship*, 1961

LANDSTRÖM, B.   *Ships of the Pharaohs*, 1970

LESLIE, R. C.   *The Sea Boat. How to build, rig and sail her*, 1892

LINDER, E.   'Naval warfare in the El Amarna Age' in BLACKMAN, D. J. (ed) *Marine Archaeology*, pp. 317–22, 1973

LLOYD, A. B. 'Triremes in the Saite Navy', *Journal of Egyptian Archaeology*, 63:268–79, 1972

McGRAIL, S. 'Models, Replicas and Experiments in Nautical Archaeology', *Mariner's Mirror*, 61:3–8, 1975A

McGRAIL, S. 'The Brigg Raft Re-excavated', *Lincolnshire History and Archaeology*, 10:5–13, 1975B

McGRAIL, S. Unpublished study of the dugout canoes of England and Wales, undated

McGRAIL, S. and GREGSON, C. 'Archaeology of Wooden Boats', *Journal of the Institute of Wood Science*, 7(1):16–19, 1975

McGRAIL, S. and McKEE, J. E. G. *The Building and Trials of the Replica of an Ancient Boat: The Gokstad Faering*. NMM MM + R No. 11, 1974

McGRAIL, S. and SWITSUR, R. 'Early British Boats and their Chronology', *IJNA*, 4:191–200, 1975

McKEE, J. E. G. *Clenched Lap or Clinker*, 1972

McKEE, J. E. G. Unpublished study of East Sussex and Chesil Bank beach boats, undated

McKEE, J. E. G. 'Flatners', *Mariner's Mirror*, 56:232–4, 1970

McKEE, J. E. G. 'Weston-super-Mare Flatners', *Mariner's Mirror*, 57:25–39, 1971

MacPHERSON, N. 'Notes on antiquities from the Isle of Eigg', *Proceedings of the Society of Antiquaries of Scotland*, 12:594–6, 1877/8

MacPHERSON RICE, W. 'Account of an Ancient vessel recently found under the old bed of the River Rother, Kent', *Archaelogia*, 20:553–65, 1824

MARCH, E. J. *Inshore Craft of Britain*, 2 vols, Newton Abbot, 1970

MARSDEN, P. R. V. *A Ship of the Roman Period from Blackfriars in the City of London*, Guildhall Museum, undated

MARSTRANDER, S. *Østfolds jordbruksristninger: Skjeberg*, 2 vols, Oslo, 1963

MARTIN, C. J. M. 'The Spanish Armada Expedition 1968–70' in BLACKMAN, D. J. (ed) *Marine Archaeology*, pp. 439–62, 1973

MESSENGER, A. H. 'Notes on the New Zealand Scow', *Mariner's Mirror*, 55:461–5, 1969

MOLL, F. 'History of Wood Preserving in shipbuilding', *Mariner's Mirror*, 12:357–74, 1926

MOORE, A. *Last Days of Mast and Sail*, Oxford, 1925. Reprinted Newton Abbot, 1970

MORRISON, J. S. 'Review of Casson (1971)', *IJNA*, 1:230–3, 1972

MORRISON, J. S. and WILLIAMS, R. T. *Greek Oared Ships, 900–322 BC*, Cambridge, 1968

MORSE, E. W. *Canoe Routes of the Voyageurs*. Reprinted from the *Canadian Geographical Journal*, May, July and August 1961 for the Quetico Foundation of Ontario and the Minnesota Historical Society, St Paul, Minnesota and Toronto, Ontario, 1962

MORSE, E. W. *Fur Trade Canoe Routes of Canada, Then and Now*, Ottawa, 1968

MORTON NANCE, R. 'The Ship of the Renaissance', *Mariner's Mirror*, 41:180–92 and 281–98, 1955

NEEDHAM, J. *Science and Civilisation in China*, 4, Part 3, Cambridge, 1971

NICHOLLS, R. V. *Archaeological Reports No. 17* for 1970–1:85, no. 28, fig. 14, Hellenic Society, 1970–1

NICOLAYSEN, N. *Viking Ship discovered at Gokstad in Norway*, Kristiania, 1882. Republished Farnborough, 1971

NIELSON, C. *Danske bådtyper*, Copenhagen, 1973

OLSEN, O. and CRUMLIN-PEDERSEN, O. 'Skuldelev Ships', *Acta Archaeologica*, 38:73–174, 1967

OWEN, D. I. 'Excavation Report', *IJNA*, 1:197–8, 1972

PARKER, W. J. L. *Great Coal Schooners of New England, 1870–1909*, Mystic Seaport, Connecticut, 1948

PARRY, J. H. *The Discovery of the Sea*, 1975

PETERSEN, J. 'Vikingetidens Redskaper', *Skrifter utgitt av Det Norske Videnskaps-Akademi i Oslo*, Oslo, 1951

PHILIPSEN, J. P. W. 'Utrecht Ship', *Mariner's Mirror*, 51:35–46, 1965

PRINS, A. H. J. *Sailing from Lamu*, Assen, Netherlands, 1965

PRYNNE, M. 'Some general considerations applying to the examination of the remains of old ships', *IJNA*, 2:227–33, 1973

RÅLAMB, Å. C. *Skeps Byggerij eller Adelig Öfnings Tionde Tom*, 1691. Reprinted Stockholm, 1943

ROBERTSON, F. L. *Evolution of Naval Armament*, 1921

ROSENBERG, G. 'Hjortspringfunnet', *Nordiske Fortidsminder*, 3, Copenhagen, 1937

RUDOLPH, W. *Inshore Fishing Craft of the Southern Baltic from Holstein to Curonia*, NMM MM + R No. 14, 1974

SALISBURY, W. (ed) *Treatise on Shipbuilding* issued as Occasional Publication No. 6 by the Society for Nautical Research, 1958

SANDISON, C. *Sixareen and her racing descendants*, Lerwick, 1954

SAVORY, J. G. *Prevention of decay of wood in boats*, Forest Products Research Laboratory Bulletin No. 31, 1966

SAWYER, P. H. *Age of the Vikings*, 2nd edition, 1971

SHAW, A. 'Bridgwater Flatner', *Mariner's Mirror*, 55:411–5, 1969

SJØVOLD, T. *Oseberg Find*, Oslo, 1969

STENTON, F. M. *Bayeux Tapestry*, 1957

SWINEY, H. W. and KATZEV, M. L. 'The Kyrenia Shipwreck' in BLACKMAN, D. J. (ed) *Marine Archaeology*, pp. 339–55, 1973

TAYLOR, J. du PLAT, *Marine Archaeology*, 1965

THOMAS, A. V. *Timbers used in the Boatbuilding Industry*, Forest Products Research Laboratory Industrial Survey No. 6, 1964

THORVILDSEN, K. *Ladby-Skibet*, Copenhagen, 1957

TORNROOS, B. *Båtar och båtbyggeri i Ålands östra skärgård 1850–1930*, Abo, 1968

TRAUNG, J-O. (ed) *Fishing Boats of the World*, 3 vols, 1955–67

van der HEIDE, G. D. 'Archaeological Investigations on New Lands', *Antiquity + Survival*, 1:221–52, 1955 van der HEIDE, G. D.   'Ship Archaeological Investigations in the Netherlands' in *Aspects of the History of Wooden Shipbuilding*, NMM MM + R No. 1:24–31, 1970

VILLIERS, A. J.   *Sons of Sinbad*, New York, 1940

WARINGTON-SMYTH, H.   *Mast and Sail in Europe and Asia*, 1906

WASKONIG, D.   'Bidliche Darstellungan des Hulk', *Altonaer Museum in Hamburg*, pp. 139–66, 1969

WEIBUST, K.   'Holmsbuprammen', *Norsk Sjøfartsmuseum 1914–1964*, pp. 87–96, Oslo, 1964

WHITE, E. W.   *British Fishing Boats and Coastal Craft*, 1950

WILSON, D. M.   'Anglo Saxon Carpenters' Tools' in CLAUS, M. (ed)   *Studien zur Europäischen vor-und Frühgeschichte*, pp. 143–50, Neumünster, 1968

WORCESTER, G. R. G.   *Sail and Sweep in China*, 1966

WRIGHT, E. V.   'The Boats of North Ferriby' in *Three Major Ancient Boat Finds in Britain*, NMM MM + R No. 6:3–7, 1972

WRIGHT, E. V.   *A Handbook on the Ferriby Boats*, in preparation

ZACKE, A. and HÄGG, M.   *Allmogebåtar*, Stockholm, 1973

Glossary

Boatbuilding terms are not standardised in Britain: Essex will interpret a word differently from Wessex. In addition, the same parts of a boat or the same boatbuilding technique may be known by different names in different counties. This glossary, therefore, defines the terms as they are used in this text, and is based on the glossaries in Sean McGrail's *Building and Trials of the Replica of an Ancient Boat* and Eric McKee's *Clenched Lap or Clinker*.

baulk   a tree trunk which has been roughly squared.

bevel   a surface which has been angled to make a fit with another.

blind fastening   one in which the point of the nail does not protrude through the timber.

bottom boards   lengths of timber fastened together and laid over the bottom of a boat as flooring.

brail   rope used to bundle a fore-and-aft sail rapidly. It may be rigged singly or with others, generally on boomless sails that have their peaks extended by a sprit or a standing gaff, which are not readily lowered.

breasthook   stemlock, fore hook. In wooden ships a stout knee fitted internally across the bows, holding the sides together. In boats this knee is at gunwale level.

carvel build   there are several definitions in use; in particular, this term is sometimes taken to be synonymous with skeleton build with flush-laid strakes. The term is confusing and ill defined and is not used here.

caulk   to insert material between two members *after* they have been assembled, and thus make the junction watertight. (see **luting**)

chine beam   longitudinal strength member fitted at the turn of the bilge and into which the planking is rabbeted and fastened above and below. If an angle is formed, this is known as a hard chine, and is usual in 'V'-bottom designs.

clench   rivet. To deform the end of a fastening so that it will not draw out—usually done over a rove.

clinker build   a form of boatbuilding in which the strakes are placed so that they partly overlap one another—usually upper strake outboard of lower strake, but occasionally the reverse arrangement is found.

construction plan   a scale drawing of a boat with a longitudinal section, horizontal plan, and several transverse sections. The position and nature of the scarfs, and other important constructional details and scantlings, may also be given.

cove   scotia. A hollow shaped moulding. May be used to hold the luting between two strakes.

cramp   clamp, gripe. A device for holding elements of a boat together temporarily.

crook   a curved piece of wood which has grown into a shape useful for boatbuilding.

dagger plate   a metal retractable device on the centre-line for combating leeway.

dolly   a metal billet held against the head of a boat nail whilst it is being clenched.

double-ended   a boat which is (nearly) symmetrical about the transverse axis—pointed at both ends. It would not be normal usage to describe a pram as double-ended.

drop-keel   centre board or centre plate. A wood or metal retractable device on the centre-line for combating leeway.

fair (n)   a line is fair when it passes through its guide marks without any abrupt changes in direction. The lines of a boat are fair when the level lines, half breadths, buttock lines and diagonals, being themselves fair, all correspond.

fair (v)   to render a set of lines eyesweet and mutually true on a ship's draught.

feather-edge   tapering to nothing.

floor   a transverse member—often a crook—extending from turn of bilge to turn of bilge, and set against the planking.

frame   a transverse member made up of more than one piece of timber, usually extending from sheer to sheer and set

against the planking. (see **rib** and **timber**).

futtock   any of the timbers used to make up a frame in a wooden ship. More exactly, not the floor or top timbers.

garboard   the strake next to the keel or keel plank.

grommet   strand(s) of rope layed up in the form of a ring.

gunwale   a longitudinal member fitted round the inside top edge of the sheer strake of an open boat. In open boats, mainly positional—the timber or arrangement of timbers that make up the sheer line.

hog   a longitudinal strength member of a boat fastened to the top of the keel to provide a landing for the inner edge of the garboard between the forward and aft deadwoods. Also a form of distortion which causes the ends of a boat to drop.

horn   to check the squareness of a mould, relative to the boat's centre-line.

joggle   to cut out a notch in a piece of timber so that it will fit close against another member.

keel   the main longitudinal strength member, scarfed to the stempost forward and the sternpost aft.

knee   a naturally grown crook used as a bracket between two members set at about right angles to each other or more.

land   that part of a strake which is overlapped by the strake immediately above it.

lay-off   to draw out the lines of a boat full size.

lines   the interrelation of sections in different planes which show the shape of a boat's hull. They usually consist of (a) sheer plan with longitudinal sections, (b) half breadth plan with waterlines or horizontal sections, (c) body plan with transverse sections. Diagonal lines, longitudinal section lines on the half breadth plan, and waterlines on the sheer plan, enable the three plans to be related to each other and checked for fairness. Lines converted to numbers are known as a Table of Offsets.

loom   that part of an oar inboard of the point of pivot; it includes the grip. The section of an oar between the loom and the blade is called the shaft.

luting   traditionally, luting is a plastic substance such as paint used between two adjacent members. In this text the term is used to describe any material inserted between two members *before* they are assembled. (see **caulk**)

mast step   fitting used to locate the heel of a mast.

moisture content   the weight of water in a specimen of wood expressed as a percentage of the weight of oven dry-wood. Thus the figure can be greater than 100%.

moulds   transverse wooden patterns taking their shape from the body plan. (see **lines**)

mould loft   loft with a levelled floor on which the lines of a vessel are drawn out full size and faired.

moulding   a pattern or linear decoration cut into a length of timber.

pay   cover caulking in seams with a layer of hot pitch. Loosely but commonly used—to coat a ship's bottom with tar.

plank   a component of a strake that is not all in one piece.

rabbet   rabet, rebate. A groove or channel worked in a member to accept another, without a lip being formed.

rays   layers of parenchyma cells in horizontal strands running out from the centre of a tree towards the circumference.

rib   a simple form of frame. This term may be more appropriate than frame, when applied to small open boats.

rove   roove. A washer-like piece of metal, which is forced over the point of a nail before it is clenched.

scarf   scarph, scarve. A tapered or wedge shaped joint between pieces of similar section at the join.

scrive or scrieve board   the floor of the mould loft or (more frequently) a board erected in the open air for the same purpose.

shake   a crack or split forming in wood, usually during drying or seasoning. Examples are: cup shakes—curved clefts between the growth rings; heart shakes—splits radiating from the centre of a tree.

sheer   sheer line. The curve of the upper edge of the hull.

sheer strake   the top strake of planking.

shell construction   a method of boatbuilding in which the shell (ie the watertight envelope of stems, keel and planking) is built or partly built *before* the ribs and other internal strengthening members are fitted. (see **skeleton construction**)

shrouds   ropes leading from the masthead to the sides of the boat to support the mast athwartships.

skeleton construction   a method of boatbuilding in which a framework of stems, keel *and ribs* is first erected, or partly erected. This skeleton is then clothed in a 'skin' of planking. Skeleton and shell construction merge into one another with the use of 'intermediate methods' of uncertain age.

spall   a light batten used during building to brace parts of the boat from floor, rafters or other strong point.

Spanish windlass   a simple rope and rod device for forcing two elements closer together, and holding them there.

spile   to transfer a curved line on to a pattern which, when laid flat, will give the shape to cut the lower edge of a plank.

station   the horizontal position of the transverse sections on the lines. They are used as datum lines when building from drawings, and moulds are generally made of transverse sections at some or all of these stations.

stealer   a tapered plank or plate worked

into the entry or run of a vessel to preserve the general lie of the strakes without making the ends too thick or thin.

Stockholm tar   a blackish semi-liquid prepared by the destructive distillation of various trees of the Pinaceae family.

stocks   set-up. The temporary wooden support on which a boat is built.

strake   a single plank or combination of planks which stretches from one end of a boat to the other.

stretcher   an athwartships length of timber against which a rower braces his feet.

template   a shaped pattern of an element or section of a boat, made of plywood or

hardboard, etc.

thole   a pin projecting upwards at sheer level to provide a pivot for an oar. Strictly thole-pin, but frequently used as above.

thwart   a transverse member used as a seat.

timber   an element of a frame or rib. May also be used generally referring to any piece of wood used in boatbuilding. One piece ribs or frames, especially those steamed or bent into place, are frequently called timbers.

trenail   treenail, trunnel. Wooden peg or through fastening used to join two members. It may be secured at each or either end by the insertion of a wedge.

Index

Adams, George, 34–8, 43, 197, 273
Admiralty Islands, 143
Africa, 99, 108, 125, 128, 129
Åkerlund, Harold, 181–2
Alalia, battle of, 158
Albion, 238
Alexander, 172
Alfred, King, 223
Algonquin Reserve, 125
Alma, fig. 200
Als boat, 81, 119, 121, 178, 182, 215, figs. 33, 70, 144
Althiburus, mosaic of, 155–6
Ancholme river, 111, 114
Andersen, Capt. Magnus, 235
Andersen, Neils, 48–50, 56
Andersen, R. C., 289
Anderson, Eric, 231
angel, of Edward IV, 285, fig. 202
Angles, 180, 182, 186
Anglo-Saxons, 183, 186, 246
Antwerp, 196
Apollonia, 158
Appledore, 274, 285
Apulian rhyton, 169
Arab *baggala*, 148, fig. 103
  bhum, fig. 102
  influence, 29
  vessels, 147
Arabian Sea, 148
Årby boat, 178, 226–7
Archaeological Research Centre, 111

Aristophanes, 165, 168
Aristotle, 165
Asia, 129, 177, 269
  Minor, 157
Äskekärr ship, 23
Assam, 175
Assyrian reliefs, the, 157
Athenian *triereis*, 169
Atlantic, 252
Attic triakontor, fig. 112
Australia, 125

baggala, a, 148, fig. 103
Baker, Stanley, 38
balam, the, 137, fig. 89
Ballinderry, 110
Baltic, 29, 138, 149, 193–6, 198, 218, 268
Bangladesh, 25, 32, 51–6, 73, 75, 77, 85–6, 99, 134, 138, 145, 151, 175, 198, 283, 294
  boat, building of, 51–3, 61, figs. 13–17
  cargo boat, figs. 18, 101
  extended dugout, fig. 126
  'reversed clinker', fig. 42
  river boat, 60, figs. 19, 41
Banks, Sir Joseph, 27–8
Banks dory, 197, 259, 269, 272, figs. 131, 186
Bantry, 122
  boat, fig. 75
barge, Bridgwater, 265

double-ended, 265
  Norfolk, 192
  Thames, 281
bark boat, 25, 92–4, 124–8, 129, fig. 46
bark canoes, 124
  Australian, 125, 128
  building of, 125, 127–8
barquentine, Canadian, 65
  French fishing, fig. 187
Barset boat, 178, 187–8
Basch, Lucien, 21, 158
basket boat, 92, 117, fig. 15
Bass, G. F., 21
bateau, lumberman's, 272, fig. 189
Bath, Maine, 271
  N. C., 34
Bayeux Tapestry, 214–15, 246, figs. 143, 163
Bayonne, 259
beach boat, 255, fig. 174
Beals Island, fig. 10
Belgium, 204, 223
Belisarius' ship, 169
Bengal, Bay of, 137
Beothuk canoe, 125, fig. 77
Bergen, 77, 207, 227, 238, 250, 252, fig. 167
Bevaix, 70
bhum, a, 148, fig. 102
Bideford, 285
Birka, coin from, 200, fig. 133
Biscay coasts, 29, 288, 289

Björke boat, 82, 178, 180, 182, fig. 34

Black Sea, 158, 202, 207

Blackfriars boats, 21, 70

Blagdon's boatyard, fig. 11

Block Island boats, 255, fig. 173

boats, ancient, discoveries of, fig. 117

recording building traditions of, 30

boats, clinker-built, 37, 39, 75, 77, 134, 137, 146–7, 174–188, 201, 203, 204, 207–8, 219, 223, 245, 250, 252, 255, 256–7, 259, 261, 264–5, 268, 283, 286, 289, 292, 298, figs. 144, 171–3, 185, 194, 195, 206

construction of, 178, figs. 115, 126, 128

Cornish, 38, 42, 46

fastening strakes of, figs. 7, 8

pram, 48–50

'reverse', 86, figs. 39, 42

boats, edge-joined, 51–3, 58, 60–1, 63, 65, 68, 70, 72–3, 80, 106, 116, 119, 134, 139, 141, 145, 148, 151, 161, 165, 175, 178, 203, 234, 255, 268, 287, 292, 294, 296, figs. 26, 91, 206

flat-bottomed, 34–5, 37–9, 45, 48, 68–70, 78, 97, 103, 106, 108, 147, 192–201, 204, 250, 261, 264, 265, 268–70, 272–4, 279, 281, 286, figs. 19, 22, 127, 128, 185, 195, 196

in art, 29–30, 119, 121

in literature, 29, 167, 202, 236–8

non-edge joined, 58, 60–1, 63–6, 68, 70, 72–3, 116, 147, 151–2, 250, 261, 265, 279, 285–9, 292, 294, 296, 298, 300, figs. 20, 21, 206, 208

plank-built, 94, 100, 106, 111, 116, 118, 119, 121, 138, 141, 144–6, 148, 150, 193, 204, 220, 259, 279, figs. 70, 92

round-hulled, 108, 118, 121, 138, 145, 147, 190–3, 196, 197, 204, 250, 252, 259, 265, 279, 283, fig. 129

sewn, 134, 137, 147–8, figs. 86, 87, 104

'V'-bottomed, 274, 278–9, fig. 197

boat-building, use of drawings, 57–8, 298

use of half models, 296, 298

Venetian, 289

bohatja, the, 104

Bonaventure, Quebec, 256

Borden, 47

botter, 265–6, fig. 181

Boy Albert, 255, fig. 174

Brahmaputra, 145

Brazil, 25, 99, 131

making a dugout in, fig. 81

Bremen, 261

cog, the, 70, 261, 286, fig. 177

Bremerhaven, 261

Breton, a, 292

Brewington, Marion, 21, 152

Bridgwater barge, 197, 265, fig. 184

'Bridgwater boats', 197, 265, fig. 184

Bridgwater river flatners, 25, 78, 265, fig. 183

Brigg boat, 22, 30, 111, fig. 64

construction of, 114

Britain, 73, 75, 95, 109, 111, 116, 134, 174, 175, 180, 186, 202–4, 207, 212, 214, 218, 219, 221, 230, 237, 241, 250, 255, 256, 265, 274, 281, 287, 289, 296–8

British boatbuilding, 61–2

Columbia, 144

fishing boats, 232

Museum, 21, 186, 225–6

Broighter gold boat, 121, fig. 73

Brøndsted, Johannes, 208

Bronze Age boats, 109–11, 113–14, 118, 119, 121, 122, 156, 160, 167, figs. 67, 71

Brotiog Cenarth, 122

Brown's Creek, 45–6

Bruce-Mitford, Rupert, 21

Bruges boat, 178, 195, 197, 259, fig. 130

bugeye, log, 150–2, 279

Burness Corlett & Partners, 223

Bygdøy, 78, 210, 227

Byzantine Age, 167

merchantmen, 156

Caergwrle bowl, 122, fig. 74

Caergwrle Castle, 122

Calypso's island, 158

Cambridge, 158

Camden, Maine, 64

Canada, 125–8, 219–20, 255, 274, 294, fig. 172

Canoe, building of, 27–8, 151, figs. 1, 105

dugout, 151–2

fur traders', 127, fig. 80

Maori war, 143, fig. 96

single outrigger, 143, figs. 97, 100

Canute, King, 218

Cape Breton, 45, 47, 255

'Cape Fear' skiff, fig. 191

Cape Gelydonia Bronze Age ship, the 160, 162, 163

Cape Islander, 46–7

building of, 46

Cape Sable, 47

Cape Tormentine, 47

caravela, 292

Cardiff, 122

cargo ship, Skuldelev, 83–4, 218, 220, 223, 252, figs. 37, 146, 147, 148, 149

Viking, 29

Carolina skiff, building of a 34–7, 39, 60

Sounds, 281

Carthaginian navy, 172

carvel, 75, 76, 292, 298

Casson, Lionel, 21, 156, 163, 168–9, 171

Castletown, 255

Catalonia, 259

caulking tools, 294

method of, 294, 297–8, fig. 205

Ceylon, dugout from, 144, fig. 98

Chapelle, Howard I., 21, 273, 274

Charles A. Dean, fig. 21

Charlton, 43

Chebacco boats, 255

Cheops ship, the 161–2, fig. 111

Chesapeake Bay, 21, 141, 279

log bugeye, 150–2, fig. 106

log canoe, 150–2, 285, fig. 105

oyster fishery, 150, 274

skipjack, 279

Chesil Beach, 265

China, 32, 58, 100, 102–4, 139

Chinese boats, 97, 99–104, figs. 53, 54

Chittagong balam, 137, fig. 89

dugout base, 134

sampan, 100, fig. 52

Christensen, Arne Emil, 20, 21, 61, 78, 211, 236, 238, 244–5, 298

Chronicle of Zeeland, 292

church boat, Swedish, 215, fig. 145

Churchill, Hudson Bay, fig. 76

Cimon, 171

City of London, 287

Clark, David, 300

Clenched lap or Clinker, 76

Clevedon, Somerset, 274

Clovelly, 25

Cobb, Butler & Co's yard, fig. 211

Cobb, F., 301

coble, the, 255, fig. 168

cog, the, 39, 70, 86, 147, 197, 200, 250, 252, 259, 261, 264–5, 278, 283, 286, 287, 289, 292
   the Bremen, 70, 261, 286, fig. 177

Connecticut, 47, fig. 173

Continental gun boat, fig. 188

Cook, Capt. James, 27

Copacabana, 132

Copenhagen, 214, 216
   University of, 292

coracle, Welsh, 92, 122, fig. 68
   Euphrates, 165

Corcyra, 167

Cork, County, 122

Corinth, 167

Corinthians, 170

Cornish working boat, 38–45

Cornwall, 39, 297, 298

Crumlin-Pedersen, Ole, 21, 78, 134, 180, 196, 200, 211, 213, 218, 220, 221, 236, 240, 243, 244, 246

curragh, Irish, 92, 116, 122, figs. 69, 75

Dacca, fig. 41

Dahshur boats, 109, fig. 62

Danish National Museum, 21, 23, 218, 231, 257

Dark Age, the, 186

Dean shipyard, R. L., fig. 21

De Bello Gallico, 29

Delabole Quarries, 39

de la Morandiere, Charles, 272, 278

Demosthenes, 165

Denmark, 25, 30, 78, 175, 180, 182, 186, 193, 190, 200, 204, 207, 214–16, 218, 220, 230, 243, 246, 250, 264, 268, 274, 300

Development of the boat, the, 24, 29, 55, 58, 68, 73, 77, 91–2, 99, 104, 119, 131, 138–9, 141, 144, 146, 149, 167, 177, 188, 193, 196, 197, 202, 211, 221, 234, 250, 261, 268, 272, 285, 288

Devon, 285

Dipylon vase triakontor, 165, fig. 112

Donegal, County, 117

Dorset, coast of, 265, 272

dory, the, 269–73
   Banks, 197, 269, 272, figs. 131, 186, 187
   North American, 75, 78, 80, 269, 270, fig. 31
   Portuguese, 25

dory-building shop, 78, 197, figs. 131, 186

double-ended barge, 265
   boat, 68, 148
   dory, 272
   ship, 252

dragger, wooden, fig. 210

dragon ship, a, 218

dugout, the, 24, 38, 58, 69, 75, 81, 82, 94, 97, 102, 106, 116, 118, 121, 129–52, 174, 178, 180, 181, 183, 279, 287, figs., 33, 34, 47, 84, 198
   boats of Brazil, 25, 131, fig. 81
   canoe, 151–2, 279
   Ceylonese, 144, figs. 82, 98
   expanded, 26, 102, 134, 137, 141, 146, 149, 175, 180, 182, 190, 191, 193, figs. 83, 85–9
   extended, 130, 134, 149, 180, 182, 190, 191, 193, figs. 83, 85–9, 91, 92, 98, 126
   Indian, 151
   monoxylous, 158
   outrigger, 143, 144, fig. 100
   sailing, 144, fig. 100
   Shalish, 144, fig. 99
   Tepuke, 144

Dumas, S., 21

Dutch vessels, 265

Duval, P. M., 155

East Coast boat types, 21

East German coast, 193
   19th century boats of, figs. 128, 129

East Weymss, 114

Edward IV, angel of, 285, fig. 202

Egypt, 21, 81, 99, 106, 162, 197

Egyptian punt, fig. 61
   vessels, 108–9, 162, 163
   construction of, 161–2, 165–6

Egyptians, the, 72, 157

Eigg, Isle of, 237–8

Elbing, Seal of, 261, fig. 176

Ellmers, Detlev, 70

Eskimo kayak, 116, 122, fig. 76

Essai sur la Construction Navale des Peuples Extra-Européens, 101

Euphrates coracles, 165
   quffas, 166

Evelyn, John, 236

evolution of the boat, see development

faering, Gokstad, 77–8, 197, 234–6, 241, figs. 28–30

'Farmer's Daughter' skiff, fig. 192

Faversham, 186, 223

femboring, 257

Fenwick, Valerie, 22, 223

Ferriby boats, the, 21, 22, 81, 111, 113, fig. 32
   construction of, 114

Ficoronian chest, 171

Fitzwilliam Museum, 158

flatner, the, 25, 78, 265, figs. 183, 193

Flintshire, 122

Florentine, a, 259

Foochow pole junk, 104, 106, fig. 58

Food and Agriculture Organisation, 26

Forest Products Research Laboratory, 238

Formosan rafts, 100, fig. 53

Fort Chipewyan, 127

fourern, 230

Fowey, Port of, 298

France, 29, 193, 198, 204, 207, 212, 219, 268, 272, 288, 289

Frau Minna Petersen, fig. 205

Frederikstad, 120, 121

French barquentine, fig. 187
   fishermen, 270, 272

Friendship, Maine, 269

Frisian vessels, 200, 259, 283

Frisians, 186, 201

Frost, Honor, 21, 158

Funen, 214

galeass, a, fig. 206

galley, building of, a, 289
   the oared, 167 72
   war, 155

Ganges, the, 266

Gardner, John, 21

Gascony, 259

Gaspé schooners, 255, fig. 171
   skiffs, 275, 278, fig. 195
   Peninsula, 275

Genesis, 239

Genoa, 259

Geometric vases, 167

Georgetown, P. E. I., fig. 197

Georgia, 273, 274

Germany, 180, 182, 186, 204, 218, 223, 250, 261, 264, 268, 283

German, 259, 292

Gibraltar, Straits of, 259

gig, Cornish, 255, fig. 169

goelette, St. Lawrence, 278

Gokstad faering, 197, 227, 232, 234, 244, fig. 29
   ship, 77, 78, 83, 178, 212–16, 219, 220, 221, 223, 227, 234, figs. 35, 139, 140, 144, 149

Gotland, 246
    stone carvings, 200, 209, fig. 132
Grace Dieu, 286
Graeco-Roman, 287
Graveney boat, 21, 22, 25, 83, 178,
    186, 200, 203, 221, 223–6, 227, 232,
        236, 255, 261, figs. 36,
        150–5
    Marsh dyke, 226
*Great Coal Schooners of New England,
    The*, 300
Great Galley, the, 292
Gredstedbro boat, 178, 182–3, 185,
    186
Greek civilisation, 155
    merchantmen, 155–6, fig. 113
    ship, fig. 108
    shipwrights, 169
Greeks, the, 72
Greenland, 29, 202, 207, 219–20
Greenwich, 22, 235
Gulf of Mexico, 127
Gulf of St. Lawrence, 45, 48

half model, the, 296, 298
Hamble river, 286
Handbook of Hardwoods, 236
Hanseatic League, 259
Hardanger, 227
Hasslöf, Olof, 21, 66, 73, 292, 298
Hedeby, coin from, 200, fig. 133
Heimskringla, the, 236, 237
Helen Barnet Gring, fig. 21
Henry V, 286
Heraclion Museum, 159
Herodotus, 158, 161, 162, 165–6,
    167, 171, 287
Hinks, Alan, 274
Hipponax, 158, 167
Hjortspring boat, *see* Als boat
holkadikon ploion, 165
holkas, 165
Holland, 192, 198, 204, 218, 223,
    250, 265, 268
Holmsbu, 49
Homer, 29, 156, 157, 159, 162–3,
    171
Hong Kong, 104
holrikjekta, 252, figs. 166, 167
hora, fig. 27
Hornell, James, 20, 21, 66, 97, 132
Hudson Bay, 123
Hueng-ho river, 102
hulk, the, 49, 84–6, 146, 151–2, 192,
    250, 283–5, 286, 289, 292, fig.
    39
hulls, shape and structure, 23
Humber, river, 109, 114, 118, 121

Iberian Peninsula, 285, 289
Ibrahim Hyderi, 76
Iceland, 177, 202, 207, 219–20
Icelandic sagas, 29, 220
Iliad, the, 163
Immaculé Conception, fig. 187
Imperial College, London
    University, 239
India, 73, 97, 175, 265
Indonesia, 29, 125
Indus, the, 68, 104, 287
    punt, fig. 59
    river boat, 68–9, figs. 22, 23
Innes, H. A., 272
Ionian Greeks, 171
Ireland, 116, 117, 118, 121, 129,
    207, 212, fig. 73
Irish curragh, 92, fig. 69

jagt, fishing, 174, fig. 116
Jane Banks, fig. 205
jangada sailing raft, fig. 51
Japan, 58, 102, 138, 139, 143, 174,
    294, 298
Japanese boatbuilding, 138, 139,
    141, 297, fig. 207
Jean Richard, The, 278
jegt, Nordlands, 252, fig. 167
Jenkins, Geraint, 122
Jersey skiff, 272
Jessie A. Bishop, fig. 211
Jodrell Laboratory, 237
Johansen, Kristian, 49
Johnson, Odd, 121
Johnstone, Paul, 114, 118, 121
Jonathan's Cave, 114, fig. 67
Jonesport, Maine, 47
Julian a Breton, 292
Julius Caesar, 29
junk, the, 104, 106
Jutes, 186
Jutland, 180, 182

Kabul river, fig. 24
Kalmar, 250, 252
Kalnes rock carvings, 121, fig. 71
Kapel Avezaath, 70
Karachi, fig. 208
karve, 209, 220
Kaupang, Norway, 49
Kayak, 116, 122, fig. 76
Kenada-wan, 143
Kennebunkport, Maine, 300
Kent, 186, 223, 246, 264
ketch, coasting, 298, fig. 209
ketch-rig, 281, fig. 206
Ketelhaven Maritime

    Archaeological Museum, 192,
        fig. 127
Keying, 104
Kiel, Seal of 261, fig. 175
Klåstad ship, 211
knarr, 220
Knivsvik, 49
Kobe University of Mercantile
    Marine, 139
Kongsviken, fig. 206
Krefeld, 70
Kühn, Kurt, 138, 193
Kuwait, 148
Kvalsund boat, 178, 187, fig. 123
Kyrenia ship, the, 160

Lachine, 127
Ladby ship, 178, 214–16, 218, 220,
    figs. 141, 144
Lake Athabasca, 127
    Champlain, 271
    Neuchatel, 70
    Siljan, 215, fig. 145
    Titicaca, 98
Lal Mian, 50–3, 55–7
Lamu Archipelago, 148
Landström, Bjorn, 106, 161
lapstrake, *see* clinker
Lawrence Allen dory shop, 78, 197,
    fig. 131
Levy, Dr. John, 239
liburnian, a, 158
Lilybaeum, 156
Limavady, 121
Lincolnshire, 114
Lobito Bay raft boat, 99, 100, fig.
    48
lobster boat, 45–7, 58, 255, 274,
    figs. 9, 10
log bugeye, 150–2, 279
Long Island Sound oyster fishery,
    150, 273
Long Serpent, the, 237, 238, 245
'long ship', 155, 163–5
longships, 214, 215, 218, 220, 234,
    252
Low Countries, the, 192, 196, 198,
    200, 223, 259, 265, 283
lug, dipping, 232, 255
Lunenberg, N. S., 78, 80, 197, fig.
    131

McGrail, Sean, 22, 24, 31, 111, 129
McKee, Eric, 22, 24, 40, 41, 75, 76,
    78, 80, 119, 203, 223, 226, 265,
    274

MacMurray, Campbell, 19
MacPherson, N., 238
Machias, Maine, 301
Magdalen Islands, 275
Mahdia wreck, 167
Mahone Bay, fig. 210
Maine, 47, 269, 270, 271, 272, 274,
    275, 299, 300, 301
Man, the Isle of, 207, 255
Manus, 143
Manx schooner, fig. 170
Maori war canoe, 143, fig. 96
Mariners' Mirror, 238, 289
Mariners' Museum, Newport News,
    24, 134, 274, figs. 51, 66, 84
Maritime Ethnology, 292
Maritime Museum, Bath, Maine,
    fig. 189
  Bremerhaven, 261
  Oslo, 257
Marsala, 156, 168, 169
Marsden, P., 21
Marstrander, Prof. S., 121
Martin, Colin, 21
Maryland oyster fishery, 141,
    150-1, 279
Massachusetts, 255, 270
Mastermyr, 246, 247, fig. 162
Mataro ship, fig. 203
Matsuki, Prof. Satoru, 139, 141
May, Bob, 43, 44
Medinet Habu reliefs, the, 157
Mediterranean, 21, 29, 64, 72, 118,
    155, 158, 162, 202, 207, 259,
    268, 285, 287, 288, 289, 292
meia lua, a, 114-15, fig. 66
Meiji Restoration, 141
Merchant Schooners, The, 296, 298
merchant ship, Greek, fig. 113
  vessel, 13th century, 250
Mere, 37
Middle East, 73
  Kingdom, 108, 162
Millom Castle, 297
Minoan seal stones, 156
Mississippi, 127
Moesgård, 243
Moll, F., 238
Montreal, 127
Morrison, John, 72, 287
moulds, use of, 61-2, 65, 72-3, 245,
    298, fig. 208
mtepe, 148, fig. 104
Mulroy Bay, 117
murina, the, 137, fig. 90
Museum of History & Technology,
    Washington, 21
  London, 21

Mycenaean ship, 107
Mymemsingh, 86
Mystic Seaport, 21, fig. 173

Nance, R. Morton, 289
Narayanganj, fig. 18
National Film Board of Canada,
    278
  Maritime Museum, Greenwich,
    19, 21, 23, 24, 25, 38, 94, 101,
    111, 112, 122, 129, 131, 141,
    148, 181, 186, 209, 218, 223,
    225, 226, 227, 230, 240, 241,
    258, 272, 274, 291, 294, 298,
    figs. 8, 12
  Museum of Wales, 122
  Trust, 298
Nautical Museum, Castletown, 255
Needham, J., 97, 104
Netherlands, boats of the, 39, 70,
    265
New Bideford, P. E. I., 35, 65
  Brunswick, 46-7
  England, 255, 270, 272, 281, 300
  Jersey, 275
  Kingdom, 162
  Shoreham, Seal of, 289, fig. 201
  Zealand scow, 281
Newfoundland, 125, 202, 270, 272,
    273, 278
Newhaven sharpie, the, 273-4, fig.
    190
Nile nuggar, 109, fig. 63
Nord-fjord, 252
Nordlands boat, 231-2, 257, 258,
    fig. 157
  jegt, 252, figs. 166, 167
Norfolk barge, 192
Normans, the, 214
Norsk Sjøfartsmuseum, 187
North Africa, 158
North America, 58, 95, 97, 116,
    174, 196, 198, 202, 207, 255,
    268, 270, 272, 273, 278, 281,
    288, 296, 298
North American Banks fishery, 270
  dory, 75
  Indian bark canoe, 124-8, figs.
    77, 78
  building of a, 125, 127
  dugout, 144, fig. 99
  lobster boat, 45-7, 60, figs. 9, 10
  Atlantic banks, 270
  fishermen, 270
  Carolina Sounds, 37, 274, fig. 2
  China, 104
  East Polder, 192, fig. 182

Ferriby, Yorks, 111, fig. 65
  Island, 281
  Lincolnshire, 111
  Sea, 186, 212, 236
Northern Europe, 23, 25, 29, 46,
    58, 66, 69, 73, 75, 77, 86, 97,
    109, 111, 119, 121, 134, 146,
    174, 177, 178, 179, 180, 182,
    186, 187, 196, 197, 201, 203,
    207, 234, 236, 238, 241, 245,
    250, 259, 265, 287, 292, 296,
    297, 298
  clinker-built boats of, 144
  discoveries of Ancient boats, fig.
    117
Norway, 23, 25, 30, 48, 55, 77, 119,
    121, 178, 182, 187, 188, 204,
    207-8, 209, 211, 220, 227, 230,
    238, 245, 248, 250, 252, 257,
    298, 300, fig. 72
Norwegian clinker-built pram,
    48-50, 84, 86, fig. 38
  tradition, 213
Nova Scotia, 45, 47, 78, 80, 197,
    198, 255, 270, 300, fig. 210
nuggar, the, 109, fig. 63
Nugget, 45, 255
  lines, fig. 5
  structural drawing, fig. 6
Nydam oak boat, 178, 180, 181,
    182, 183, 185, 186, 213, figs.
    118, 119, 144
  softwood boat, 182, 183, 186,
    187, 211, fig. 120

Oder, the, 150
Odysseus' boat, building of,
    159-63
Olsen, Olaf, 21
Ontario, 125
Oseberg ship, 178, 208-16, 220-1,
    223, figs. 136-8, 144, 149
Oselver boat, 77, 227, 230, 238, fig.
    156
Oslo, Norway, 20, 48-50, 78, 121,
    187, 210, 212
Ottawa valley, 124-5
  bark canoe, fig. 78
Otto Mathiasen, fig. 116
ottring, 231-2, fig. 157
Outer Banks, 34
Owhiti, fig. 199
oyster boat, 45
  fishery, Long Island Sound, 273
  Maryland, 141, 150-1, 279
  North Carolina Sounds, 274
  Truro river, 141

Pacific, 27, 143
Pakistan, 67–9, 76, 106, 108
  cargo vessel, 286, 294, fig. 102
Palace of Placentia, 285
Pamlico river, 34, fig. 2
  Sound, 34
Papyrus raft, 108–9, fig. 60
Par, Cornwall, 293
Paris, Seal of City of, 252, fig. 164
Parker, Capt. W. J. L. 300, fig. 207
Parret, river, 265
patalia, the, 265, 268
pavilionpoon, 265, fig. 180
Peat Princess, the, fig. 4
Pechili trading junk, 104, fig. 57
Peggy, 255, figs. 170–1
pentekontors, 158, 163, fig. 113
Peoples of the Sea, the, 157
Perkins, Tom, fig. 209
Persian Gulf, 148
Persians, the, 171
Peshawar valley, boat building of,
  68–9
  cargo boat, fig. 24
Philadelphia, fig. 188
Phoenicians, the, 72
plank ends, the problem of the,
  80–8, 146, 149–50, 219, 223,
  227, 283, figs. 6, 32–42, 101
planks, splitting logs into, 241–4,
  figs. 159–61
ploion strongulon, 165
Plutarch, 171
Plymouth, 48
Poland, 250
Polynesians, 27
Pomerania, 150
Poole, Seal of, 85
Port Hill, 45, 46, 294
Porth Gaverne, 39
Portland, Maine, 274
Portmadoc, 293
Portugal, 25, 29, 114, 198
Portuguese fishing boats, 114–15,
  270, 272, 292
pram, a, 48–50, 60, 103
  building of a, 48–9, fig. 11
Prince Edward Is., 35, 45, 48, 65,
  255, 279, 294, figs. 172, 197
Procopius, 169
Prynne, Major-General Michael,
  289
Ptolemy Philopator, 172
Punic ship, a, 156, 158, 168–9
punt, Indus, building of, 106–8,
  figs. 59, 107
  Egyptian, fig. 61
punts, 106, 279

Pylos ship, the, 156, fig. 107

Quebec, 255, fig. 171
quffas, 166
quinquereme, 172

raft, the, 24, 92, 94, 97–115, 129,
  287
  boat, the, 58, 69, 70, 92, 94,
    97–115, 281, fig. 43
  reed, 118, fig. 49
  boats of S.W. Africa, 25, fig. 48
  the papyrus, 106
  a skin, fig. 50
Raiatea, Island of, 27–8
Rålamb, 77
ram, a, fig. 109
reed-bundle raft boats, 118, fig. 49
replicas, full-sized boat, 30–1, 116,
  121, 214–15, 223, 226–7, 232,
  235–6, 241, 247, fig. 141
Reygersbergen, Jan, 292
Rhine, the, 70, 190, 196
Richmond Bay, P.E.I., 35, 45
Rio de Janeiro, 25, 32, 132
Rockland, Maine, 299, 310
Roman civilization, 155
  merchantmen, 155–6
  navy, 172
  period, the, 165
  Republic, 172
Romans, the, 72, 239
Roskilde fjord, 21, 214, 215, 216,
  220, 221
Rostock, 150
Rother barge, fig. 178
  river, 264
'round' ship, 155, 159–63, 165–7,
  fig. 110
rowing boat, first evidence of, 181
Royal Botanic Gardens Kew, 237
  Naval College, Greenwich, 285
  Ship of Cheops, the, 106
Rudolph, Dr. Wolfgang, 138, 149,
  193
Rügen, 150
Russia, 202, 207

St. Lawrence goelette, 278, fig. 196
  Gulf of, 278
St. Malo, 272, fig. 187
St. Pierre et Miquelon, 270, 272,
  278
sail, adoption of, 188, 200–1, 208,
  figs. 132, 133
  development of, 289
Saïte Pharaoh Necho, 167
Salamis, 171

sampan, a, 99, 100, 102, fig. 52
  'chicken', 106, fig. 56
  'duck', 104, fig. 55
San Francisco, 281
  Maritime State Park, 281, fig.
    200
Sanxton Hubbard, fig. 106
Sarazin, 125
Sarre, 246
Savannah, fig. 212
Savannah, Georgia, 274
saveiro, the, 115
Saxon migrations, 174, 177, 180,
  186
  ship, 27, 174, 236, 251
  tools, 246
Scandinavia, 118, 119, 121, 174,
  175, 227, 237, 241, 244–6, 256,
  283, 288, 298
Scandinavian boatbuilders, 240
  boats and ships, 29, 223
  clinker tradition, 200
  dockyard, 72, fig. 25
  expansion, 23, 202, 207–9, 216,
    219
  framing, 119
  raiders, 39
  settlement, 29
  tradition, 121, 193, 203, 211,
    221–2, 245, 250, 255
Scandinavians, the, 77
  learn to sail, 200–1
Schleswig, 186
schokker, fig. 179
schooner, a Cornish, 65
  a three-masted, fig. 205
  rig, 274, 281
  scow, 281, fig. 200
schooners, American, 65, 272, figs.
  21, 211–13
  fishing, 270
  Gaspé, 255
  Portuguese, 272
Scilly Isles, 255
Scotland, 129, 212, 300
scow, New Zealand, 281, fig. 199
  sailing, 281
  schooner, 281, fig. 200
  sloops, 281
scows, 279, fig. 198
Seal Cove, 274
Shalish dugout, 144, fig. 99
shallops, 255, fig. 172
Shamrock, 298, fig. 209
Shansi, 102
Shapwick, 37
sharpie, the Newhaven, 273–4, fig.
  190

shell construction, 49, 51–3, 58, 60–1, 64–6, 68, 72–3, 77, 80, 124, 146–7, 149, 150, 162, 165–6, 168, 178, 227, 245, 255, 287, 294, fig. 26
Shetland, 188, 230, 238, 245, 257, 258
Ships & Shipyards, Sailors & Fishermen, 180
Shropshire, 116
Siberia, 125
Sicily, 169
'Sister ship', the, 158
sixerns, 238
Skaw, the, 22, 177, 202
skeleton construction, 46, 58, 60, 64–6, 68, 70, 72–3, 92, 116, 124, 141, 147, 151–2, 174, 279, 205, 287, 289, 294, 296, 298, 300, fig. 21
described, 296–7
Skeps Byggerij eller Adelig Ofnings Tionde Tom, 71
skiff, Cape Fear, fig. 191
Carolina, building of a, 34–7, 39, 197, 273
Farmer's Daughter, fig. 192
Gaspé, 275, fig. 195
Jersey, 272
Magdalen Islands, 275
New Jersey, 275
oyster, 275, fig. 194
powered, 34–5, fig. 2
rowing, 34
Staten Island, 275
skin boat, the 24, 69, 92, 94, 97, 116–24, 129, 132, 182, 203, fig. 44
skipjack, oyster-dredging, 279
Skuldelev finds, the, 21, 178, 214–21, 227, 236, 243–4, 246
Wreck 1, 83–4, 220, 223, 252, figs. 37, 147, 148
Wreck 3, 218, 220, 223, figs. 146, 149
Wreck 5, 215
Slav areas, 29
sloops, 281
smack, trading, 39, 65, 298
smack's boat, building of a, 43–4, 46, 60
smooth-skinned boats of Clovelly, 25
Society Islands, 27
Solomon Islands, 144, fig. 100
Solomons, Maryland, 151
Somerset coast, 198, 265, 274
Levels, 37, 193, 265

turf boat, 37–8, 43, 193, 197, figs. 3, 4
South America, 29, 108, 125, 128–9
East Asia, 97
Wales, 39
West Africa, 96
Southern America, 97
Europe, 287
Southport, Maine, 272
Søvik, A. N., 238
Spain, 29, 300
Spanish windlass, 37
squaresail, development of, 201, 210, 213, 218, 220, 230–2, 257–8, 265, 289
Staten Island skiffs, 275
Stockholm, 178, 200
Stone Age, 119
strake diagram, the, 77–8, 197, 226, figs. 29, 31, 93, 155
stresses and strains, 63–4, 70, 116, 124, 134, 141, 235, 286–8, 294, 299, 300, fig. 20
Strongman, Bob, 45–7, 56–7, 255, 279
Sturluson, Snorri, 236
Suffolk, 183
Sukkur, 68, figs. 22, 23, 59
Summerside, P. E. I., 65
Sutton Hoo, 21, 178, 183–6, 203, 215, 236, figs. 121, 122
Swat river, fig. 50
Sweden, 119, 175, 198, 207, 209, 227, 246, 250, 268, 300, figs. 145, 206
Swedish coast, 180
church boat, 215, fig. 145
lake boats, 75
shipwright, a, 73
stem boats, 86
tools, 246–7
tradition, 213
Switzerland, 70
Sylhet, 86, figs. 42, 126
Syracuse, 170

Teifi, river, 117, 122
Tepuke dugout, 144, fig. 100
Terminology, standard, 23–4
tessarakonteres, 172
Thames barge, 281
embankment, 21
15th century find, 223
Themistocles, 171
Theoline, fig. 213
Theophrastus, 168–9
Thomas, A. V., 238
Thomas, J. C., 122

Thorberg, 245
Three-masted ship, 289, figs. 204, 205
three-plank boat, 102
Thucydides, 171
Tignish, 256
Tokugawa Shogunate, the, 141
Tokyo Bay, 143
Tønsberg, 208
Tregaskes, Jack, fig. 205
Tregaskes' yard, Par, 293
triakontor, 165, fig. 112
trials, replica, 31, 116, 121, 214–15, 223, 227, 232, 234, fig. 141
trieres, 158, 167–9, 171, 172, fig. 114
trierika ploia, 172
Troy, 163
Truro river oyster fishery, 141
Tryggvason, Olaf, 237, 245
Tune ship, 178
turf boat, building of a, 37–9, 46, 60, 193, 197, 265, figs. 3, 4
Turkey, 63
two masted rig, 152
Tyrrhenian warship, 158, fig. 108

umiak, the, 122
United States, 55, 65, 127, 150, 274, 294
schooners, fig. 21
University Museum of National Antiquities, Oslo, 20, 210
Upsala, 227
Utrecht ship, 49, 141, 178, 190–2, 285, figs. 124, 125
Utrecht boat, 70
Uttar Pradesh, 175, 265, 268

van der Heide, G. D., 21
Velius, the Chronicler, 292
Veneti, boats of the, 29
Venice, 259
Victory, H.M.S., 286
Viking Age, the, 22–3, 75, 119, 182, 188, 202–4, 206–32, 234–48, 250
boatbuilders, 238, 244–5, 248
shipbuilding, 22, 25, 27, 208, 234
tools, 247–8, figs. 162, 163
wrecks, 243
Viking boat, 77
cargo vessel, 29
construction of, 218–19, 234
coastal ship, 234
expansion, 200, 203, 207–8, fig. 134
migrations, 177
ocean trader, 234

ship, evolution of, 22, 202, 234
Ship Museum, Bygdøy, 210, 227
  Roskilde, 220
ships, 25, 27, 139, 174, 208–32,
  figs. 101, 135
  sails and rigging of, 23, 202,
  213, 230–2
Vimose, 246
Virginia coal trade, 300
  skiffs, 275
Vistula, the, 150
Voyageurs' cargo canoe, 127, fig. 80
  Highway, 127, fig. 79

Wales, 116, 117, 129
Ward Jackson, C. H. 297
Washington, 271

Waters, David, 104, 105
Wei Hai Wei, 102, 105
Wei river, 102
Welsh coracle, 92
Wens, the, 218
West European, 75, 292
  Germany, 70, 198, 259
  Hay, 36, 38
  Indies, 301
Weston-super-Mare flatner, 274,
  fig. 193
wherries, 272, 278
William the Conqueror, 247
Winchelsea, Seal of Corporation of,
  252, fig. 165
Winchester Cathedral font, 85, 283,
  fig. 40

Woodbridge, 183
Wright, C. W., 21
Wright, Edward, 21, 111, 112

Yamato-gata, 143, figs. 93–5, 207
Yangtze, 104
Yangtze-Kiang, 100
Yarmouth, 255
Yassi Adda, 63
Yellow river, 102
Yorkshire, 111
Yverdon, 70

Zeeland, Chronicle of, 292
Zierikzee, 292
zugian oarsmen, 171
Zuyder Zee, 21, 69
Zwammerdam, 70